M000317667

Emerging Practices in International Development Evaluation

A volume in
Evaluation and Society
Jennifer Caroline Greene and Stewart Donaldson, *Series Editors*

Emerging Practices in International Development Evaluation

edited by

Stewart I. Donaldson
Claremont Graduate University

Tarek Azzam
Claremont Graduate University

Ross F. Conner
University of California–Irvine

INFORMATION AGE PUBLISHING, INC.
Charlotte, NC • www.infoagepub.com

Library of Congress Cataloging-in-Publication Data

A CIP record for this book is available from the Library of Congress
http://www.loc.gov

ISBN: 978-1-62396-183-1 (Paperback)
       978-1-62396-184-8 (Hardcover)
       978-1-62396-185-5 (ebook)

*To all of those committed to improving the quality of life
and expanding opportunities for poor and vulnerable populations
throughout the world.*

CONTENTS

ACKNOWLEDGEMENTS

The editors are deeply grateful for the financial support provided by the Rockefeller Foundation for this project. Special thanks to the chapter authors for their thoughtful analyses and reflections on how to improve international development evaluation practice. The editors greatly appreciate the leadership and guidance provided Nancy MacPherson and Penny Hawkins of the Rockefeller Foundation, the support from the IAP *Evaluation and Society* series co-editor Jennifer Caroline Greene and IAP publisher George F. Johnson, and the outstanding editorial support from Edith Ramirez at Claremont Graduate University.

ACKNOWLEDGEMENTS

PREFACE

With its mission of promoting the well-being of humanity, the Rockefeller Foundation aims to expand opportunities for poor and vulnerable populations through more equitable growth, and strengthening resilience to acute crises and chronic stresses. Just as the Rockefeller Foundation's approach to philanthropy has evolved over the years, so too has its approach to evaluation. With a strong focus on evaluative knowledge generation, capacity development, field building, and innovation, the foundation's evaluation office is committed to supporting evaluation practices that are rigorous, innovative, inclusive of stakeholders' voices, and appropriate to the contexts in which the foundation works.

The impetus for this volume of Emerging Approaches in International Development Evaluation comes from reflecting on many years of experience, successes, and failures in development evaluation in Asia and Africa and from recent work supported by the Rockefeller Foundation on Rethinking, Reshaping, and Reforming Evaluation. This work has been presented and discussed at a number of different forums during the past few years, including the IDEAS Symposium. It has highlighted the challenges that development practitioners, evaluators, and policymakers face, as never before, with the complexity and pace of change in an increasingly interdependent world. Increasingly, problems are interdisciplinary and systemic in nature (e.g., climate change, health, livelihood), and solutions often lie at the intersection of disciplines and sectors and across systems and geographies on a local, national, and global scale.

Emerging Practices in International Development Evaluation, pages xi–xiii
Copyright © 2013 by Information Age Publishing

Effective implementation at scale is now more likely to be funded, managed, and governed by coalitions, alliances, networks, and new partnerships with government, private sector, and civil society. In some countries, philanthropy and private impact investing funds account for more development funding than traditional aid donors. This in turn gives rise to (the need for) new forms of accountability by multiple players—funders, governments, private investors, and beneficiaries alike. Advancements in technology have transformed, and, to some extent, democratized the way information is accessed, shared, and used. Data collection and analysis are no longer the exclusive domain of experts. All of these changes have profound implications for international development evaluation.

There is widespread recognition in the development community and philanthropy that conventional evaluation needs to evolve quickly to keep pace with these changes and challenges, and to take advantage of the opportunities they present, for example, with new information technology. As noted by Shiva Kumar and Zenda Ofir in Chapter 2, there is a growing feeling, especially in developing countries, that evaluations need to be more useful and responsive to the needs of policymakers and key stakeholders. Many conventional evaluations focus too narrowly on a particular project or program and account only for inputs (funds and staff) and outputs. They often fail to adequately understand what leads to successful and durable development outcomes that transform the lives of people. They often omit drawing broader lessons for policymakers and the field or fail to include the voices of those most affected. In sum, they argue that conventional evaluation methods do not adequately reflect and take account of the needs and circumstances of developing countries, and far too often do not empower developing country evaluators. Some regional evaluation associations are taking steps to ensure evaluations are more context relevant, as illustrated by the recent "Made in Africa" campaign of the Africa Evaluation Association.

While some progress has been made to address both asymmetries in development evaluation and the challenges that complexity poses for development and evaluation, much of this has yet to be translated and widely adopted into development evaluation practice.

We hope that the concepts, frameworks, and ideas presented in this volume are a useful contribution to the ongoing efforts at rethinking, reforming, and reshaping international development evaluation. They come from leading thinkers and practitioners in development, evaluation, research, and academia who have recognized that development evaluation must evolve if it is to respond to the challenges of the 21st century and play a meaningful role in social and economic transformation.

We are grateful to all the authors for generously sharing their wisdom, ideas, and expertise to help reshape the practice and governance of development evaluation, and to Claremont Graduate University for so capably convening, facilitating, and producing the collective wisdom of this dedicated group.

We look forward to continuing this journey with all of you.

—Nancy MacPherson
Managing Director, Evaluation
Rockefeller Foundation
New York, NY

CHAPTER 1

SEARCHING FOR APPROACHES TO IMPROVE INTERNATIONAL DEVELOPMENT EVALUATIONS

Stewart I. Donaldson, Tarek Azzam, and Ross F. Conner

The need for high-quality evaluation is an important factor in many international development projects. These projects often have ambitious outcomes that are not easy to measure and evaluate. Such outcomes include the project's ability to build capacity, influence policy, form networks, help other organizations perform, foster innovation, and enhance sustainable development. Each of these outcome areas involves its own set of evaluative focuses, approaches, methods, and challenges. To better understand the evaluation issues in these six areas, the Rockefeller Foundation provided a grant to Claremont Graduate University (CGU) to convene a workshop with a small group of key global evaluation leaders in these areas.

The workshop was held at the Rockefeller Foundation in March 2010. The primary purpose of the meeting was to contribute to the conceptual knowledge and practice in the international development context; a secondary purpose was to strengthen collaboration among and between the

Emerging Practices in International Development Evaluation, pages 1–10
Copyright © 2013 by Information Age Publishing
All rights of reproduction in any form reserved.

TABLE 1.1

Outcome Area	Presenters	Affiliation
Organization Performance	Charles Lusthaus & Katrina Rojas	Universalia
Capacity Development	Peter Morgan	Independent Consultant
Policy Influence	Fred Carden & Colleen Duggan	International Development Research Center
Networks & Partnerships	Heather Creech	International Institute for Sustainable Development
Coalitions	Jared Raynor	TCC Group
Sustainable Development	Steve Bass & Alastair Bradstock	International Institute for Environment and Development
Innovation	Steve Rochlin & Sasha Radovich	AccountAbility

participants and their organizations, all of whom shared an interest in the evaluation of these areas. Publications that are produced from the meeting are intended to enhance learning in development and philanthropy by advancing concepts that can guide practitioners and support understanding in international development evaluation. To achieve these ends, each participant or participant pair prepared a paper about a specific outcome area that described the best practices, approaches, and principles that guided evaluation in that area. Table 1.1 lists the presenters and their topics.

At the workshop, each presenter or team shared the main ideas from their prepared papers, then engaged the others in an extended discussion of evaluation issues. To bring a local, developing country perspective, one discussant from Africa (Ofir) presented ideas about realities and constraints in evaluation work generally in developing regions and areas. The workshop concluded with a special half-day session for Rockefeller Foundation staff to hear from presenters and to share their perspectives on the six outcomes areas and their evaluation, based on their work in the field with Rockefeller grantees.

Following the meeting, each presenter prepared a short 'guidance note' to highlight the main issues related to evaluation in each outcome area. These notes offer a broad perspective on how to approach the evaluation of each outcome area and are also designed to offer a quick overview to practitioners who are conducting evaluations in development contexts. The guidance notes are provided in the Appendix in Chapter 10.

OVERVIEW

Each chapter author in this volume was asked to discuss the terms and definitions used to describe their topic as a first step to understanding the methods, measures, and designs commonly used. The authors were also encouraged to highlight strategies for increasing utilization of evaluation findings and candidly describe reoccurring challenges they face when conducting evaluations. As a prelude to the ideas and issues discussed in each chapter, we provide a brief summary of each chapter below.

USING A DEVELOPING COUNTRY LENS IN EVALUATION

In Chapter 2, Shev Kumar and Zenda Ofir point out that the societies and institutional systems of developing countries tend to be more vulnerable and less predictable and more easily destabilized than those of developed countries. Developing countries, or large swathes of their populations, tend to be poor. Resources, opportunities, exposure to new ideas, and the "freedom to choose" that others take for granted are lacking. Those already powerful—within and outside these countries—continue to be so through domination of natural and material resources and of the intellectual discourse (including on development).

Getting good and sustained results in developing countries is more complicated and unpredictable than in developed countries, and when development is driven from outside, even with the best intentions, the chance of success diminishes. Approaches such as theories of change (TOCs) often overly simplify ideas about development designs and are likely to hide potential reasons for success or failure. Development contexts should therefore be well understood, especially where development strategies are not aligned with a society's most deeply ingrained values, norms, and ways of working. The misunderstanding typically occurs when planners fail to recognize privilege and power differentials or fail to address (dis)empowerment. Understanding the asymmetrical nature of power, who holds it, how it is used, and the relationships between ever-increasing numbers of actors is critical. It is challenging to establish evaluation as a credible, empowering, useful, and respected practice in areas where evaluation is not a tradition or part of the culture, where power differentials are marked, where it has in the past served the interests of a few (usually external) agencies, or where those in power have the motivation to disregard the results.

The current move to emphasize complexity has the unfortunate sideeffect that nothing appears predictable. Yet much can be done when designing and implementing development initiatives to enhance the chance that development will be sustained. Evaluation has to increase its focus on this aspect. It is too often completely neglected or insufficiently considered.

EVALUATING ORGANIZATIONAL PERFORMANCE

Evaluation has historically not utilized the organization as the unit of analysis. However, in Chapter 3, Charles Lusthaus and Katrina Rojas describe advances in the assessment of organizational performance that may prove useful to evaluations in the international development context. By using assessment tools that have been traditionally employed in the fields of management or organizational behavior, evaluators are able to address the growing needs of donor agencies who strive to understand the performance and capacity of their grantees' organizations.

Lusthaus and Rojas make a case for the inclusion of organizational performance assessments (OPAs) in the field of evaluation. An OPA is the process of collecting information according to a rigorous methodology with the goal of improving organizational performance. Common measures of organizational success can range from financial data to indicators of motivation or the environmental setting.

Organizational performance assessments contain several stages that reflect processes used in program evaluation. In the initial stage of the OPA, it is important to select an appropriate conceptual framework and decide who will conduct the OPA (internal vs. external). Appropriate frameworks may be adopted from the field of management, like the McKinsey 7-S, or from generic evaluation matrices. The authors delineate the framework used by their organization, Universalia, which is targeted towards the assessment of organizations in international development. The OPA matrix can be used to organize key questions, relevant indicators, and data collection methods. Care should be taken to avoid potential obstacles in order to facilitate the use of OPA results in capacity building, dialogue with partners and funders, and planning for the future.

Despite the potential value of OPAs for informing funding practices of donor agencies, fostering learning within the evaluand's organizations, and improving the performance of those organizations, there are several challenges that can inhibit the success of an OPA. The absence of industry standards and accepted methodology are two potential obstacles. It can also be challenging to recognize the early indicators of positive organizational performance, given that many indicators of success develop over an extended timeframe. Regardless of the challenges, the application of OPAs in evaluation, such as the framework proposed by Universalia, can serve as a visible step towards improving our understanding of development organizations and the factors that contribute to their success.

EVALUATING CAPACITY DEVELOPMENT

Capacity development is a concept that has been defined in many different ways. At its core, capacity development represents "the processes of change that, both intentionally and indirectly, contribute to the emergence of capacity over time." In Chapter 4, Peter Morgan describes capacity development as a nonlinear process that is highly dependent on uncontrollable contextual factors operating in complex environments. Thus, the evaluation of capacity development poses many methodological and measurement challenges to the evaluator.

Each capacity development process requires unique factors such as time, common language/vision, and stakeholder commitment. An evaluator should work with stakeholders to determine if these critical factors are present and to help set the standards and methods for measuring their progress. This approach to capacity development evaluation can help ensure that the evaluation is (1) selecting the most appropriate time scale for capturing CD outcomes, (2) selecting applicable quantitative and qualitative indicators, and (3) relevant and potentially useful to the stakeholders involved.

Peter Morgan also recognizes that many uncontrollable factors can influence capacity development outcomes. These factors create a complex network of causes and effects that often blurs the relationship between the CD activities and the intended outcomes. He suggests that a Complex Adaptive Systems (CAS) approach to evaluation offers a set of ideas that can guide the evaluation. At its core CAS acknowledges that system changes around capacity development are often unpredictable and that no pattern remains for long. This requires evaluators to focus on continuous formative evaluation rather then a summative type of evaluation. This approach allows evaluators to contribute to the constant transformation of capacity development and offers insights about the process.

EVALUATING POLICY INFLUENCE

Fred Carden and Colleen Duggan discuss ways to evaluate policy influence in Chapter 5. Policy influence is often an incremental process requiring the correct combination of contextual factors and researcher actions to occur. It is recognized that policymakers are not waiting for evidence in order to act but are often responding to many different factors at the same time. Knowledge is only one input, and ideology and politics play important roles. Influence from a research perspective is often indirect and may require expanding policy capacities both for researchers and decision makers. This means increasing the capacity of researchers to think about the policy process in relation to their research and as well increasing the capacities of decision makers to make use of knowledge, especially knowledge that might not fit their preconceived notions of what is correct and what is politically feasible.

To influence policy and build capacity, a researcher/evaluator needs to account for the stability of the government or program, foster trusting relationships with potential policymakers, and anticipate upcoming needs and interests. Another component to policy influence is an awareness of a government's ability to act on the research supported policies. In addition, an evaluator should understand the influence of correct timing and constant communication of research supported policies to decision makers. Comparative case study methods along with a realistic synthesis represent viable methods for studying and measuring policy influence. The comparative case studies offer contextual lessons on the factors contributing to policy influence and the process of reaching influence, while the realistic synthesis can offer a broader (or more generalizable) perspective on how or why policy influence occurred.

EVALUATING NETWORKS AND PARTNERSHIPS

In their essence, networks and partnerships are often described as the relationships between individuals and organizations who have come together to address a set of issues. The relationships created through these interactions can affect their ability to function and succeed in their efforts. To better depict networks and partnerships, the language of relationship should be emphasized and networks should be described by the types of relationships that they have amongst each other and the level of formality that exists between members. Thus, defining these partnerships as interorganizational relationships (IOR) is a more accurate description of how they function.

Through the IOR framing, Heather Creech discusses how evaluators can utilize relationship-based measures and outcomes to evaluate the effectiveness of networks and partnerships in Chapter 6. An IOR evaluation could examine the network's governance structure, financial management systems, and the transaction costs associated with their functioning as a way to determine the network's viability and functioning. From an outcomes perspective, an IOR evaluation could focus on the network's ability to change an issue or accomplish a stated goal through the use of a mixed methods approaches that also capture the interactions between network members. By highlighting the relationship development process as part of the evaluation, the evaluation can offer a clearer understanding of the factors that affected the successes or failures of the network/partnership and provide ways to improve the relationships or even argue for their need to dissolve the relationships.

EVALUATING COALITIONS

Relationships between organizations can range from informal networks to formalized partnerships, like a merger of two companies. Coalitions, which require a common goal to which two or more organizations have committed, represent an alternative to such formal or informal types of relationships. Although some coalitions do establish legal status, organizations that participate in a coalition generally retain their own autonomy when allying with another organization. While coalitions may incorporate multiple groups with varying interests, the key gauge of their success is their level of agreement on a common outcome. In Chapter 7, Jared Raynor provides a look at the evolving role of coalitions within the international development context, and offers his perspective on the opportunities and challenges of evaluating these interorganizational partnerships.

Raynor distinguishes between the concepts of "coalition" as a strategy used to accomplish some means, versus "coalition" as a unique entity. When evaluating a coalition, it is important to establish early on whether it is being used as a strategy or an actor to correctly identify the evaluation's unit of analysis. The web of relationships inherent to coalitions should also be seriously considered. Any imbalance in power or influence can complicate the collection and analysis of evidence. Additionally, evaluation results can serve to expose existing inequalities, potentially jeopardizing the future of the coalition. Given this context, formative evaluations, as opposed to summative evaluations, are often the most appropriate choice when assessing coalitions, as the goal of many evaluations is often to improve coalition performance instead of replicating findings.

Successful coalitions tend to possess strong leadership capacity, management capacity, adaptive capacity, and technical capacity to achieve intended goals. Evaluative indicators of coalition success could include the coalition's progress towards achieving its stated goals (e.g., policy adoption/blocking, increased public awareness) and ability to increase its legitimacy and relevance (e.g., increased membership, visibility, responsiveness). Mixed-methods approaches are effective tools to measure the progress of coalitions and can be used to adequately account for contextual factors and provide concrete evidence of success.

EVALUATING SUSTAINABLE DEVELOPMENT

The definition of "sustainable development" (SD) simultaneously encompasses the needs of current generations and the ability of future generations to meet their own needs. This broad definition can be applied to SD evaluations within economic, environmental, and social contexts. In Chapter 8, Alastair Bradstock and Steve Bass describe the evolution of sustainable development, from the coinage of a commonly accepted definition by the Brundtland Commission Report in 1987 to widespread emphasis on the concept in contemporary society. The authors present a compelling argument for the evaluation of sustainable development initiatives, while recognizing that there are substantial challenges to such evaluation endeavors.

Despite the proliferation of sustainable development indicators, several obstacles remain in evaluating sustainable development. For example, evaluations of sustainable development may be threatened by lack of accepted evaluation frameworks or inadequacies of data and methodology. The multiple spatial (e.g., global vs. local) and temporal (e.g., short-term interests vs. ongoing outcomes) levels of sustainable development can also complicate evaluation endeavors. Institutional resistance to assessment, stemming from unfamiliarity with evaluation practices or fears about the results, may also inhibit the evaluation process. Successful frameworks for evaluating sustainable development must address these challenges within the economic, environmental, and social contexts.

Bradstock and Bass center their discussion on three pillars of sustainable development: the aforementioned economic, environmental, and social areas. In many cases, they suggest that input from local stakeholders can inform the selection of proper indicators and methods in these three overlapping spheres. The authors also reference alternatives to indicator-based monitoring that capture information from the input/process level. Evaluators should design evaluations of sustainable development so that they achieve maximum use in varied ways. Ideally, evaluation results will inform improvements in program design and implementation as well as decisions made by donor agencies or program managers. Additionally, the evaluation process can serve as a learning experience for program staff.

EVALUATING INNOVATION

Innovation for Development (I4D) is an emerging concept that involves the application of new ideas, methods, or devices to produce changes that benefit vulnerable populations. In Chapter 9, Steve Rochlin and Sasha Radovich outline their vision of innovation within the developing world while focusing on the value of evaluating I4D in order to maximize their funding, dissemination, and sustainability. The authors organize innovations into four types: product, process, market, and organizational. They characterize innovation according to scope, differentiating between radical additions to a field or improvements upon existing entities. The identification of an innovation's type and scope provides a conceptual structure for designing the evaluation.

Innovation evaluation in developing countries requires awareness of the contextual factors that contribute to the innovation, as well as the identification of the factors that could potentially impede the implementation of innovation. Innovation evaluations can provide grant makers with some understanding of the grantees capacities.

Given that innovations for development strive to provide creative solutions for people in developing countries, there are a host of factors specific to the development environment that complicate evaluation efforts. Considerable challenges may be reflected in the existing infrastructure of the organization or country, such as availability of labor skills, policy influence, local governance, and gender disparities. However, Rochlin and Radovich indicate that involving local stakeholders in the evaluation can stimulate the identification of untapped opportunities in the form of knowledge, skills, or ideas. Additionally, stakeholder involvement increases the potential for organizational learning. Ideally, the grant-maker would utilize evaluation results to support grantees and to improve and disseminate the I4D. It is important that the grant-maker moderate its expectations of the I4D outcomes, as innovations often develop over an extended timeline. Scaling up an I4D and solidifying its sustainability can also be lengthy processes that may involve trial-and-error and substantial risk.

The Rockefeller Foundation's evaluation matrix, which addresses the relevance, effectiveness, influence, sustainability of program outcomes, impact, and risk management of grantees, can be modified to suit the specific needs of evaluating innovation for development.

FUTURE DIRECTIONS FOR INTERNATIONAL DEVELOPMENT EVALUATION

In the final chapter (Chapter 10), we explore the previous chapter authors' contributions to furthering the understanding of emerging ideas and evaluation practices aimed at improving outcomes for international development initiatives. In Chapter 10, we examine some of the common themes across Chapters 2–9, illustrate the challenges and opportunities of searching for common definitions, highlighting the evaluation methods that have been recommended, and exploring the challenges noted for undertaking evaluation in developing countries. These analyses are followed by a discussion of possible next step for improving international development evaluation and for keeping this conversation moving in productive directions. This final chapter ends with an appendix providing specific guidance notes written by the chapter authors for practitioners working in the field of international development evaluation.

We think you will find valuable ideas, concepts, methods, and practical guidance to improve international development evaluation practice in the chapters ahead. It is our hope that you find this conversation useful and a springboard to future conversations about how best to use evaluation to achieve development outcomes and to improve the quality of life in developing countries.

CHAPTER 2

EVALUATION IN DEVELOPING COUNTRIES

What Makes it Different?

Zenda Ofir and A. K. Shiva Kumar

There is a growing feeling, especially in developing countries, that most evaluations are neither useful nor responsive to the needs of policy makers and other stakeholders. For a start, many conventional evaluations, by focusing too narrowly on a particular project, end up accounting for inputs and a few scattered outputs, outcomes, or impacts. They fail to consider unpredictable development trajectories or to draw realistic or significant lessons for program, strategy, and policy improvements. Knowledge and lessons learned are seldom synthesized and presented in a manner that can be used beyond a particular project or program. Such evaluations also fail to offer an understanding of change that is sustainable and transformative and of progress that is enduring. Why is this so? Part of the explanation can be found in the failure of conventional evaluation methods to take note of both the needs and circumstances of developing countries. Developing countries[1,2] have important characteristics that should shape development evaluation practice, and yet they are often ignored or underplayed in meth-

Emerging Practices in International Development Evaluation, pages 11–24
Copyright © 2013 by Information Age Publishing
11

odology guidelines, to the detriment of credible and useful evaluation and effective development.

In this chapter, we argue that a developing country lens should be applied for determining the evaluation focus and to understand the importance of the intervention and its evaluation. We end with some suggestions for future evaluation practices that follow from using a "developing country lens." By adopting development evaluation practices, we would be adding much-needed credibility and value to our practice.

FRAMING THE EVALUATION

Attention is seldom given to the broader frameworks or sets of values that determine the focus of development evaluations. There are three distinct streams of thought that have shaped development dialogue and thinking in recent years: the human development approach, the human rights approach, and the human security approach to development.

Defined broadly as a widening of choices, an enhancement of capabilities and an expansion of freedoms, the human development approach calls for a focus on people and what they cherish and value in life.[3] In the human development framework, human deprivations are viewed as a denial of freedoms, including economic, civil, social, cultural, and political. Human poverty is traced to inadequacies and inequalities in the distribution of opportunities, between women and men, across regions, between rural and urban areas, and within communities. Evaluating progress entails more than monitoring trends in economic variables such as economic growth and expansion in outputs, which are no doubt important. The evaluative question is whether or not the benefits of economic growth have contributed equitably to tangible improvements in the lives of people.

The idea of human development has been enriched by the human rights discourse. The human rights and human development approaches share a common vision and a common purpose. Amartya Sen (1999) explains the complementarities in this way:

> [F]reedoms depend also on other determinants, such as social and economic arrangements (for example, facilities for education and health care) as well as political and civil rights (for example, the liberty to participate in public discussion and scrutiny) ... Viewing development in terms of expanding substantive freedoms directs attention to the ends that make development important, rather than merely to some of the means that, inter alia, play a prominent role in the the process. (Sen, 1999, p. 3)

The state is principally obligated to ensure universal access to basic social and other services and to create the enabling environment for the assurance of human rights. From a rights perspective, human poverty stems from a denial of basic entitlements to education, health, nutrition, and other components of decent living.[4] Importance is given to both moral consensus and legal obligations. By underscoring the importance of accountability, transparency, and rule of law, the human rights approach calls for adopting democratic methods of implementation that give primacy to participation, protection, and empowerment of the poor. Therefore, from a human rights perspective, the evaluative questions are whether the process of development has been fair, just, and respectful of the rights of individuals, and whether the benefits of growth have reached the most marginalized and socially disadvantaged groups in society.

Both the ideas of human development and human rights have been complemented in many ways by the idea of human security. The Commission on Human Security (2003) gives this definition of human security:

> to protect the vital core of all human lives in ways that enhance human freedoms and human fulfilment. Human security means protecting fundamental freedoms—freedoms that are the essence of life. It means protecting people from critical (severe) and pervasive (widespread) threats and situations. It means using processes that build on people's strengths and aspirations. It means creating political, social, environmental, economic, military, and cultural systems that together give people the building blocks of survival, livelihood, and dignity... Human security is comprehensive in the sense that it integrates these agendas. Human security in its broadest sense embraces far more than the absence of violent conflict. It encompasses human rights, good governance, access to education and health care, and ensuring that each individual has opportunities and choices to fulfill his or her own potential. Every step in this direction is also a step towards reducing poverty, achieving economic growth, and preventing conflict. Freedom from want, freedom from fear, and the freedom of future generations to inherit a healthy natural environment—these are the interrelated building blocks of human, and therefore national, security. Human security also reinforces human dignity. People's horizons extend far beyond survival, to matters of love, culture, and faith. Protecting a core of activities and abilities is essential for human security, but that alone is not enough. Human security must also aim at developing the capabilities of individuals and communities to make informed choices and to act on behalf of causes and interests in many spheres of life. That is why human security starts from the recognition that people are the most active participants in determining their well-being. It builds on people's efforts, strengthening what they do for themselves. (p. 4)

The human security, human rights, and human development approaches are fundamentally concerned with the lives of human beings and the freedoms people enjoy. Human development is about an expansion in people's capabilities and choices before them to lead valuable lives. It focuses on expanding opportunities for people so that progress is just and combines growth with inclusion and equity. Human security, on the other hand, complements human development by addressing "downside risks" that threaten survival, healthy life, livelihoods, and the dignity of human beings. Respecting the universality and interdependence of civil, political, social, and economic rights of all people is at the core of protecting human security. Human security is deliberately protective. People's ability to act on their own behalf and on behalf of others is the second key to human security. Given these two dimensions, the evaluative questions become: How well has the intervention protected people against downside risks? How well have people been empowered to exercise choices, avoid risks, and demand improvements in the system of protection?

These approaches require that the goals of development policy should be to end human deprivations, reduce inequalities, eliminate injustices, minimize vulnerabilities, and get rid of the sense of powerlessness that haunts the lives of the poor. Hence, any programmatic or policy initiative must be judged and evaluated in terms of the contribution to improving the quality of people's lives, promoting equity, enhancing security, reducing discrimination, and empowering people.

CONTEXT IN DEVELOPMENT
AND IN DEVELOPMENT EVALUATION

In any evaluation it is important to consider context. This becomes even more important in the case of developing countries. The societies and institutional systems of developing countries tend to be more vulnerable and hence less predictable and more easily destabilized than those of developed countries. They are often old civilizations with rich cultures that have over time either evolved or been eroded through their own actions or foreign intervention. And often, as a result of a globalization, they have had to align with others' notions of "success" and "development." Confusion and intergenerational tension about how their ingrained values, norms, and knowledge systems relate to the modern world are frequently exacerbated by a sense of victimization, of dependence on uncontrollable forces, and a struggle to cope. Developing countries, or large proportions of their populations, also tend to be poor. They lack sufficient resources, opportunities, exposure to new ideas, and the "freedom to choose" that others take for granted. Those who are already powerful, both within and outside these countries, often continue to be so through domination over natural and material resources, the media, and the intellectual discourse.

All these factors work together to limit the capacities of developing countries and frequently also the resolve of individuals, including leaders, institutions and societies to cope and thrive, especially in a world dominated by Euro-American perspectives, models, and power. They tend to induce or exacerbate feelings of inadequacy, disempowerment, and marginalization that have sometimes been embedded over generations. The effects on the psyche of an individual, institution, or nation are often underestimated: confidence, exposure, opportunity, hope, and the ability and freedom to develop suitable strategies based on previous and evolving values, beliefs, and norms are major factors in success. The effects are even more pronounced in states designated as "fragile." In spite of recent global power shifts, the least powerful remain the most vulnerable and exposed to exploitation.

Individuals, communities, or nations respond differently to such triggers. Some are passive; some turn inwards; some lash out; some become resolute and move forward with the conviction that positive change is possible, either on their own or on others' terms. A struggle for power, sometimes by any and even unsavory means, over the ability and means to control their own circumstances easily ensues.

Recent economic development success stories have important lessons. They illustrate among others that it is crucial to have national policies and strategies deeply rooted in an understanding of a country's comparative strengths and niche globally and regionally, while drawing from its own values, norms, and innovations as well as international experiences to inform home-grown solutions.

Such models of development do not necessarily find favor among institutions that are used to power and control. This can intensify power struggles among actors at local, national, regional, and global levels—a major reason why politics and power relations at and between these different levels play such an important role in development.

IMPLICATIONS OF THE DEVELOPMENT CONTEXT FOR EVALUATION

Several implications for development evaluation follow:

One, getting good and sustained results in developing countries is *more complicated and unpredictable* than in developed countries. When development is driven from outside, even with the best intentions, the chance of success diminishes. Theories of change that reflect overly simple ideas about development designs are likely to hide potential reasons for success or failure.

Two, globalization has encouraged "glocalization." *Deep cultural differences persist*, sometimes less visibly underneath what seems the same and sometimes more visibly than decades ago. The role and evolution of culture in development contexts should therefore be well understood, especially where development strategies are not aligned with a society's most deeply ingrained values, norms and ways of working.

Three, *capacity and other constraints*, among individuals and institutional systems, and in evaluation, are usually more serious and pervasive in developing than in developed countries. When capacities have to meet notions of performance and worth outside the society's own culture, this can greatly affect their successful application and sustainability.

Four, development easily goes wrong when planners fail to understand and recognize *privilege and power* differentials, or fail to address *(dis)empowerment*. Understanding the asymmetrical nature of power—who holds it, how it is used, and the relationships between ever-increasing numbers of actors—is critical for sensitive, useful evaluation.

Development evaluation is unlikely to be effective and, most importantly, sustained without due attention to these considerations. It is therefore imperative that evaluation is sensitive to and sheds light on these issues.

RECOMMENDATIONS FOR EVALUATION PRACTICE

Using a "developing country lens," we make the following list of suggestions for evaluation practices. This list is not exhaustive, nor would all issues or illustrative questions be relevant to everyone. It is based on the arguments above and the experience and perspectives of the authors, reflecting their own values. We present this list in order to promote awareness, understanding, and emphasis on the specific context of developing countries; to encourage constructive debate; and to share insights among those using and developing evaluation methodologies and guidelines. Tables 2.1 and 2.2 summarize these points.

1. **Contextual responsiveness and systems approaches:** Development efforts are based on interventions that range from often too simplistic quick fixes to integrated, complex policies, strategies, and programs. The latter usually includes the capacity strengthening of individuals, institutions or governance systems, often imperative for enduring development success. It recognizes the complexity of change and the importance of context.[5] Change therefore needs to be deeply understood if improvement, transfer or scaling up is to be done successfully.

2. **Culture, multicultural validity, and theories of change:** Culture impacts all aspects of development and of evaluation, and yet it is seldom at the center when designing and testing theories of change. Conversations about validity in evaluation seldom include multicul-

TABLE 2.1 Applying a Developing Country Lens to Evaluation: Key Issues, Assumptions and Illustrative Questions [a,b]

Key Issue	Assumptions	Illustrative Questions
Contextual responsiveness and systems approaches	• "Context" has different dimensions such as economic, technical, political, legal and sociocultural, which should be considered during evaluation. • Development that has a good chance of being sustained requires a sound understanding of change in a specific context given a certain set of circumstances, actors, and relationships. Evaluation should contribute to this understanding without trying to "oversimplify" or "complexify."	• Will the proposed evaluation approach and methods help to understand better the complex nature of change in this context? • Will it provide an opportunity to interrogate the assumptions underlying the theory of change, and illuminate the factors that influenced success or failure? • Are the proposed evaluation approach and methods sufficiently sensitive to context? • Are the proposed evaluation approach and methods sufficiently considering diversity—racial, ethnic, cultural, linguistic, geographic, gender, political, and more?
Culture, multicultural validity, and theories of change	• Theories of change and evaluation rarely focus sufficiently on the sociocultural values, beliefs, and knowledge that underlie the assumptions we make about change. • Development (and evaluation) that considers the relevant cultural features of a given society is likely to be more effective. • Biases embedded in cultural diversity threaten validity, and can be found in all aspects of evaluation—yet this dimension is frequently ignored. • Developed and developing regions have real differences in values, beliefs and knowledge systems (refer to Table 2.2). This means that reigning paradigms around development and evaluation, and who has the power to determine these, become very important.	• Do the evaluation definitions, approaches, and methods sufficiently consider different value systems and other sociocultural aspects? • Whose values, norms, or knowledge systems underlie the evaluation approach and methods? Is this appropriate? • Will the proposed evaluation approach and methods adequately illuminate threats to validity as a result of biases embedded in cultural diversity?

(continued)

TABLE 2.1 Applying a Developing Country Lens to Evaluation: Key Issues, Assumptions and Illustrative Questions (continued)

Key Issue	Assumptions	Illustrative Questions
Privilege, power, and (dis) empowerment	• Power asymmetries will influence and in many cases harm development efforts. These asymmetries tend to be more pronounced in developing countries with vulnerable or fragile institutions, communities, and individuals. It is therefore imperative to consider the role of power in development efforts— and hence also in evaluation. • Better ways have to be found to understand and analyse the influence of power on development success, focusing on the relationships between actors that direct, participate in, and influence development interventions, as well as on evaluation processes themselves. This includes smarter engagement with the politics embedded in aid-driven development that often also shape evaluation. • Development interventions should empower individuals, communities, institutions, and societies. It should be at the core of development efforts that are to lead to enduring (sustainable) development results. It should also be at the core of evaluation practices—in terms of both assessing the extent to which interventions empower or disempower, and ensuring that evaluation processes themselves empower. • This implies engaging with the relationship between power and cultural values, beliefs, and practices. Perceptions around power and empowerment will often differ from one society to another.	• Are the proposed evaluation definitions, approaches, and methods sufficiently sensitive to issues of power in the development intervention? • Is enough done to challenge how power is treated in the theories and frameworks underlying development interventions? • To what extent does cultural context have to be considered when assessing the influence of power asymmetries?

(continued)

TABLE 2.1 Applying a Developing Country Lens to Evaluation: Key Issues, Assumptions and Illustrative Questions (continued)

Key Issue	Assumptions	Illustrative Questions
Dealing with constraints	• Culture, power, and capacity intersect. When capacities to be developed have to meet notions of performance and worth outside that society's own culture, this can greatly affect their performance. And when individuals or nations have felt disempowered for generations, many continue to lack confidence and voice. Evaluation content and processes have to take this into account. • Many resources, most notably the book RealWorld Evaluation (Bamberger, Rugh, & Mabry, 2012), have been successful in focusing evaluators' attention on the many constraints evaluators face in developing countries where systems are fragile, communities vulnerable, and development trajectories unpredictable. • Developing country evaluators are also often constrained by insufficient experience in evaluation in complex contexts, the limited visibility of their profession and greater exposure to risk in authoritarian governance systems.	• Do the evaluation approaches and methods show sufficient awareness of the constraints that may affect success, and how to deal with these? • Do the evaluation definitions, approaches, and methods sufficiently highlight and interrogate the challenges posed by unrealistic expectations and unpredictable development trajectories? • Do the evaluation definitions, approaches, and methods sufficiently deal with relevant cultural or societal practices that might marginalize vulnerable groups?

(continued)

TABLE 2.1   Applying a Developing Country Lens to Evaluation: Key Issues, Assumptions and Illustrative Questions (continued)

Key Issue	Assumptions	Illustrative Questions
Evaluation that is empowering, useful, and respected	• The evaluation profession needs to change the image of evaluation in developing countries so that it is seen as useful and empowering. • External or independent evaluation as well as learning-oriented monitoring and self-evaluation are needed, and they should be in dialogue with each other. • More effort should go into the development of evaluation frameworks, models, and standards rooted in non-Western value systems and ways of thinking and knowing.	• Is it necessary to streamline or transform the evaluation definitions, approaches, and methods to be more beneficial and empowering to developing country stakeholders?
A focus on sustained (enduring) development	• It is essential for evaluation to attend to issues of sustainability (of ideas, models, capacities, results, institutions, or systems) in a thoughtful and thorough manner if an intervention is to be designated as "successful." • Determining impact should be accompanied at all times by efforts to determine whether the intervention has a good chance to lead to sustainable benefits—otherwise it cannot be seen as a success.	• Have the evaluation definitions, approaches, and methods been designed with a sufficient emphasis on all relevant dimensions of sustainability? • Are there unintended negative outcomes or impacts that might neutralize the positive benefits from the intervention?

[a] In this table a development policy, strategy, program, and/or project is referred to as an "intervention."

[b] Many of the issues and questions raised in this chapter and table are equally relevant for monitoring and self-evaluation.

TABLE 2.2 Dimensions on Which Organizations in Developed and Developing Countries Differ

Dimensions	Developed Countries	Developing Countries
Characterization of economic and political environment		
Predictability of events	Relatively high	Relatively low
Difficulty of obtaining resources from the environment	Relatively easy	Relatively difficult
Characterization of socio-cultural environment		
Uncertainty avoidance	Relatively low	Relatively high
Individualism-collectivism	Relatively high individualism	Relatively low individualism
Power distance	Relatively low	Relatively high
Characterization of internal work culture		
Causality and control of outcomes	Internal	External
Environment orientation	Collegial/participative	Authoritarian/paternalistic
	Context independent	Context dependent

Source: Adapted from Kanungo and Jaeger, 1992, p. 8.

Note: This table lists some of the important dimensions that make for considerable differences in context between many developed and developing countries. They will of course not hold true in all instances.

tural validity.[6] Its low profile significantly diminishes our understanding of why development succeeds or fails.

3. **Privilege, power, and (dis)empowerment:** Privilege and power are central to, yet invisible in most theories about how change happens and results are achieved and measured. Much in development and evaluation does not work because such issues are not considered and the lingering and ongoing disempowerment of individuals, systems, communities, and nations is not addressed. Measuring real change in all its complexities is difficult and time-consuming. This situation is thus increasingly challenging with the renewed focus on reductionist, simplistic "quick fix" technical solutions and linear ideas of change, and which usually do not focus on power, empowerment, or sustainability. Evaluation needs to expose rather than support this trend.

4. **Dealing with constraints:** The constraints normally affecting individuals, institutions, and evaluators are magnified in developing, and especially in fragile, countries. These constraints can have a dire effect on the pace and quality of development. Development trajectories therefore need to be much more carefully considered. More attention should be paid to identifying and strengthening processes and systems that may enhance the chance of impact. The current tendency to focus almost exclusively on measuring impact means that too little is understood about how to "manage for impact."

5. **Evaluation as a respected and useful practice:** It is challenging to establish monitoring and evaluation as a credible, empowering, and useful practice in environments where evaluation is not a tradition or part of the culture, where power differentials are marked, where it has in the past served the interests of a few (usually external agencies or the ruling elite), or where agencies in power have the motivation and means to disregard the results. This has to be addressed with more vigor by those who theorize about, commission, and conduct evaluation.

6. **Sustaining development:** A major reason for development failure is the lack of focus by policymakers, planners, and evaluators on development that can endure. The current trend to emphasize complexity has the unfortunate side-effect that nothing appears predictable. Yet much can be done when designing and implementing initiatives to enhance the chance that the development benefits will be sustained. Evaluators have to focus more on understanding resilience, transformative change, and other influences on sustainability. These aspects are too often neglected.

CONCLUDING COMMENTS

In sum, we argue that evaluators should be more sensitive to, and innovative around, challenges that are typically more pronounced in developing than developed countries. Development trajectories and transformative change in developing contexts are more difficult to predict. Contexts in which interventions play out vary enormously, often in ways invisible to the observer. Communities are typically heterogeneous. Sociocultural beliefs and practices differ markedly within countries, while the practice of democracy differs from country to country. Very significant differentials in privilege, power, and confidence complicate evaluations and the politics that surround them. It is important to factor in the political economy of change that addresses issues of entrenched vested interests and the inherent preference for status quo. It is also not easy to define and measure outcomes in these highly complex and diverse environments. For example, how do we define empowerment, capacity strengthening, or sustainable livelihoods in different cultures—often in one country—and in an equitable manner for groups with different degrees of vulnerability? How do we convincingly capture growth in inner strength, in aspects such as self-esteem and confidence—changes that make a major difference among the disempowered? And how do we prevent dire negative consequences or negative outcomes in our complex and fluid environments? Compounding these dimensions are the many common constraints that limit the effectiveness of development evaluation—limited data, information, financial resources, evaluation, and civil society engagement and participation.

There is a dire need in the development evaluation community for *more visible* creativity and innovation in addressing in practice the aspects outlined above. This is a challenge especially for indigenous evaluators in countries where the evaluation profession is relatively new. We need to draw from the most useful and credible international theories and practices in development and in evaluation, and build where appropriate on indigenous knowledge and value systems, experiences, and wisdom. We need to collaborate across many disciplines, engage unconventional thinkers and practitioners, and influence evaluation commissioners and users to address critical issues that might otherwise not receive sufficient attention. How else can development evaluation achieve its potential?

NOTES

1. Nations where all or large groups of the population have a low level of human development, including low levels of material well-being and limited capabilities to enjoy a long and healthy life in a safe environment. They usually lack continuous, self-sustaining economic growth and score relatively low on the human development index. Many dislike the "inferiority" implied in the term and the perceived need to "develop" according to Western notions.

2. It is admittedly controversial to define characteristics across "developing countries" as a group; some of the statements may hold more true for certain parts of the world. While caution is needed, it does not negate the need to reflect on the issues in this document.

3. For a set of papers on human development, see Fukuda-Parr and Shiva Kumar (2009).

4. For a comprehensive discussion see, in particular, United Nations Development Programme (2000). *Human Development Report 2000.* Oxford University Press, New York; Commonwealth Human Rights Initiative (2001). *Millennium report—Human rights and poverty eradication: A Talisman for the commonwealth.* New Delhi; and Centre for Development and Human Rights (2004). *The right to development: A primer.* Sage Publications, New Delhi.

5. Some of the resistance to the widespread use of randomized control trials stems from their insufficient focus on complexity and contextuality.

6. "Multicultural" validity refers to the correctness or authenticity of understandings across multiple, intersecting (socio)cultural contexts, and focuses attention on how well evaluation captures meaning across dimensions of cultural diversity. It considers (i) the role of culture in the theoretical foundations of the evaluation; (ii) the cultural appropriateness of the design and tools; (iii) the relationship and interactions between and among participants in the evaluation process; (iv) the local knowledge and lived experience of

the stakeholders; and (v) the potential social consequences of the insights, judgements, and actions resulting from the evaluation (Kirkhart, 2010).

REFERENCE

Bamberger, M., Rugh, J., & Mabry, L. (2012). RealWorld evaluation. Working under budget, time, data, and political constraints. (2nd ed.). Sage Publications, Inc.

Centre for Development and Human Rights (2004). *The right to development: A primer.* Sage Publications, New Delhi.

Commission on Human Security (2003). Human security now. Commission on human security/UNOPS (United Nations Office for Project Services), New York.

Commonwealth Human Rights Initiative (2001). *Millennium report—Human rights and poverty eradication: A Talisman for the commonwealth.* New Delhi.

Fukuda-Parr, S. & Shiva Kumar, A. K. (2009). Handbook of human development: Concepts, measures, and policies. New Delhi: Oxford University Press.

Hood, S., Hopson, R., & Frierson, H. (2005). The Role of culture and cultural context: A mandate for inclusion, discovery of truth and understanding in evaluation theory and practice. Greenwich, CT: Information Age Publishing, Inc.

Kanungo, R. N. & Jaeger, A. M. (Eds.).(1990). Management in developing countries. London and New York: Routledge.

Kirkhart, K. E. (2010). Eyes on the prize: Multicultural validity and evaluation theory. *American Journal of Evaluation, 31*(3), 400–413.

Sen, A. (1999). *Development as freedom.* New Delhi: Oxford University Press.

United Nations Development Programme (2000). *Human Development Report 2000.* Oxford University Press, New York

CHAPTER 3

ORGANIZATIONAL PERFORMANCE ASSESSMENT

Charles Lusthaus and Katrina Rojas

ORGANIZATIONAL PERFORMANCE ASSESSMENT

Over the past decades, the evaluation community has focused almost all of its attention on evaluating projects and programs. The Organization for Economic Cooperation and Development—Development Assistance Committee (OECD-DAC), which is the most common reference point for international development evaluation criteria, terminology, and standards, has given little guidance on assessing organizations. Their materials refer to "development interventions" as a general term to indicate the subject of the evaluation, and while this may refer to an activity, project, program, strategy, policy, topic, sector, operational area, or institutional performance (OECD-DAC, 2010), the thrust of the guidelines is the project and program. Thus, in development evaluation practice, the "organization" as a unit of analysis remains a black box.[1]

In the United States and Canada,[2] evaluation practice has also focused largely on evaluating projects and programs. The majority of sessions at any evaluation conference, such as the Canadian Evaluation Society (CES) and American Evaluation Association (AEA), and listserves do not focus on the organization as the unit of analysis. For example, at the 2009 Annual

Emerging Practices in International Development Evaluation, pages 25–73

AEA conference, only eight out of 621 sessions (1.3%) discussed issues specifically related to organizational assessment, and most of these focused on some dimension of organizational capacity building.

In contrast to this lack of attention to evaluating organizational performance, donors are increasing their investments in organizations such as government ministries, international financial institutions (IFIs), other multilateral organizations, NGOs, and research institutions. Many bilateral and multilateral donors are moving away from project funding to more program and institutional funding, and they are raising concerns about the tools available for understanding these organizations to which they are entrusting considerable funds. Donor agencies that invest in multilateral organizations as a way of fulfilling their missions are increasingly attempting to gain a deeper understanding of the performance of these organizations, not only in terms of their contributions to development results, but also in terms of the capacities they have in place to support results achievement.

Although organizational assessments are being considered as a key tool within the broad continuum of public sector performance management, unlike project and program evaluations, they are not yet institutionalized within government policies. Linking the assessment of the performance of an organization to the assessment of the projects and programs that it carries out appears to be a logical step for performance improvement—a step that will catapult the importance of organizational assessment as a useful tool for evaluators.

UNDERSTANDING ORGANIZATIONS AND THEIR PERFORMANCE—AN EVOLUTION

Early studies about organizations assumed that they existed to serve a purpose (Clegg et al., 2006) and that the role of management was to support this purpose by strategically gathering and applying resources in an efficient manner. However, experience showed that organizations did not serve one single purpose, but had multiple goals and subgoals (Quinn & Rohrbaugh, 1983), some of which supported the original organizing purpose, while others did not. Furthermore, those studying organizations suggested that organizations are social constructions, and that managers, staff, and people observing organizations construct their own meaning of what an organization is and how it ought to perform.

In practice, it was found that an organization's goals were constantly being displaced by the actors of the organization. They were displaced in a variety of ways: Time changed people's perceptions of the goals; leaders sometimes changed the goals; organizational events caused a shift in priorities; and sometimes changes in the environment, law, or political situation inadvertently acted as counterproductive forces and inhibited the achievement of objectives. Given this complexity, how were organizations and their constituents to know if they were moving in the right direction? How were they to measure performance and the factors associated with good performance?

Caplow argued that "every organization has work to do in the real world and some way of measuring how well that work is done" (Caplow, 1976, p. 90). His concept of organizational performance was based on common sense and the notion that organizations need a way of concretely identifying their purpose and assessing how well they are doing in relation to it. According to Caplow, each organization does have a sense of what it is doing and ways of assessing success; in other words, it has an institutional definition of its own purpose.

Since it was clear to most people and managers that organizations that did not make money went out of business, private firms used the common-sense concept of profit as a way to judge their performance. Thus, at the simplest level, measuring the profit of an organization was a way of assessing how well the organization was doing. Profit is indeed an important and valid aspect of performance in the private sector, and many managers use profitability as a metaphor for an organization's success. In government and nonprofit organizations, however, ideas about what constituted success were much less clear. We all knew that schools helped children learn and that many foundations wanted to reduce poverty, but there was no root concept equivalent to profit that could be used to access their success.

Creating methodologies to assess profitability as a primary objective in the private sector was congruent with prevailing ideologies shaping management practices at the time. Management theorists in the early part of the century tended to focus on devising scientific or engineering methods of increasing financial gain (Taylor, 1947). In support of such management objectives, organizational assessment focused on identifying ways to improve the efficiency of workers. By "engineering" optimal ways for people to behave in specific organizational production systems, managers aimed to produce more goods for less money, thereby increasing profits.

Starting in the 1940s, more abstract and generic conceptions of performance (Table 3.1) began to emerge in the discourse on organizational performance (Likert, 1958). Gradually, concepts such as "effectiveness," "efficiency," and "employee morale" gained ground in the management literature and, by the 1960s, were considered to be major components of successful organizations (Campbell et al., 1970). Managers understood an organization to be performing if it achieved its intended goals (effectiveness) and used relatively few resources in doing so (efficiency).[3] In this new context, profit became just one of several indicators of performance. The implicit goal shaping most definitions of organizational performance was the ability to survive. Thus, organizational assessment focused on the extent to

TABLE 3.1 Overview of Definitions: What is an "excellent," "successful," or "performing" organization?

Author	Definition	Year	Emphasis
Weber	Some believed that the most efficient organizational form was bureaucracy. The assumption was that the more bureaucratic the organization, the better performing and efficient it would be.	1947	Use of resources (efficiency)
Georgopoulos & Tannenbaum	The extent to which an organization as a social system fulfilled its objectives	1957	Fulfilling its objectives (effectiveness)
Yuchtman & Seashore	The ability to exploit its environment in the acquisition of scarce and valued resources to sustain its functioning	1967	Exploiting its environment and sustaining its functioning
Cf. Price	Most research and discussion on organizational performance within the social sciences has been devoted to a study of the conditions under which organizations achieve different levels of effectiveness.	1968	Effectiveness and its necessary conditions
Peters & Waterman	Eight attributes to characterize the distinction of excellent companies: a bias for action, close to the customer; autonomy and entrepreneurship, productivity through people, hands-on and value driven, stick to the knitting; simple form and lean staff, simultaneous loose-tight properties (these build on the 7-S model described in chapter 3)	1982	Organizational capacities
Harrison	Special emphasis is given to models for examining organizational and division-level factors, such as organization-environment relations and the fit between organizational structures and technologies. This emphasis reflects the growing recognition in organizational studies of the powerful impact of such factors on organizational effectiveness.	1987	Emphasis on externalities and their impact on performance
Kilmann	Organizational success is a matter of creating and maintaining high performance and satisfaction for both internal and external stakeholders over an extended period of time.	1989	Emphasis on perspectives in assessing Performance

(continued)

TABLE 3.1 Overview of Definitions: What is an "excellent," "successful," or "performing" organization? (continued)

Author	Definition	Year	Emphasis
Kaplan & Norton	The balanced scorecard is a strategic management system. It provides a summary of performance and performance measures that originally related to financial performance, customer knowledge, internal business processes, and learning and growth (these have been adapted by organizations in different sectors). The balanced scorecard approach to metrics is widely used as part of a strategy for managing performance.	1996	Performance as a multidimensional idea that must be measured and managed
Hervé Corvellec	An organization's performance is a series of meaningful statements recounting what has been achieved in and by the organization within a given period of time. As an account of organizational activity, the performance of an organization is a tale, a narrative.	1997	Organizational achievements (effectiveness, efficiency)
IDRC/Universalia	When an organization balances effectiveness, efficiency and relevance while being financially viable.	2002	Performance as a multidimensional idea
Greene	There is a difference between the activity of performance and the result of performance. The definition of performance should only include the activity of performance.	2007	Emphasis is on inputs rather than results
Stannard-Stockton, Sean	A high performance non-profit is a very well run organization. It has outstanding leadership, clear goals, an ethic of monitoring performance and makes adjustments as needed, and it is financially healthy.	2009	Performance associated with capacities and financial viability

which an organization was able to meet its goals within reasonable resource parameters and in doing so make a profit.

Gradually, it became clear that organizational assessment needed to go beyond the measurement of these rather simplistic ideas (Levinson, 1972). A host of factors emerged as important components to be factored into the assessment equation: the present and future utility of the organization's products and services, productivity, systems, quality, customer satisfaction, innovation, and relevance. Organizational assessment was gradually becoming more holistic, attempting to integrate as many aspects of an organization as possible (Gaebler & Osborne, 1992; Harrison, 1987; Levinson, 1972; Meyer & Scott, 1992). Furthermore, assessing organizations was more complex than originally thought. Evaluating or assessing the performance of an organization was anything but a mechanical venture. For example, when Peters and Waterman (1982) searched for excellent organizations, they found organizations that met their constructed criteria, but it is less than certain that they were in fact excellent organizations, performing well.

It is clear from engaging in such assessments that assessing organizations and their performance is a murky business in the profit world and even more so in the not-for-profit world where there are few industry-wide agreed-to criteria of organizational success. Few government agencies, not-for-profit organizations, and foundations go out of business, and few of these same organizations have success criteria that they identify, monitor, and use for decision making over time.

What we have found is that at best we can provide ways of understanding and constructing frameworks and methodologies for helping those adventurous souls in the government, not-for-profit, and foundation world explore their performance through frameworks that can be supported by systematic assessments.

DEFINING ORGANIZATIONAL PERFORMANCE ASSESSMENT

Thus, the question still remains, what is organizational performance assessment? Immordino (2010, p. 7) describes it as "a systematic process for examining an organization to create a shared understanding of the current state of the elements that are critical to the successful achievement of its purpose." In our own practice, we have defined it as a systematic process for obtaining valid information about the performance of an organization and the factors that affect performance. It is a type of evaluation in which the tools of organizational assessment are used to judge the level of performance.

An organizational performance assessment (OPA) differs from other types of evaluations (such as policy, program, and project evaluations) because the assessment focuses on the organization as the primary unit of analysis (i.e., the performance of an *organization*, not the performance of a project, a program, or a policy). It is conducted to help investors or funders make investment decisions and identify possible areas for improvement. Breaking our definition down into its component parts helps identify the key principles of OPA.

First and foremost, OPA is a systematic process or series of actions aimed at answering a set of questions about an organization. It provides a structured framework for collecting, analyzing, and evaluating information that is organizational in nature.

Process

In the OPA context, "process" means a sequence of steps and a planned methodology. The process used for conducting the assessment is in many ways as important as the results obtained. It is the emphasis on process in OPA that helps to ensure that the assessment is responsive to the context in which the organization operates, taking into account culture, power relationships, and other variables.

While the process may vary along a number of dimensions, it always involves people working together to better understand the performance and functioning of an organization within its own context. It provides a way to involve members of the organization in seeking the needed information and may also involve them in other components of the assessment processes. The success of the process, and of the relationships created in the course of conducting an assessment, can influence the degree to which the organization will take ownership of the OPA and any changes that may ensue. Thus, the process is inextricably linked to the extent to which the assessment is used, creating a feedback loop.

Systematic

In an OPA, "systematic" means having a structured way of collecting information in which decisions are made carefully and conscientiously about the scope and depth of information that is available, how it is to be obtained, and how it will be used. Stakeholders must have confidence that the information provided in an OPA is trustworthy. It should be collected, processed, and analyzed using the same standards as any other applied social science activity, and should provide the best evidence available to answer the questions posed.

Improving Performance

In addition to knowing how well an organization is performing, we want to know what it can do to improve its performance. Here again, there are a wide range of ideas and concepts (hypotheses, if you will) that can be identified through an OPA as ways to improve performance. For example, is having a clear strategy known to all organizational members a quality that supports improved organizational performance? While there may be any number of changes that an organization can make to try to improve performance, one of the purposes of engaging in OPA is to identify the changes that are feasible. The underlying premise of the authors is that the purpose of organizational assessment is to provide a perspective on the organization that might improve the organization and its performance. This approach to performance and performance improvement takes into account the broader context or systems that the organization is a part of.

In short, an organizational performance assessment should be an ordered, systematic method of gathering data on the performance of the organization, its environment, and the various component parts that support the performance and functioning of the organization.

FRAMEWORKS AND MODELS

Overview

A number of models and frameworks for organizational diagnosis and assessment have been developed and applied over the years. Many of these link the use of assessment to *organizational development,* traditionally conceived as an "effort planned organization-wide and managed from the top, to increase organizational effectiveness and health through planned interventions in the organization's processes using behavioural science knowledge" (Immordino,2010, p. 10)[4] An OA thus often feeds into a change process that aims to identify areas in which the organization can initiate improvements in order to reach a higher level of performance; however that may be defined as more effective, more efficient, and so on.

In this section, we provide an overview of frameworks and models that have been recognized as good practices or approaches to organizational assessment at different times. These generations of frameworks, so to speak, can be broadly classified into three types:

1. Models/frameworks that identify best practices or standards associated with "strong performance" or "organizational excellence"

2. Models/frameworks that aim to explore relationships among variables or concepts, some of them based on empirical evidence
3. Results frameworks, which provide an implicit definition of organizational performance that focuses on results achievement

These models or frameworks have generally had their origins in North America, although several of them have been adapted for and tested in developing country contexts. At least one of them has been designed with the developing country context in mind (IDRC/Universalia). All of the models/frameworks face some limitations in relation to addressing the full complexity of the systems that organizations are a part of.[5]

Models and Frameworks that Identify Best Practices

Most models and frameworks that have been used in this field identify a set of organizational practices that are associated with strong organizational performance or organizational excellence. These are often developed into what are referred to as "capacity checklists."

Seven-S Framework

The Seven-S Framework (also known as the McKinsey 7-S Framework) was one of the first models of organizational assessment to be popularized almost thirty years ago (Pascale & Athos, 1981; Peters & Waterman, 1982). It was one of the first to incorporate a holistic or "systems" perspective in which the interrelationships of key components are seen to determine overall system performance. It was also one of the first popular models to give sustained attention to organizational "software," such as human behavioral factors (management style, shared values, staff, and skills) as part of a systematic approach to organizational assessment. The Seven-S Framework (see Figure 3.1) looks at the following seven variables:

- Structure
- Strategy
- Skills
- Style
- Staff
- Shared values
- Systems

However, the original model focused more on activities inside the organization than outside (i.e., it did not look at how the environment affected the organization). Nor did it address a wide variety of organizational issues

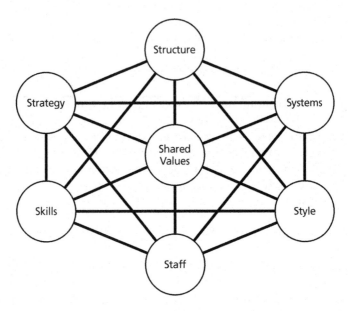

Figure 3.1 Seven-S framework. *Source:* http://www.mindtools.com/pages/article/newSTR_91.htm

such as sustainability, access to financing, power and control, clients and beneficiaries, and many others. Although the model describes the organizational variables and recognizes the importance of the interrelationships among them, it does not explain how each dimension affects the other (Burke & Litwin, 1992). The Seven S Framework is used widely in the international development community and, in adapting the framework, several of these concepts—such as sustainability and relationship to external environment—have been incorporated.[6]

Malcolm Baldrige Model

This model, which is the basis for the Malcolm Baldrige National Quality Award (MBNQA) in the United States,[7] provides standards for organizational excellence that can be applied from sector to sector. In general terms, the framework suggests that organizational excellence requires:[8]

- Leadership—Examines how senior executives guide the organization and how the organization addresses its responsibilities to the public and practices good citizenship
- Strategic planning—Examines how the organization sets strategic directions and how it determines key action plans
- Customer focus—Examines how the organization determines requirements and expectations of customers and markets; builds

relationships with customers; and acquires, satisfies, and retains customers

- Measurement, analysis, and knowledge management—Examines the management, effective use, analysis, and improvement of data and information to support key organization processes and the organization's performance management system
- Workforce focus—Examines how the organization enables its workforce to develop its full potential and how the workforce is aligned with the organization's objectives
- Process management—Examines aspects of how key production/delivery and support processes are designed, managed, and improved
- Results—Examines the organization's performance and improvement in its key business areas: customer satisfaction, financial and marketplace performance, human resources, supplier and partner performance, operational performance, and governance and social responsibility. The category also examines how the organization performs relative to competitors.

Models and Frameworks that Explore Relationships between Concepts or Variables

The Causal Model of Organizational Performance and Change, or the Burke & Litwin Model

This model emerged from the authors' desire to create a guide for both organizational diagnosis and planned management organization change (Burke & Litwin, 1992). It suggests linkages that hypothesize how performance is affected by internal and external factors. It provides a framework to assess organizational and environmental dimensions that are keys to successful change, and it demonstrates how these dimensions should be linked causally to achieve a change in performance. The model links what could be understood from practice to what is known from research and theory.

The model revolves around 12 organizational dimensions that draw on the variables put forward by other models. Although presented here as a simple list, the model is complex and aims to depict relationships between variables and explicitly account for variables at different levels of an organizational system, from group and local work unit ideas to the individual level (Burke & Litwin, 1992):

- External environment
- Mission and strategy
- Leadership
- Organizational culture

- Structure
- Management practices
- Systems
- Work unit climate
- Task and individual skills
- Individual needs and values
- Motivation
- Individual and organizational performance

Universalia/IDRC Organizational Assessment Framework

As noted above, Universalia sees performance as a multidimensional idea, defined in our framework as the balance between effectiveness, relevance, efficiency, financial viability (see Figure 3.2). Each of these concepts is defined and draws on definitions used in the literature. The underlying assumption is that organizations do not exist in a vacuum. They are affected by a number of external and internal factors. In designing the Universalia/IDRC framework, we reviewed the literature to identify the factors that seemed to drive change in organizations. Three key ideas emerged from this review: (1) organizations change because of their external environment, which is the notion of "adaptation" that is often referenced with

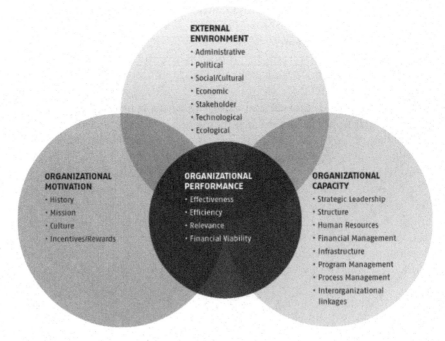

Figure 3.2   The Universalia/IDRC framework.

regard to drivers of change; (2) organizations also change as their internal resources change (financial, human, technology, etc.); and (3) organizations change when there are fundamental shifts in values that affect climate, culture, and ways of operating.

This exploration led Universalia/IDRC to posit that performance is a function of an organization's enabling environment, organizational motivation, and capacity. The framework aims to understand the relationship between these factors and the organization's level of performance. Only in understanding these factors will improvement come from organizational assessment.

The framework includes an assessment of "capacities" that are also considered in the frameworks and models described above, but explicitly adds the concepts of external environment and internal motivation (or organizational culture) as key factors that drive performance in an organization.

The Universalia/IDRC organizational assessment framework (Figure 3.2) explores the relationships between the factors that affect performance and the actual performance of an organization, but there still is limited empirical evidence to help understand if and how those factors affect performance. For example, we assume that having clear strategic plans/inclusive planning processes will have positive effects on performance. Based on experience, we can say that this is a supportive factor, but we do not have the empirical evidence to back this up. Nor do we have the kind of evidence that would help to define the crucial variables in the performance equation for different types of organizations.

Models and Frameworks Focused on Results and Metrics

Organizational Results Frameworks

The frameworks noted above emerged from reflection on the nature of organizations and organizational excellence and performance, and the factors that are believed to relate to performance. However, there is another basis for assessing the performance of organizations that emerges from the changing culture of public administration and its increasing emphasis on accountability for results and outcomes.

Through federal legislation in the United States (Accountability Act, 1993) and Canada (Federal Accountability Act, 2006), central agencies are holding departments accountable through departmental and results frameworks. This approach is characterized by measuring progress towards the results that are sought, having the flexibility to adjust operations to better meet these expectations, and reporting on the outcomes accomplished (Mayne, 2001). This has led to growing emphasis on results frameworks—in Canada, for example, the Results Management and Accountability Framework (RMAF) —as a basis for measuring, reporting on, and assessing organizational performance. In other words, an organization is assessed based on the outputs, outcomes, and impacts that it achieves.

Internationally, there has been a continued emphasis and increased momentum on managing for results. Policies and frameworks in the international context provide explanations of the importance of results-based management (RBM) for ensuring that management practices optimize value for money and the use of human and financial resources. Donor agencies that invest in multilateral organizations as a way of fulfilling their missions are increasingly trying to gain a deeper understanding of the performance of these organizations, both their contributions to development results and the capacities in place to support results achievement. From the perspective of these donors, many multilaterals are improving their results frameworks and data-gathering systems, but these are not yet developed enough across organizations to be used as the basis for a systematic effectiveness assessment (MOPAN, 2010). As a result, performance information is sought through other means, such as the approach adopted by the Multilateral Organization Performance Assessment Network (MOPAN), which aims to draw on perceptions and secondary data in order to assess organizational performance in terms of systems, behaviors, and practices (or organizational capacities) that are viewed to be important in achieving development results. In 2012, MOPAN also began to explore questions related to the actual results achieved by these organizations.

The Balanced Scorecard

The Balanced Scorecard (Kaplan & Norton, 1996) emerged from concerns about performance measurement approaches in the corporate sector that focused exclusively on financial measures. The unidimensional focus was seen to limit an organization's ability to develop a future strategy that could create future economic value. Thus, a scorecard that looked at how an organization was doing from different perspectives—initially conceived as financial, customer, internal business process, and learning and growth perspectives—became the pillar of an approach to managing and measuring organizational performance. The Balanced Scorecard provided a framework that could be used for strategy/planning as well as for monitoring and assessment.

The Balanced Scorecard has been one of the driving forces in emphasizing the importance of measuring performance. Indeed we have seen growing efforts to develop "numbers" that explain performance and that enable comparison or tracking of performance over time or across organizations. Graham Brown (2007) recognized the need for a more evolved scorecard with metrics that more accurately measure complicated dimensions of an organization's performance. In his critique of the first generation of scorecards, he noted the lack of measurement of ethics—for example, and the absence of external factors that could have an impact on the organization's success.

CONDUCTING AN ORGANIZATIONAL PERFORMANCE ASSESSMENT

Overview

This chapter provides an overview of the steps involved in an assessment of organizational performance, which include selecting a conceptual framework, deciding who will conduct the OPA, determining the issues and key questions, identifying appropriate measures/indicators, deciding on data collection methods, and constructing an organizational performance assessment (OPA) matrix.

Selecting a Conceptual Framework

It is important to begin with a coherent conceptual framework for conducting the OPA and analyzing the OPA data. As noted in previous sections, there are a number of models or frameworks that can be used to conduct an organizational performance assessment. Any of the models described can be used. It is important for the evaluator to consider which framework or combination of frameworks will be most appropriate for the organization that will be assessed and the cultural context in which it operates.

Deciding Who Will Conduct the Organizational Performance Assessment

One of the first considerations in designing an organizational performance assessment is to decide who will conduct the assessment—the organization itself (a self-assessment), an external consultant, or a combination of the two? Each approach has potential advantages and limitations. This decision will have implications for how the process is conducted and who is involved in making subsequent decisions about the exact methods and measures to use in the process. The decision about how to conduct the assessment must take into consideration issues of culture, power relationships within the organization and in the broader system in which it operates, and capacity or other constraints.

Self-Assessment
Self-assessment is an approach to organizational performance assessment (OPA) in which the organization itself has considerable control over the assessment (see Table 3.2). When an organization engages in a self-assessment, it manages the assessment either on its own or with the support of

TABLE 3.2   Self-Assessment Processes: Strengths and Limitations

Strengths/Benefits	Limitations/Considerations
• Encourages ownership and engagement in a learning process • People in the organization have easy access to data • Enhances sense of dignity and self-respect • Increases perception of the fairness of the process • Increases acceptance of feedback because it promotes self-reflection • Increases commitment to recommendations • Reduces background research on the organization by providing current information about the organization and existing data • Cost benefits: does not require time-consuming procurement negotiations, and may not need to draw on a separate budget line	• The independence of the assessment may be questioned by external stakeholders concerned about the validity of findings • The external concern that hard issues may not be tackled • The process requires a great deal of managerial time • Because the players are involved with the content of the assessment and have some stake in the organization, sensitivities can be strong. A clear definition of the roles and of the process at the outset can help ease tensions. • The notion of self-assessment is not necessarily accepted in all cultures, and group discussions of the issues may be uncomfortable for people in some cultures or organizations.

an external facilitator or coach who helps to guide the assessment process. Donors often have input into a self-assessment process, but the assessment questions, data collection, analysis, and report are done by the organization or under the management of the organization.

External Assessment

The most common situation occurs when donors hire external consultants to conduct independent OPAs. In an external assessment, the donor is responsible for the overall management of the assessment, and both the donor and the organization being reviewed define the basic issues and questions to be explored, but it is the external assessor or evaluator that is responsible for making judgments about the organization's performance and for ensuring the independence of the final product (Table 3.3). While stakeholder input is sought throughout the OPA process, the external consultant determines the methodology and manages the data collection, analysis, and reporting.

External consultants should strive to design a participatory approach to the OPA from the outset. There are many benefits to a participatory organizational assessment process. For the organization, the participation of stakeholders throughout the OPA gives them greater opportunities to develop a sense of ownership and commitment to the assessment and its results and provides greater opportunities for organizational learning, improvement, and even for generating support from other donors. For a do-

TABLE 3.3   External Assessment Processes: Strengths and Limitations

Strengths/Benefits	Limitations/Considerations
External assessments are often viewed as more independent and objective	Fewer opportunities for the organization to develop leadership/ownership for the OPA process and results
External assessments improve the range of issues addressed and the reliability of findings	Requires more time for contract negotiation, orientation and supervision
The donor can specify requirements for consultant expertise	Time spent on site may be limited by costs
External consultants:	External consultants:
• can focus exclusively on the OPA (as they are not distracted by other organizational work)	• may not know the organization, its policies and procedures, or the available data
• can help to save time and handle very sensitive issues	• may be perceived as adversaries, arousing unnecessary anxiety
• are more likely to be available for intensive work within required timeframes	• may not be aware of constraints on feasibility of recommendations, and are not contracted to follow up on them
• may bring fresh perspectives and state-of-the-art knowledge	External consultants require that partners invest time in supporting and assisting them during the process
External consulting teams enriched with local consultants can obtain a much better sense of the issues in the sub-regions, adapt data collection tools to the context, and lower the overall costs of the study.	

nor agency, a participatory OPA gives the donor information that can help it in due diligence and decisions about investing in the partner organization. However, participatory processes can be more time consuming and therefore more costly to implement, so this needs to be factored into the budget for the assignment.

Mixed Models

There are also a wide variety of mixed models that integrate different aspects of the assessment approaches described above (Table 3.4). For example, an organization may carry out a self-assessment with assistance from an independent evaluator who can provide a suitable methodological framework, coach an internal team to develop appropriate tools, participate in and give advice on data collection and analysis, and review and comment on overall findings and/or reports.

Determining the Issues and Key Questions

The performance issues or criteria to be explored by the OPA provide the basis for the design of an appropriate methodology. What is an accept-

TABLE 3.4   Mixed Models for Assessment: Strengths and Limitations

Strengths/Benefits	Limitations/Considerations
• Can combine benefits of self-assessment (especially organizational buy-in, active participation in the OPA process, and acceptance and ownership of OPA findings) with the benefits of an external OPA (i.e., independent and objective, ability to address sensitive issues not mentioned to colleagues or supervisors, experience in design and facilitation of OPA processes). • Can broaden the issues and perspectives covered in the assessment and thus increase the possibility that findings will be used.	• Not as independent and objective as an external assessment • Can be more time consuming than external OPA or self-assessment as more players are involved and need to be brought 'up to speed' • Needs to be managed carefully to avoid becoming a 'token' participatory approach (e.g., if intent is to include self-assessment components, these need to be carefully planned and managed).

able definition of performance in the organization's broader culture? What are the main performance issues in the organization? The definition of these issues will be based on the context for the organization and conceptual approach that is chosen for the OPA. In other words, the identification of the issues and questions must be context-specific. Some examples of performance issues and key questions, based on the Universalia/IDRC framework, are provided in Table 3.5.

As in other types of evaluation, there is a need to further break down the key questions into subquestions that will help to understand these issues. In the Universalia/IDRC framework, for example, there is a compendium of potential questions that relate to each of the elements that comprise performance (effectiveness, relevance, efficiency, financial viability) and the factors that affect the organization's performance (capacity, motivation, and the environment). In preparing an assessment framework, one can refer to this checklist of subquestions (included in Appendix A) that may be relevant to include but will need to be tailored to the organization assessed.

TABLE 3.5   Examples of Performance Issues and Key Questions

Performance Issue	Examples of Key Questions to ask in an OPA
Effectiveness	How effective is the organization in working towards its mission?
Relevance	How relevant is the organization to its stakeholders?
Efficiency	How efficient is the organization in the use of its human, financial, and physical resources?
Financial Viability	Is the organization financially viable?

Once a satisfactory set of questions has been developed to explore the key issues, these should be prioritized according to:

- Resource levels—the time required and resources available to answer the question
- Purpose of the OPA—if the organization has determined that the primary purpose is accountability, for example, then the prioritization might favour questions that will help to respond to this aim.
- Stakeholder interest—since some questions may be more important to one set of stakeholders than another, the selection of questions will need to reflect a balance of stakeholder needs.

Identifying Appropriate Measures/Indicators

Performance measures and performance indicators are essentially synonymous. As defined by Harbour (2009, p. 10), a performance indicator is a "comparative performance metric used to answer the question, 'How are we doing?' along a specific performance dimension and associated performance goal." There is no one set of best practice measures or indicators that can be used for assessing the performance of organizations. In an OPA, the important element to keep in mind is that these must be measures of *organizational* performance.

Simply stated, indicators should provide concrete, simple, and reliable measures to answer assessment questions. Indicators can be quantitative or qualitative. In general, quantitative indicators are numeric representations (e.g., the number of refereed research articles written as a result of a project). Qualitative indicators are less tangible and not always easy to count and are often based on perceptions of a situation (e.g., descriptions of the ways people found the research useful).

In Appendix B, we have provided examples of indicators for each of the performance dimensions in the IDRC/Universalia framework, as well as a guide on performance indicators for municipalities, which was developed several years ago to help the Federation of Canadian Municipalities implement organizational performance self-assessments. In all the organizations we worked with, the most difficult part of the diagnosis was identifying indicators. Sometimes this was because of an abundance of suggested indicators and the difficulty of weeding out the ones that really mattered—that answered the assessment questions. Indicators are not the starting point. To develop a good indicator, you first need a clear picture of what you are trying to measure. Then, you will want to consider the relevant data you need, the possible sources of data (there may be many), and the availability and feasibility of getting it. Finally, you may want to consider some of the more subtle implications of indicators:

- Measuring something can give it importance—Measuring an organization can change organizational activities, for better or for worse. For example, if the number of experiments conducted by researchers is used as a performance indicator in an OA of a research institution, some may see this as encouraging quantity over quality of research. Or, if the number of people served in a community is used as an indicator in the OA of a social service agency, this might lead some to believe that they should try to increase the numbers and reduce the time spent with each person.
- Measuring complex dynamics may require a set of indicators—It can be challenging to develop adequate indicators to measure the complex dynamics in an organization. Simple indicators may not always fit the bill and may need to be combined. Most organizations develop a set of carefully considered indicators and modify them over time as they analyze their results.
- Indicators may be interpreted in different ways by different stakeholders—What seems like a straightforward indicator to the assessment team may sometimes point out an organizational paradox or give conflicting signals. For example, an indicator that measures diversification of funding as a measure of financial viability could be seen as both positive and negative. On the positive side, diversification is an indication that the organization is not overly reliant on one donor. However, others may think of this measurement in a different way, as having multiple donors (each with its own priorities, expectations, systems, and evaluation and reporting requirements) can lead to fragmentation and increased costs in managing multiple donor requirements.

In developing indicators for an OPA, it is worth considering some emerging trends with regard to good organizational measures of performance. The Balanced Scorecard approach is generating growing organizational experience in the definition of metrics that can be used to measure organizational performance. These metrics, however, often fall short of providing what organizations need to know (Graham Brown, 2007). For example, most measures on scorecards are measures of the past (e.g., financial measures), measures that may lack integrity or are too easy to manipulate, or measures that do not provide an accurate reflection of what is really going on (e.g., customer satisfaction or human resource metrics that are still rudimentary).

The problem with single measures is that they do not offer enough information either to tell an organization how it is really performing or to diagnose the causes of decline (or improvement) in performance. Thus, Graham Brown (2007) proposes greater use of "analytics" or composite measures, which focus on a particular aspect of performance and are made up of a series of submetrics. The challenge in designing an OPA is to identify what composite measures are important and determine their submeasures.

Deciding on Data Collection Methods

OPAs follow in the tradition of *case study* or *multiple case study* methodologies. A case study is a qualitative form of assessment that draws on both qualitative and quantitative data and relies on multiple sources of information. Organizational performance assessments are expected to reflect on multiple sources of data to gain insight into the organization. The choice of the methods is dependent on the specific circumstances for the organization and its stakeholders. We have used the following methods in carrying out organizational assessments:

- Document review—For most OPA questions, some type of documentation is available. This includes reports, file data, memoranda, staff lists, policy handbooks, meeting minutes, Board handbook (usually a collection of board policies, roles and responsibilities, etc.), previous studies, audits, assessments, reviews, and so forth.
- Stakeholder interviews—Stakeholders are prime sources of data for OPAs. The evaluators should propose to interview a range of respondents who have knowledge about the organization. These individuals are critical to enhancing the validity of the conclusions that will be drawn.
- Surveys—Surveys are often used to gather data from a large number of people (including internal and external stakeholders). In defining the methodology, it is important to clarify the nature of the survey (objective, target audience), the expected response rate, and any potential limitations to using a survey.
- Site visits/observation—Typically, an OPA requires site visits so that the assessment team can directly observe facilities, physical artefacts, and interactions among staff. Observational evidence can be very helpful in understanding data collected from other sources.

Constructing an OPA Matrix

Finally, the components identified above (issues and questions, measures/indicators, and data collection methods) should be articulated in an Organizational Performance Assessment matrix like the one shown in Table 3.6.

TABLE 3.6   Outline for an Organizational Performance Assessment Matrix

Organizational Performance Assessment Matrix

Issue	Major Questions	Sub-Questions	Indicators	Data Sources	Data Collection Methods
Organizational capacity					
Organizational motivation					
External environment					
Performance					

MAKING OA USEFUL

Using Organizational Performance Assessments

Using OPAs to improve the performance of an organization is not only beneficial to the organization, it is critical to the future of organizational assessment as a recognized tool for the evaluator's toolbox. Furthermore, when the results of organizational assessments are under-used, resources are wasted and it throws into question why the assessment took place to begin with. In this chapter we look at what OPAs are used for, and the factors that support the use of OPA results.

What Organizations Use OPA Results For

Ideally, organizations use the results of assessments to help make strategic decisions for the future. They also often need to use assessments and evaluations to justify past behavior for accountability purposes. Almost 20 years ago, Universalia (1991) explored the utilization of organizational assessments among 69 Canadian nongovernmental organizations (NGO) in the Canadian International Development Agency's (CIDA) NGO Division. Many of the results have been replicated in various other settings. The study found that organizational assessments had two major consumers: the NGO and the funder. It is interesting to note that while the NGO respondents almost

TABLE 3.7 Uses of Organizational Assessment

Areas in which OA Results were used	Explanation
Capacity building	The most frequent response was that the NGOs used the assessment to build their capacity, often by bringing Board members and staff together to discuss the OA recommendations.
Validate their work	NGO respondents generally perceived that they were doing good work and used parts of assessment to communicate their worth to their stakeholders.
Dialogue with funders	NGOs saw the assessment as an opportunity to negotiate different or better funding arrangements.
Dialogue with partners	The NGOs participating in the study were Canadian NGOs who were supporting overseas NGOs. The Canadian NGOs saw this as an opportunity to discuss difficult issues with their partners.
Future Planning	Almost all NGOs integrated the OA results into strategic planning exercises.

always saw the funder as the primary consumer of assessment results, the funders often identified the NGO as the primary consumer.

Over 90% of the NGO respondents indicated that they used the results of the organizational assessment or were planning to use them. Table 3.7 shows a summary of their responses.

Factors that Support the Use of OPA Results

We have identified some important characteristics of organizational assessments and the settings in which they take place that support the use of OPA findings and recommendations.

Planning to Use the Results of an OPA

Like other evaluation activities, we have learned over the years that it is not enough to complete an OPA report, submit it to the organization and/or client, and assume that utilization will somehow take care of itself. Instead, our lesson is that if we want OPAs to be used, utilization must be planned for from the outset of an assessment and considered throughout the implementation and after reports are submitted and disseminated and debriefed.

At the outset of the assessment, this means deciding on approaches and processes that will ensure the confidence of major stakeholders and support their ownership of OPA results, and also ensuring that sufficient resources are allocated to implement the recommendations. We have found that utilization of OPA results is enhanced when:

- The purpose of the assessment is clear; stakeholders understand the purpose and benefits and agree that the OPA is a valuable exercise
- The main focus of the assessment is learning rather than accountability
- Internal leadership is identified for the assessment—Leaders or "champions" within the organization who have the vision, interest, and influence to guide other people in the organization can be a key to the use of OPA results.
- Stakeholders are involved the OPA process—Through involvement in the negotiation and planning stages of the assessment, the commitment of the organization can be developed or enhanced. Participation in the assessment tends to increase the likelihood that the findings will be used.
- Stakeholders see the assessment as relevant, credible, transparent, of high quality, and the findings have face validity.
- The assessment team is able to communicate the intent of the assessment, their approach, and the assessment results to senior staff and board members.
- The report is timely—OPA reports that are submitted six months later than expected may not be useful. It is important to consider the planning cycle of the organization.
- There is a process in place and resources allocated for following up on and implementing OPA recommendations.
- Recommendations are realistic and feasible—The financial climate can significantly influence the utilization of OPA results. This means that the financial situation of the organization and the financial implications of the recommendations should be taken into account.

CHALLENGES FOR ORGANIZATIONAL PERFORMANCE ASSESSMENT

As OPA is an emerging area within the evaluator's toolkit, there is no literature that reflects on the challenges. This in itself is a challenge. In this section we identify challenges that need to be addressed. Some are conceptual, some are methodological, and all are interrelated.

Challenge 1: Importance of Organizations and of Evaluating Organizations

It seems that we need a better debate on the importance and role of organizations in solving social problems. Are organizations a critical part of solving social problems? Should ministries, departments, and government agencies be evaluated as social instruments used to solve social problems? Is the same true for foundations? What about the World Bank? What role do NGOs and other voluntary organizations play? What are the forums for this debate? As noted in the introductory sections of this chapter, there has been limited emphasis on organizations in the field of evaluation. Why is that? Why is it that there have been limited new approaches or contributions to understanding organizations and organizational performance in the last few years? If the notion of "generations" of frameworks is appropriate, the field is due to have a new generation of OPA frameworks that address some of the other challenges noted below, yet we still see limited efforts in this area.

Challenge 2: Lack of Methodologies, Measures and Tools to Assess Complex Organizations and a Lack of Industry Standards to Make Judgments

Over the past ten years, one of the most difficult aspects of assessing organizational performance has been the lack of progress in developing trustworthy ways of understanding the complexity of organizations. Clearly there is a wide assortment of methodologies that can be brought to bear on this. Some answer the OPA questions using tools from appreciative inquiry. Others use tools associated with complexity theory. New approaches to results-based management and outcome mapping have provided some insight into methodologies, tools, and measures for assessing organizations. But there has been relatively little work done in exploring these approaches and identifying what works and under what circumstances.

For example, Universalia is presently engaged with a network of 16 bilateral donors who are interested in evaluating the multilateral architecture—that is to say, all multilateral organizations. The donor governments participating in this network are spending millions of dollars to support organizations whose role it is to solve global economic and social problems. Yet the donors do not feel that they are receiving sufficient information on the performance of organizations such as the World Bank, UNICEF, UNDP, WHO, and so forth. For this network, an annual assessment process helps fills the gap in information. But the challenge they faced in developing an assessment framework was: what to assess?

The group chose the Balanced Scorecard as the framework for their assessment and selected a series of key performance indicators in the areas of operational management, knowledge management, relationship management, and strategic management. The indicators were selected because the group felt they provided indications of the kinds of practices, behaviors, and systems that would enable an organization to perform (and thus ultimately contribute to development results). However, these choices were made in a context in which insufficient work has been done on both the content and methodology for assessing these complex organizations.

A similar limitation exists with respect to developing industry standards for assessing the effectiveness of many of the organizations we work with. What performance standards should we expect of a foundation, an aid agency, or a research centre? While progress is being made with respect to standards for service organizations that provide health and education and in the philanthropy sector, in many areas the only standards available are those that relate to general management practices (e.g., ISO standards, operational audit standards). Thus, we still have limited understanding of makes a "good" development NGO, development bank, or humanitarian organization.[9] We also recognize that there are complex factors in developing industry standards (e.g., availability, cost, scope, upkeep, and cataloguing). The challenge today is to increase the types of organizations that have some criteria for determining the quality of their performance.

Challenge 3: Providing Concepts That Can Help Organizations Respond to Demands for Greater Organizational Accountability

Accountability is not new to those involved in evaluation. Throughout most of the 20th century, accountability and performance measurement in the public sector centered on financial accounting (focusing on questions of how much money was spent and on what items), and improved organizational performance was defined primarily in terms of efficiency. Today, however, accountability has a broader meaning and includes the results of actions. Performance has come to mean useful products and services and understanding whether constituents are satisfied with the way tasks have been performed (Romzek & Dubnick, 1987) as well as efficiency. Current performance assessment efforts are called Managing for Results. This latest management reform attempts to link measures to mission, set performance targets, and regularly report on the achievement of target levels of performance. Organizations attempt to show their constituents what they are getting for their dollars, how efficiently and effectively their tax dollars are spent, and how expenditures benefit beneficiaries.

However, while organizations today talk about their accountability, they rarely report on performance in a way that fully meets expectations for accountability. When one looks at organizational reports, one finds information on some of the organization's programs and projects but not on the organization as a whole. In the not-for-profit world, we lack performance concepts for describing accountability. For example, we have fewer performance concepts to discuss the Rockefeller Foundation than we have to discuss General Motors (e.g., in terms of profitability, market share, customer satisfaction, productivity, and so forth).

Challenge 4: Adjusting to New Organizational Types

The global problems facing the world have led many organizations to seek new organizational configurations in order to confront the complexity of the issues they need to address. Among the organizations that develop and implement assistance programs, some new forms of organizations have emerged, geared to making global development more effective. These include new global movements, coalitions, networks, virtual structures, public–private partnerships (PPP), and so forth.

While the OPA framework has been used to evaluate these new organizational types, the framework has been applied most often to more traditionally structured organizations with defined boundaries and similar life-cycle patterns (i.e., they grow, mature, decline, and eventually pass away). The newer organizational structures are more fluid and dynamic and are continually reinventing themselves. As such, they may have different needs, priorities and sensitivities— which may require a different OPA model.

Also, some of the processes identified in the OPA framework may need to be assessed in different ways in newer organizational structures. For example, coordination and communication processes are touched on in the OPA framework, but are not central to it. Network organizations, however, are highly dependent on coordination and communication to maintain relationships, and have inherently high transaction costs for these processes. Should efficiency be of paramount importance when trying to solve problems that are interorganizational in nature? Another issue is that these newer forms of organizations are problem-focused rather than goods- and service-focused. Does such a focus require a different understanding of performance assessment?

Challenge 5: Heightened Concern for Organizational Social Responsibility

While the concept of corporate social responsibility (CSR) began as a way for large private sector organizations to integrate economic, social, and environmental imperatives into their activities, the donor community is gradually incorporating the concept of social responsibility into their operations to influence the processes they seek to change. The question remains, should organizations be judged by the level of social responsibility they exhibit?

Today, as citizens and stakeholders are asking organizations to move beyond their typical narrow focus and demonstrate their concerns and responsibilities for society as a whole, there is increasing pressure for organizations to better understand and assess their social responsibility. Where does this idea fit when one explores the performance of an organization? Graham Brown (2007) has done some initial exploration of this idea in relation to the Balanced Scorecard. He argues that a new Scorecard Architecture should include the dimension of "leadership/social responsibility," based on the fact that ethics and social responsibility are no less important than financial results in terms of their effects on the strong performance, or demise, of an organization. However, few organizational performance assessment frameworks incorporate such an idea, nor is there any serious exploration of this concept in most of the organizational assessment literature.

In an OPA framework, should "social responsibility" be added as a performance element, with subquestions about responsibility for promoting gender equality, environment, human rights, and community development? For example, what is the carbon footprint of the organization? To what extent is it engaged in practices that support or undermine human rights? How much support does it provide to the community within which it operates? Does it have a coherent way of promoting gender equality? Universalia has worked with clients in trying to incorporate some of these elements into the Universalia/IDRC framework. An example of this is provided in Appendix C, which presents a collaborative effort between Universalia and the gender specialists at CIDA to integrate gender equality concepts and programming tools into the OPA framework.

Challenge 6: Having Valid Data to Answer the Questions Posed by the OPA

Over the past 25 years, we have worked extensively with government and various not-for-profit organizations. We have found that they have significantly improved their financial information systems and are now in much better position to explore some issues of efficiency. While some progress has been made, most of our encounters with organizations suggest that their data systems for generating information on their results, their stakeholders, or any other organizational performance issue is still at an early stage of development. For example, even though we have been working in the area of results-based management for almost 15 years, few international organizations have a way of discussing (let alone judging) their outcomes as an organization either quantitatively or qualitatively. Thus, we are always implementing an OPA with suboptimal data. This raises an additional challenge in terms of the ethics of making judgments based on incomplete data. We are asked to make judgments about the adequacy of the performance of an organization, but are often dealing with incomplete information.

NOTES

1. In physics, a black box is a system whose internal structure is unknown, or need not be considered.
2. Clearly, from a Universalia perspective, the notable exception in Canada has been IDRC and CIDA. Both of these organizations have recognized the importance of assessing organizations since the early 1980s.
3. At the time, "morale" was considered to be a component of broader efficiency indicators.
4. Original reference is to Richard Beckhard (1969).
5. For more information on these frameworks see the Reflect and Learn web site—www.reflectlearn.org—a website dedicated to organizational assessment that has been supported by the International Development Resource Centre (IDRC) and the Rockefeller Foundation.
6. See, for example, UK Department for International Development (DfID). (2003). *Promoting Institutional and Organizational Development: A sourcebook of tools and techniques.* London, UK: Author.
7. The Malcolm Baldrige National Quality Award was signed into law in the United States in August, 1987. During his term as Secretary of Commerce, Malcolm Baldrige was a proponent of quality management. The award program was designed to stimulate quality improvement processes in private companies as well as the public sector. The Baldrige Award is given annually by the President of the United States to businesses and to education, healthcare, and nonprofit organizations that apply and are judged to be outstanding in seven areas of organizational excellence.
8. The criteria are adapted in different ways in the literature but generally comprise these elements, which are taken from the National Institutes of Standards and Technology website http://www.nist.gov/public_affairs/factsheet/baldfaqs.htm:
9. For humanitarian organizations, however, the Humanitarian Accountability Partnership has established standards that are used to certify organizations based on their accountability framework, quality of management, and quality of service.

APPENDIX A: EXAMPLES OF OA QUESTIONS

The following questions were taken from the IDRC/Universalia Framework. Lusthaus, C., Adrien, M.-H., Anderson, G., & Carden, F. (1999). *Enhancing organizational performance: A toolbox for self-assessment.* Ottawa, ON: IDRC, pp. 53–56.

Issue	Questions	Subquestions
External Environment	Does the stakeholder environment support the organization?	• To what extent are the community and partners involved in the organization? • Does the government value and support the organization's efforts? • Do donor agencies support the organization? • Do organizations involved in similar work support the organization?
	How is the organization affected by political and governance issues in the country?	• Does the political ideology of the government support the kind of work the organization does? • Does the organization have access to government funding? • Does the organization play a role in influencing national or sectoral development policies? • Do government policies and programs support the organization?
	How is the organization affected by the social/cultural environment?	• Has the organization effectively integrated cultural norms into its operations and programming? • Are equity and diversity in the workplace an accepted social value?
	How is the organization affected by the economic environment	• Do economic policy and the general economic situation support the organization's ability to acquire needed technologies and resources? • Is adequate support provided by the government and donors to the organization and the sector?
	Are the technology and resources needed to carry out the organization's work available?	• Is there adequate physical infrastructure for the organization to carry out its work (e.g., power, telecommunications, transport)? • Does government facilitate the acquisition of technology? • Is there an adequate level of human resource development to support the implementation of new technologies?

(continued)

Issue	Questions	Subquestions
	How is the organization affected by existing rules, regulations and legal requirements?	• Is the organization able to function appropriately within the existing sectoral rules and regulations? • Does the organization have administrative and legal autonomy from other organizations and groups it is involved with? • Are the organization's objectives and activities unduly influenced by government, donors and other organizations?
	How is the organization affected by ecological and environmental challenges?	• Will the organization be severely impacted by the occurrence of natural phenomena? • Are environmental conditions workable or do they represent a constraint? • Do pollution issues impact on the organization's work?
Organizational Performance	How effective is the organization in achieving its objectives, commitments and targeted results?	• What performance indicators are identified in the organization's mission statement, mandate, charter, other documents, etc.? • Is data available that can be used to measure effectiveness? • Are programming priorities identified? • What indications demonstrate that the organization is achieving its objectives, commitments and targeted results?
	How efficient is the organization?	• Does the organization identify ways to assess its efficiency? • Are there adequate indicators and data available to assess the efficiency of the organization? • What indications demonstrate that the organization is utilizing its human resources, financial resources, and physical facilities efficiently?
	Is the organization relevant and will its relevance be maintained over time?	• Are the key stakeholders satisfied with the way the organization is performing? • Are there adequate indicators and data to assess relevance? • Has the organization adapted to changing political, economical or societal dimensions? • Do key stakeholders agree with new and/or proposed programming?
	Is the organization financially viable?	• To what extent is the level of funding suitable for the mission and priorities of the organization? • Has there been continued and sustained support from existing sources of revenue? • Are there adequate funds to support existing programs, operating costs, and capital requirements? • To what extent has the organization obtained the funds it has requested?

(continued)

Issue	Questions	Subquestions
Organizational Motivation	What are the memorable milestones, successes, and/or crises in the organization's history?	• How has the organization's history affected performance?
	To what extent does a mission and vision drive the behavior of the organization and its members?	• Does organizational behavior demonstrate alignment/congruence between mission/vision and goals? • To what extent have staff bought into the organization's mission and vision? • Is the mission and vision updated?
	What aspects of the organization's culture contribute to the mission execution?	• Are the organization's values defined and applied? • Is morale good? • Is there high commitment to performance? A positive attitude towards change? • Does training reinforce the organization's values?
	Does the incentive/reward system encourage or discourage the performance of the organization's members?	• Do people feel rewarded for their work? • Are people adequately compensated? • Do non-monetary rewards support good organizational behavior? • Is the incentive system managed adequately? Reviewed regularly?
Organizational Capacity	To what extent does strategic leadership affect the organization's performance?	• Do people feel goal-oriented? • Is leadership concerned about getting significant activities done well? Is leadership respected? • Are people willing to express new ideas to those in positions of power? • Does leadership welcome change?
	To what extent does strategic planning affect the organization's ability to achieve its goals?	• Is there a strategic plan? • Is the strategy known by the board, senior managers, and staff? • Is the strategy generally accepted and supported in the organization? • Is the strategy used as a way of helping to make decisions?

(continued)

Issue	Questions	Subquestions
	Is the organizational structure facilitating or hindering movement towards the mission and goals?	• Are the organization's mission and goals supported by its structures? • Are the roles within the organization clearly defined, yet flexible enough to adapt to changing needs? • Is structural authority used to further issues of equity? • Are there clear lines of accountability (individual, group, and organizational)?
	To what extent does governance affect the organization's performance?	• Does the governing structure both clarify and support organizational direction? • Does the charter provide an adequate framework for carrying out the mission of the organization and for dealing adequately with the external forces challenging the organization? • Does the governing body scan the external and internal environment in order to understand the forces affecting the organization? • Does the governing body operate effectively and efficiently?
	To what extent does the organization's ability to plan for its human resource needs affect its performance?	• Are the right people in the right jobs in the organization? • Does the organization have the ability to forecast current and future demands for human resources? • Does the organization know how and where to identify people with the skills needed to fill its needs? • Is the organization able to link its mission and goals to its human resource planning?
	To what extent does the organization have effective human resources relations?	• Are there appropriate grievance procedures inside the organization? • Are labor management relations constructive? • Are there measures and procedures inside the organization to deal with people in emotional or physical distress? • Does the organization promote loyalty and the commitment of staff?
	Is there adequate financial planning to support performance?	• Is there adequate budgetary planning? • Are members of the governing body involved in financial planning and monitoring? • Are human resources adequate to ensure good financial planning?
	Are financial systems appropriate to support performance?	• Are the finances of grants or loans properly managed? • Is there an adequate bookkeeping system? • Is there adequate staff to record financial information? • Are balance sheets and income and expense statements prepared at least quarterly? • Is there a procedure to control and record the assets of the organization?

(continued)

Issue	Questions	Subquestions
	Is infrastructure adequate to support performance?	• Does the organizational strategy identify the opportunities and constraints regarding infrastructure? • Is there an adequate transportation system to and from work for employees? • Are communications systems functioning at the level required?
	To what extent do technological resources affect the organization's performance?	• Is there adequate planning for technological requirements? • Overall, is the organization's level of technology appropriate to carry out its functions? • Is access to international information provided to all units through library and/or information management systems? • Are there adequate systems and training in place for managing the organizational technology?
	Is program planning adequate?	• Is there a written plan for each program and services area and each major project? • Are program, services, and project plans linked to the organizational mission? • Are the programs, services, and projects consistent with the mission, needs, strategies, and priorities of the organization? • Are there adequate timelines? Adequate budgets?
	To what extent does the organization implement its programming appropriately?	• Is there support for staff getting programming results, and products and services to clients/beneficiaries? • Does staff work well together to provide good products and services? • Are resources used efficiently to provide the product or service? Are schedules adhered to in a reasonable fashion?
	To what extent does the organization monitor its program and services appropriately?	• Are there monitoring and evaluation systems in place? • Is staff given feedback on program/services performance? • Are there adequate opportunities to review program and services indicators to measure progress against plans? • Are timelines monitored to reduce overruns? • Budgets reviewed?

(continued)

Issue	Questions	Subquestions
	Are there problem-solving and decision-making processes supporting the organization's capacity to carry out its functions?	Is the implementation of work at various levels of the organization smooth-flowing?
		Are decisions made in a timely manner?
		Are performance gaps and opportunities identified in sufficient time to resolve them, and to the benefit of the individuals involved and the productivity of the organization?
		Are there problem-solving and decision-making mechanisms in place?
		Are there adequate organizational problem-solving and decision-making skills on the governing board and within the ranks of senior managers?
	Are communications effective in supporting performance?	Do people in the organization feel there is adequate, ongoing communication about the organization's activities?
		Do staff members receive information related to the organization's mission and about progress in fulfilling the mission?
		Are there corrective mechanisms to remedy rumors?
		Is there adequate written communication?
	Are monitoring and evaluation linked to improved performance?	Are there policies, procedures and planning that guide evaluation and monitoring activities?
		Are resources assigned to monitoring and evaluation?
		Is data gathered through organizational monitoring and evaluation activities utilized?
	Are external linkages adequately established or pursued to support performance?	Does the organization have adequate formal and informal linkages with like-minded organizations?
		Are organizational linkages adequately supported?
		Are there fruitful, ongoing partnerships with external organizations that bring new ideas and/or resources to the organization?
		Is the organization communicating information about its work to external stakeholders, including the general public?

APPENDIX B: EXAMPLES OF OA INDICATORS

OA Indicators from Universalia/IDRC Framework

These examples of indicators were prepared by Universalia/IDRC as part of their framework for organizational performance assessment.

	Indicators
Effectiveness	• Number of clients served • Quality of services or products • Changes with respect to equality • Environmental changes • Quality-of-life changes • Service access and usage • Knowledge generation and use • Collaborative arrangements • Demand for policy or technical advice from stakeholders • Replication of the organization's programs by stakeholders • Growth indicators in terms of coverage of programs, services, clients, and funding
Efficiency	• Cost per program • Cost per client served • Cost–benefit of programs • Output per staff • Employee absenteeism and turnover rates • Program-completion rates • Overhead—total program cost • Frequency of system breakdowns • Timeliness of service delivery
Relevance	• Stakeholder satisfaction (clients, donors, etc.) • Number of new programs and services • Changes in partner attitudes • Changes in role • Changes in funders (quality and quantity) • Changes in reputation among peer organizations • Changes in reputation among key stakeholders • Stakeholders' acceptance of programs and services • Support earmarked for professional development • Number of old and new financial contributors (risk of discontinuance, leverage of funding) • Changes in organizational innovation and adaptiveness (changes appropriate to needs, methods) • Changes in services and programs related to changing client systems
Financial viability	• Changes to net operating capital over three years • Ratio of largest funder to overall revenues • Ratio of cash to deferred revenues • Ratio of current assets to current liabilities • Ratio of total assets to total liabilities

(continued)

Indicators

- Growth in terms of number of funders, amount of resources mobilized, assets, capital, and revenues
- Levels of diversification of funding sources
- Partners hired to provide services on a regular basis

Source: Lusthaus, C., M.-H. Adrien, G. Anderson, F. Carden, (1999). *Enhancing organizational performance: A toolbox for self-assessment.* Ottawa, ON: IDRC, pp. 48–50.

Examples of Indicators for Municipal Performance Assessments

These materials on indicators were prepared by the Federation of Canadian Municipalities as part of a toolkit on self-assessment for Municipal Performance Assessments. The framework was adapted from the Universalia/IDRC framework for organizational performance assessment.

Performance Measure	Measure	Indicator
Effectiveness		
Environmental Sphere This sphere includes the natural environment and refers to resources such as water, air, and green space. It deals with the physical consumption of resources and material and the efforts to optimize efficiency.	Access to safe water and sanitation Municipal bylaws geared toward environmental protection Air quality monitoring Water quality monitoring Businesses with built-in recycling Water management systems— e.g., waste land filled, waste diverted from landfill	# of days/year with air quality in the good range # of businesses with built-in recycling
Social Sphere This sphere includes all the social components that lead to the physical and psychological well-being of citizens. This includes concepts such as the achievement of social equity, meeting basic human needs, personal development, and maintaining personal health.	*Education* Access to primary/secondary education Adult literacy rate Continuing education program availability Education and training levels Local training and educational facilities Access to and use of technology	# of continuing education programs available/capita

(continued)

Performance Measure	Measure	Indicator
	Health	# of hospital beds/
	Illness quota	capita
	Health outcome indicators: mortality rates, morbidity rates, suicide rates, and low birth weights	
	Health-related behaviors: incidence of smoking, alcohol consumption, and physician-prescribed drugs	
	Elderly engaged in community activities	
	Employment	Average proportion
	Employment, unemployment, and underemployment indicators/rate (labour market stats)	of unemployed as a fraction of the workforce
	Characteristics of the labor force over time	Average annual growth rate of the number
	Replacement rate of labor force	of employed persons,
	Mobility rate	aged 15 and over
	Housing	Ratio of the median
	Housing cost and affordability	annual rent of a
	House rent-to-income ratio	dwelling unit and the
	Housing space per person	median household/
	Vacancy rates	family income
	Amount of substandard housing	renters
	Number of people in core housing need	
	Number of people without housing (homeless)	
	Social Services	
	Community stress/population at risk:	
	% of population on social assistance, employment insurance, temporary training subsidies, in shelters for the homeless	
	% of economy sustained by social programs	
	Role that social programs play in generating employment	
	% of population receiving social benefits within a specific time period	
	Safety Sphere	
	Level of safety in the community: rates of reported crime, reports of violent incidents, fatality or personal injury statistics and perceived danger	
	Accident rate	
	Road maintenance measure	
	Neighborhood planning	

(continued)

Performance Measure	Measure	Indicator
	Transportation Access to public transit Level of public transit ridership	
Equity Sphere This sphere relates to those activities that contribute to social justice and human rights extended to all citizens. It includes fairness and equal access to services by all citizens.	Recognition of ethnic practices & respect for diversity Recognition of subcommunities (ethnic, religious, age groups) Equitable distribution of income between subcommunities Level of community conviviality Distribution of personal income/poverty level	Extent to which racial, gender groups are actively represented per 1,000 population Extent to which disadvantaged groups are politically represented
Governance Sphere This sphere relates to the format, style, and effectiveness of leadership and governance within the municipality. It includes processes for ensuring citizen involvement in governance.	Public participation in decision-making Development of democratic processes such as community consultation, community-based decision-making processes % of electorate voting in local elections Committee structures/meetings; council/administration relations Citizen participation measure: voting rates, non-paid community work per capita, giving per capita Extent to which external linkages are established or pursued to support municipal performance	Voter participation rate # of registered voters as active participants % of adult population (having reached voting age) who voted in last municipal election # of participatory mechanisms (forum, meetings, etc) encouraging public participation and representation
Cultural Sphere This sphere refers to the arts, beliefs, institutions, and other human activity or thought and the opportunities to practice them in a municipality. It includes opportunities for both practicing and promoting artistic and cultural life within and outside of a municipality, as well as a commitment from government and private sector to support diverse cultural activities.	Number and frequency of cultural attractions/sites—museums, theatre, special events Historical awareness Citizen involvement Degree of pride in community/culture	# of recreational facilities/capita # of buildings in municipality on heritage or monument list # of cultural and heritage programs

(continued)

Performance Measure	Measure	Indicator
Economic Sphere This sphere includes an assessment of all the work crated in a municipality, and the processes, assets and knowledge that support job creation and economic development.	Level of stability and diversification in local economy Level of indebtedness (individual, community, nation) Average income relative to the costs of living Community affordability measure: citizen's incomes relative to cost of living Business development Consumer and business bankruptcies Labor force activity (unemployment rates, labor force working) Inflation rate Migration rate International gateway % of female administrators and managers % women in government Access to investment Level of infrastructure (electricity, roads) Access to transportation	GDP/industry Rate of inflation Rate of migration
Efficiency	Cost per citizen Cost per program service Service expenditure per capita Cost/quality ratio Number of employee hours: comparative indication of time spent on providing services to community Number of municipal employees per capita % of municipal budget in administrative cost	Total expenditure, both capital and current, public and private, on social services in dollar per person
Relevance	Surveying stakeholder/citizens level of satisfaction with regard to service Monitoring the number of calls for information/comments/complaints Level of commitment in above sphere, notably social Benchmark comparisons to measure progress of new and existing businesses (sales, investments) Word-of-mouth: business-to-business Ongoing local hiring	% of stakeholders/ citizens satisfied with services % increase of sales/ investments in local business % increase in amount of investment in municipality

(continued)

Performance Measure	Measure	Indicator
	Monitoring changing demands of funder/investor with regard to fund allocation	
	Benchmarking comparisons to assess funder/investor status— repetitive funding may imply loyalty to municipality	
	Funder/investor level of involvement in municipal operations	
	Survey whether funders are satisfied with the way municipalities are managing their expenditures and activities	
	Strong identification of citizens to their municipality and/or their jobs	
	Voluntary involvement in multiple services	
	Level of turnover	
	Property values	
	Level of education of municipal staff	
	Capacity levels of municipal staff	
	Relevance of tender call process	
Financial Viability		
	Credit rating (e.g., Moody's)	Ratio of funding growth to overall funding
	Tax base enhancement	
	Funding growth	
	Legal framework securing financial management	Ratio of cash to deferred revenues
	Cash to deferred revenues	% growth of funders in $
	Ration of largest funder to overall revenues	
	Ratio of current assets to total liabilities	
	Ratio of total assets to total liabilities	
	Growth in terms of number of funders, amount of resources mobilized, assets, capital and revenues	
	Partners hired to provide services on a regular basis (level of outsourcing)	

Municipal Corporate Management Indicators

Area	Measure	Effectiveness indicator	Efficiency indicator
1. Technical Services			
Environmental Services Department Water treatment, distribution, conservation	Water main development; Water main repair and replacement mechanisms; Water treatment mechanisms; Water conservation mechanisms	Access to reliable expertise/capacity/of water main repair/km of water main; % frequency that treated drinking water meets regional/national regulations; Water conservation rate (through effectiveness of water metering, main replacements, leak detection mechanisms)	Cost of water main repair; Total $ spent on water main repairs annually; Cost of treating a mega litre of water on an average day
Sanitation; sewage	Development of sewage system; Reliability of sewer system	Frequency that municipality/department responds to failure in sewer systems	Average operating cost (including recoveries) of maintaining one meter of sewer
Waste management; solid waste disposal, residential waste collection	Ability to manage all waste delivered to landfill sites; Quality of landfill site	Frequency that municipality/dep't meets regional/national regulations for land filling; Frequency that municipality/dep't collects all household solid wastes on schedule	Average cost to landfill one ton of material; Average direct cost of collecting solid waste from one household annually
2. Social Services			
Parks and Recreation Department	Ability of municipality to manage a diverse open space system offering a wide variety of outdoor recreation and leisure opportunities to citizens	# of users of open space and parks; User satisfaction with open space, parks, programs and services; Representative habitat types	Cost per hectare for annual growth maintenance; % increase in returns per booked hour of space; # of groups/individuals active in park maintenance, natural area preservation and restoration; Cost per program; Realized value of volunteer hours; $ value of corporate sponsorship; Rate of community support
3. Administrative Services			
Accounting and Financial Services Department	Ability to process payments for all goods and services supplied to/by the municipality	Cost as a % of total revenue; Cost per invoice processed; % of checks voided due to errors	#of transactions/payments processed per staff person; % of revenue collection vs. projected

APPENDIX C: INTEGRATING GENDER EQUALITY INTO OPA

This tip sheet is an example of guidance provided to CIDA development officers in integrating Gender Equality into an OPA.

Gender Equality	Additional Benefits of an OA
CIDA's policy on Gender Equality seeks to contribute to "equality between women and men to ensure sustainable development." The objectives of CIDA's Policy on gender equality are to: • Advance women's equal participation with men as decision-makers in shaping the sustainable development of their societies • Support women and girls in the realization of their full human rights • Reduce gender inequalities in access to and control over the resources and benefits of development. An OA can respond to CIDA's need to assess progress on the implementation of CIDA's Policy on Gender Equality. Adding gender equality components to an OA will allow CIDA to understand the extent to which gender has been institutionalized in the organization, by: • determining the extent to which gender equality has been internalized and acted upon by staff • identifying practices that have made a positive contribution to gender equality in an organization • assessing how the resources are spent on gender equality • measuring progress in implementing policies and action plans on gender quality. It will also help to identify areas where there is room for improvement.	OA can help assess the extent to which CIDA-supported organizations are contributing to gender equality. To do so, this must be explicitly written into the OA's overall scope and included in its Terms of Reference. Review the checklist below to determine how the OA can help inform both CIDA's and the organization's understanding of how well the organization integrates and contributes to gender equality results.

Examples of OA questions related to the organization's integration of gender equality

External Environment
• What are the legal, economic, technological, or political circumstances in the country that support or limit the organization in its pursuit of gender equality and achievement of gender equality results? For example, to what extent is the country meeting its obligations under CEDAW?[a] In this context, how does the organization engage with stakeholders on gender equality?
• What factors in the country's history, institutions, or ethnic, social and cultural, context may support or inhibit the organization in its pursuit of gender equality and achievement of gender equality results?
• To what extent is there political action/pressure in the country with regard to women's human rights and gender equality issues? How is this manifested? Do the constituencies have access to points of power?
• To what extent are political structures in the country representative? Are different groups able to access, be elected, and/or actively engage in these structures? How does this affect the institutional setting for the organization's work?

(continued)

Organizational Motivation

- Does the organization have a history of pursuing, rejecting, or remaining "neutral" to gender equality issues?
- Are there explicit statements referring to the pursuit of gender equality issues in the vision statement, mission statement?
- To what extent is the overall culture of the organization oriented toward the promotion of gender equality? Are there key values or principles that support or limit the pursuit of gender equality and achievement of gender equality results?
- Does the incentive system reward, encourage or discourage staff and management in pursuing gender equality?
- How do women and men from within the organization and related external organizations perceive the treatment of equality issues and is there a perception that there are equality issues that need to be addressed?
- What level of political commitment to gender equality is demonstrated by the organization's leadership?

Organizational Capacity

- How has the organization integrated gender equality perspectives in the major policy and planning documents guiding the work of the organization? (For example in strategic plans, sectoral policies, evaluations, etc.) Does the organization have an explicit Gender Equality Policy?
  - How does the organization's strategic plan integrate gender equality issues?
  - How do monitoring, evaluation, and other feedback mechanisms take into account gender equality at the project, program, and organizational levels?
- What is the extent of the organization's demonstrated commitment to pursue gender equality objectives? (For example: profile of a gender equality unit, trends regarding investments in gender equality, statements by the leadership of the organization, etc.)
- To what extent are commitments to gender equality backed by allocations or specific resources for ensuring equality in initiatives, activities, departments, programs, etc?
- To what extent do staff and management consider the priorities, roles and responsibilities of women and men in the promotion of sustainable development?
- How is the responsibility for gender mainstreaming distributed? Is it centralized or decentralized?
- Do day-to-day procedures take gender equality issues into account or are there separate procedures for addressing gender and other forms of equality that operate in isolation from regular procedures?
- How is the organization working toward gender balance in staffing throughout the organization, in particular in management positions? Do the organization's HR policies facilitate the equitable recruitment, retention, and promotion of women and men?
- Is appropriate staff development for gender equality awareness being supported and delivered, and is it effective in supporting people in fulfilling policy and procedural equality goals?
- To what extent do the organization's programs and projects apply methodologies and tools that allow them to address GE issues?
- Are gender and other equality needs being met through the delivery of actual programs and projects? Does the organization have evidence of to the achievement of gender equality results?

(continued)

- Are lessons learned and best practices gathered and used to improve the organization's performance in gender equality?
- What interorganizational linkages or partnerships does the organization use to strengthen its contributions to gender equality?

---

^a CEDAW is the UN Convention on the Elimination of All Forms of Discrimination Against Women, one of the core international human rights conventions and is second only to the UN Convention on the Rights of the Child as one of the most widely ratified/acceded human rights conventions.

Organizational Performance Questions

Effectiveness

- To what extent does organizational programming contribute to and achieve gender equality development results?
- What organizational systems are in place to collect, monitor, and track gender equality results?

Relevance

- To what extent does the organization's approach (policies and related documentation) reflect consensus reached in international documents, such as the Beijing Platform for Action and the full implementation of CEDAW?1 Is gender equality seen as an explicit development goal and as integral to the achievement of other development goals, such as the MDGs?
- To what extent does the organization's programming align with this approach?

Efficiency

- To what extent has the organization developed clear and systematic management practices to ensure achievement of gender equality results? (For example: regular investments in the knowledge of staff, operational manuals and tools, clear accountability structures, availability of expertise, partnerships and consultations with women's organizations, etc.)
- Recognizing that consultations and participatory processes may increase costs, but enable higher potential for achievement of gender equality results, how is the organization identifying, tracking, and managing the relationship between participatory process and costs?
- Does the organization leverage external resources/partnerships in order to support the achievement of gender equality results?

Financial viability

- How is the organization financing its engagement in gender equality issues? Is this funding sustainable over time?

(These questions were adapted from Tool 2 "Assessment of Core Funding" of CIDA's Framework for Assessing Gender Equality Results, 2005.)

Note: For further information, please consult CIDA, Framework for Assessing Gender Equality Results, 2005 and CIDA-CPB Frameworks for Integrating Gender Equality, 2003.

APPENDIX D: ACRONYMS

AEA	American Evaluation Association
CES	Canadian Evaluation Society
CSR	Corporate Social Responsibility
IDRC	International Development Research Centre
IFI	International Finance Institutions
IISD	International Institute for Sustainable Development
MOPAN	Multilateral Organization Performance Assessment Network
NGO	Non-governmental organization
OA	Organizational Assessment
OECD	Organization for Economic Co-operation and Development
OPA	Organizational Performance Assessment
PPP	Public-Private Partnerships

REFERENCES

Burke, W. W., & Litwin, G. H. (1992). A causal model of organizational performance and change. *Journal of Management, 18*(3), 523–545.

Campbell, J. P., Dunnette, M. D., Lawler, E. E., & Weick, K. E. (1970). *Managerial behavior, performance, and effectiveness.* New York: McGraw-Hill Book Company.

Caplow, T. (1976). *How to run any organization: A manual of practical sociology.* Hinsdale, IL: The Dryden Press.

Clegg, S., Courpasson, D., & Phillips, N (2006). *Power and organizations.* London: Sage Publications.

Federal Accountability Act (S.C. 2006, c.9).

Gaebler, T., & Osborne, D. (1992). *Reinventing government.* Reading, MA: Addison Wesley Publishing Company.

Graham Brown, M. (2007). *Beyond the balanced scorecard, improving business intelligence with analytics.* New York, NY: Productivity Press.

Harbour, J. L. (2009). *The basics of performance measurement.* New York, NY: Productivity Press.

Harrison, M. I. (1987). *Diagnosing organizations: Methods, models and processes.* Beverly Hills, CA: Sage Publications.

Immordino, K. M. (2010). *Organizational assessment and improvement in the public sector.* Boca Raton, FL: CRC Press.

Kaplan, R. S., & Norton, D. P. (1996). *The balanced scorecard, Translating strategy into action.* President and Fellows of Harvard College.

Levinson, H. (1972). *Organizational diagnostics.* Cambridge, MA.: Harvard University Press.

Likert, R. (1958). *Some applications of behavioral research.* Paris: UNESCO.

Mayne, J. (2001). Addressing attribution through contribution analysis: Using performance measures sensibly. *The Canadian Journal of Program Evaluation, 16*(1), 1–24

Meyer, J. W., & Rowan, B. (1992). Institutionalized organizations: Formal structure as myth and ceremony. In J. W. Meyer & R. Scott (Eds.), *Organizational Environments: Ritual and Rationality* (2nd ed.). London: Sage Publications

Multilateral Organisation Performance Assessment Network (2010). *MOPAN Common Approach 2009—African Development Bank (AfDB).*

Organisation for Economic Co-Operation and Development, Development Assistance Committee (OECD-DAC) (2010). *Quality standards for development evaluation.* Paris: OECD.

Pascale, R. T., & Athos, A. G. (1981). *The art of Japanese management.* Norwalk, CT: Elsevier Business Horizons.

Peters, T. J., & Waterman, R. H. Jr.. (1982). *In search of excellence: Lessons from America's best-run companies.* New York, NY: Warner Books Edition.

Quinn, R. E., & Rohrbaugh, J.(1983). A spatial model of effectiveness criteria: Towards a competing values approach to organizational analysis. *Management Science, 29,* 363–377.

Romzek, B., & Dubnick, M. (1987). Accountability in the public sector: Lessons from the Challenger tragedy. *Public Administration Review 47* (3, 1987): 227–238.

Taylor, F. W. (1947). *Scientific management.* New York, NY: Harper and Row.

United States Government Performance and Results Act of 1993 (Public Law 103-62).
Universalia. (1991) *A study of utilization of NGO evaluations.* Ottowa, ON: Author.

OTHER RESOURCES

Corvellec, H. (1997). *Stories of achievements, narrative features of organizational performance.* Piscataway, NJ: Transaction Publishers.

Georgopoulos, B., & Tannembaum, A. (1957). A study of organizational effectiveness. *American Sociological Review, 22,* 534–540.

Greene, H. (2007). *Years of management problems because of our flawed definition of performance.* Waban, MA: 21st Century Management.

Kilmann, R. H. (1989). *Managing beyond the quick fix: A completely integrated program for creating and maintaining organizational success.* San Francisco, CA.: Jossey-Bass Inc., Publishers.

National Institutes of Standards and Technology website: *http://www.nist.gov/public_affairs/factsheet/baldfaqs.htm*

Price, J. L. (1972*). Organizational effectiveness: An inventory of propositions.* Homewood: Richard D. Irwin, Inc.

Ruben, B. D. (2008). *The excellence in higher education program: Using the Baldrige framework to address the assessment, planning and improvement needs of your institution.* Hoboken, NJ: Wiley.

Stannard-Stockton, S. (2009). *A robust definition of high performance.* Burlingame, CA: Tactical Philanthropy Advisors.

Stern, G. J. (1999). *The Drucker Foundation self-assessment tool, process guide.* New York, NY: The Peter F. Drucker Foundation for Nonprofit Management.

UK Department for International Development (DfID). (2003). *Promoting Institutional and Organizational Development: A sourcebook of tools and techniques* and MDF, Monitoring, Evaluation and Learning System- Organizational Development Self Assessment (ODSA).

Weber, M. (1947). *The theory of social and economic organization.* New York, NY: Free Press.

Weisbord, Martin. (1978). *Organizational diagnosis: A workbook of theory and practice.* Boston, MA: Addison-Wesley.

Yuchtman, E., & Seashore, S. (1967). Factorial Analysis of Organizational Performance. *Administrative Science Quarterly, 12*(3), 377–395.

Universalia

Publications

Lusthaus, A., et al. (2002). *Organizational assessment: A framework for improving performance.* Ottawa, ON: International Development Research Centre/Washington, DC: Inter-American Development Bank.

Lusthaus, A., et al. (1999). *Enhancing organizational performance: A toolbox for self-assessment.* Ottawa, ON: International Development Research Centre.

Occasional Papers

Adrien, M-H, Carden, F., & Lusthaus, C. (2002). *Organizational assessment in theory and practice: From Ceremonial Assessment to Learning.*

Adrien, M-H., & Lusthaus, C. (1997). *New Horizons in Organizational Self-Assessment.*

Adrien, M-H., Sliwinski, A. & Lusthaus, C. (1998). *Planifier une auto-évaluation organisationnelle: Bilan d'une experience.*

Adrien, M-H., & Lusthaus, C. (1998). *Organizational assessment: A review of experience.*

Anderson, G., Adrien, M-H., & Lusthaus, C. (1997). *Organizational self-evaluation: An emerging frontier for organizational improvement.*

Carden, F. (1997). *Giving evaluation away: Challenges in a learning-based approach to institutional assessment.*

Smutylo, T., & Lusthaus, C. (1998). *Maximizing the benefits of self-assessment: Tools and tips.*

CHAPTER 4

EVALUATING CAPACITY DEVELOPMENT

Peter Morgan

Most of this chapter is based on my recent experiences with international development agencies (IDAs), especially donors and multilaterals.[1] Recently, most of that experience has been in fragile or conflict-affected countries including Papua New Guinea, the Solomon Islands, Sierra Leone, and Liberia. Throughout my career as a practitioner/consultant in international development, I have been mainly a consumer (and an occasional participant) of evaluations. I have usually, but not always, been underwhelmed by their actual, as opposed to their claimed, benefits.[2] Enormous amounts of elephantine huffing and puffing about methodologies, accountability and learning. Huge transaction costs as the evaluation pachyderm lumbers and staggers in circles. Or disappears into the woods. And then finally, one of three unsatisfactory outcomes usually emerges: the belated appearance of a puzzling set of conclusions that leave the survivors exhausted, angered, frustrated, or more adrift than they were before the exercise started. Or a meager analysis that actually tells us little or nothing of real substance about the issue in question. (To make matters worse, this outcome appears to please and satisfy the participants.) Or finally, some useful insights and rec-

Emerging Practices in International Development Evaluation, pages 75–104
Copyright © 2013 by Information Age Publishing

ommendations from an effective evaluation that sink without trace or result both in the international development agency (IDA) and in the country.

These patterns are, in my view, now repeating themselves with respect to the evaluation of capacity, which, despite some advances described in this paper, is still mainly rudimentary and occasionally damaging.[3] My interest is in helping to make evaluations more useful, to make practice better, to encourage better capacity development, and to prevent such evaluations from undermining the capacity, energy, and motivation of the participants. "Do no harm" in these matters is still a reasonable objective.

My sense is that the practice of capacity evaluation is at an unsettled stage at the moment. And it suffers at present from more than just gaps in methodology. If that were the problem, smart people would have come up with solutions a long time ago. But it hasn't happened. People are still confused about what capacity is and is not. Best practice in capacity evaluation seems in short supply. The focus of the analysis remains murky. Complex adaptive systems (CAS) thinking is challenging the dominance of conventional logic models based around the logical framework. Partly as a result, a variety of organizations are experimenting with new (but largely unproven) evaluation methodologies that are felt to be better suited to assessing change, uncertainty, and innovation.[4] Some analysts see both issues—evaluation and capacity—as matching up uneasily with the incentives and pressures that actually shape the behavior of IDAs. There is, as the Chinese say, danger and opportunity awaiting.

It also needs to be kept in mind that the evaluation of capacity is taking place in the context of the "official" international development industry that is becoming increasingly risk-averse. A new round of aid skepticism and funding reductions has started up again after the recent boom years. Some IDAs are losing interest in capacity issues given the lack of demonstrable progress to date. And many are becoming increasingly sclerotic and control-oriented as they descend into late middle age. Some can no longer summon up—or afford—the flexibility and imagination to make a serious contribution to capacity development. In practice, the key driving force of many donor agencies now is the struggle for domestic legitimacy and survival.

Finally, we need to approach the evaluation of capacity with a sense of modesty, curiosity, and patience. It is not an easy thing to get right for a whole series of reasons. The balance between product and process is not easy to strike. It is hard to get a consensus on the nature of the capacity and capacity development to be evaluated. Intangibles, ghosts, and hidden agendas in the countries proliferate. The time and timing issues of all the various participants are hard to match up. And untangling the behavior of complex systems change issues takes patience and contextual knowledge, both of which are in short supply everywhere. I still believe that effective evaluations of capacity can be produced. But we have a way to go to achieve that goal.

DEFINITIONS OF CAPACITY
AND CAPACITY DEVELOPMENT

Most capacity reports begin with a tedious section that tries to suggest a definition. The fact that such a section is even felt to be necessary in virtually all analyses says a good deal about the whole capacity discussion. Readers should bear in mind that a substantial number of analysts and practitioners in the aid business are skeptical about the whole concept of capacity. For the sake of brevity, I won't get into that discussion in this chapter. This section sets out the definitions used in this paper.

Capacity

Appendix A gives a sample of definitions of the term *capacity*. These have both differences and common themes. And in many ways, they reflect two of the main ways of thinking about capacity issues. Some, for example, look at capacity issues from a technical/functional perspective. They focus more on needs, constraints, and problem solving. They see capacity as more of a top-down effort to put in place the technical, organizational and logistical functions that lead, in turn, to better performance. They deal almost exclusively with formal structures and systems. This is capacity as organizational machinery. A key tactic of this approach is the application of knowledge in the form of generic, global, best practice—generalizable recipes—to specific country situations. To use a famous metaphor, this is capacity as a combination of brain and machinery (Morgan, 1986).

The second group of definitions sees capacity as having more to do with human behavior, attitudes, and values. From this perspective, capacity is about qualities such as confidence, leadership, collaboration, trust, relationships, and identity. The attention here is more on informality, the invisible, and the intangibles. It can refer, for example, to the capability to act, to learn and adapt, to exert moral authority. As such, it can also have a psychological aspect. It is usually based on a more bottom-up, customized, adaptive approach that seeks out country energy and strengths and tries to harness them in productive ways.

Inevitably, operational capacity has aspects of both these perspectives. The definition underlying the analysis in this chapter goes as follows: *Capacity is that emergent combination of individual competencies and collective capabilities which enables a human system to create value for others.* All definitions of capacity have at their core a common idea, that of abilities or the willingness, resilience, tenacity, power, and skill to do something at a certain standard over time. From a development perspective, capacity thus has to do with the collective ability of people to generate some sort of positive developmental gain over time. Some other aspects:

- Such ability can comprise the competencies of individuals or the collective capabilities of groups, networks, organizations, systems and even countries.[5] Capacity is also a relational concept emerging out of the interaction between people, groups, organizations, and institutions and their environment.
- Such competencies and capabilities can be located in public sector organizations, in NGOs, in communities or in private firms. They can be in service delivery organizations with tangible outcomes or, for example, in advocacy groups with hard-to-measure services. They can also be housed in formal structures that are recognizable or in informal network or "ghost" structures that are hard for IDAs to understand.
- The overall systems term "capacity" can also be judged in terms of resilience, legitimacy, integrity, coherence, positioning, and niche or contribution. The value of the traditional concepts of "efficiency" and "effectiveness" might merit a discussion.
- Capacity is also a potential state. Performance or results relate to delivery, production, implementation and execution. Improved capacity may not automatically lead to these kinds of outcomes. The relationships between the two need to be included in any evaluation.
- Capacity can be seen as a secondary means to primary developmental ends such as health or education. Or it can be held to be a development end in itself—that is, helping to empower people, groups, organizations, states, societies with the ability to achieve the future they want.[6] My own bias is towards the second. But whatever the choice, IDAs have to be conscious of the choice they have made and the resulting policy and operational implications including those for capacity evaluation.

Capacity Development

Capacity development in this chapter is defined as the following: *"The processes of change that, both intentionally and indirectly, contribute to the emergence of capacity over time."*

Some explanatory points:

- Capacity development can refer to a range of "macro" factors in any situation. These can take place at a variety of levels ranging from the indirect and the global (e.g., national financial crises) to the direct and the immediate (e.g., the influence of the informal networks that actually control a particular ministry). Put another way, changes to capacity are always underway regardless of what external interventions do. The game is already on.

- Any external intervention will be based, implicitly or explicitly, on some theory of change designed to induce the emergence of capacity. This could include everything from training to relationship building to infrastructure development to "unlearning." This theory of change may or may not be relevant in terms of achieving improved capacity. Monitoring and evaluation (M&E) needs to be one way of assessing this relevance and making the inevitable adaptations that will be needed as conditions change.

- In many poor countries, most formal institutions have little legitimacy for most citizens. They have likely been imposed or imported. They have ended up disconnected from the society and do not represent country values, cultural patterns, or political settlements. They are not based on indigenous values and ways of behaving. Part of capacity development thus includes trying to establish these connections and relationships.

- The actual organic processes of capacity emergence and formation take place in ways that we still do not fully understand at present. A lot of complex, multidimensional interventions in uncertain environments are involved. Most appear to be nonlinear and are not programmable in any conventional sense. In practice, they need to be seen as complex organisms or adaptive systems. Capacity development is dependent on system flows, patterns of interaction, and processes.

All of this should encourage us to think differently about the design of capacity interventions. The most effective way to address risk is not to generate ever more complex designs in a desperate effort to foresee all the difficulties. A more promising option may be to come up with more general designs and then focus more on adaptation and redesign during implementation. IDAs would, in effect, highlight projects and programs facing major risks and then shift scarce operational resources from initial design to M&E and supervision. Two caveats, of course, are (1) that the current incentive system inside IDAs including promotions and careers patterns is heavily oriented towards design and not implementation, and (2) that the capability to assess risks on the ground including the political would have to be dramatically improved.

The "long march" style of decades-long efforts to build key institutions such as universities or research institutes is no longer in favor in some IDAs. This was the pattern of the patient long-term investor who saw country capacity as a development end in itself that was a key part of any approach to sustainability. What are on the agenda now are shorter-term interventions to promote innovation, new thinking, and catalytic leadership. The pattern here is that of the venture capitalist who is far more concerned about results and impact, which are now expected early and quickly, usually in three- to five-year time frames, sometimes less. Knowledge and best practice are seen as having the power in and of themselves to induce new forms of capacity. Leadership is key. Evidence of performance needs to be generated and widely disseminated. Coming up with a strategic approach to capacity issues that fits the "new" direction appears to be a work in progress. The challenges for the "new" capacity efforts will likely be fourfold:

- First, thinking through the broad implications of new strategies for capacity issues. Being able to assess capacity "readiness" and "absorptive" capacity in country partners, for example, will assume much greater importance to help make any catalytic interventions more effective. The sensible design of exit strategies will now matter more.
- Second, being able to match preferred approaches to capacity development to the actual dynamics of particular contexts in particular countries. Low-capacity countries and most fragile states, for example, are filled with shadow and ghost structures that do not lend themselves easily to quick catalytic interventions. Achieving sustainable gains in these contexts will be a challenge.
- Third, the IDA will need to involve itself with a range of new actors, including networks, coalitions, and informal groups. This evolving pattern of relationships will have implications for activities such as capacity development and M&E.
- Fourth, the IDA will need to build its capabilities to help make these new initiatives effective. These upgrades would include more effective approaches to M&E.

CAPACITY EVALUATION METHODOLGIES

I have included in Appendix B a description of some of the main approaches to capacity evaluation. These are the following:

- Most significant change (MSC)
- Outcome mapping (OM)
- Results-based (RB)
- Complex adaptive systems (CAS)
- Development evaluation (DE)
- Contribution analysis (CA)
- Theory-based approach (TBA)

My own bias is the following:

- I have largely moved away from the mechanical logic models such as the results-based and I am now trying to master the assumptions and techniques associated with complex adaptive systems, which, from my perspective, offer much more insight into the unplannable, ambiguous, uncertain world of most capacity development interventions.
- I have also lost faith in the value of the conventional combination of "monitoring" during implementation and a final evaluation at the end of the intervention. What is now needed is a continuous process of evaluation that tracks the ongoing work and contributes to learning and adaptation.
- A methodology known as "development evaluation"[7] is designed to do that. It can offer a combination of monitoring and conventional evaluation, of both critical and creative thinking. From this perspective, evaluation design co-evolves with the unfolding dynamics of the intervention.
- I am also suggesting the need to combine different approaches to evaluation. All the ones listed above, including even the log frame methodology, can offer a way forward in different circumstances. The challenge is to combine and customize a capacity evaluation to fit a particular situation at a particular time—or to emphasize the appropriateness of any evaluation approach.
- There is a growing need to put country participants at the heart of the evaluation process. Extractive, third-party "expert"-dominated efforts do not contribute much to a legacy of evaluative thinking and acting.

DESIGNS AND USES OF CAPACITY EVALUATION FRAMEWORKS

The principles set out below reflect the points listed above, and also the assumption that an evaluation of capacity cannot only focus on capacity itself. It must start with that focus and be dominated by it. But it must also look at the interrelationships of capacity with outcomes, the influence of contextual factors and the implicit choice of any theory of change.

Some other points about evaluation guidelines:

- The need to articulate the "use-in-mind" of any capacity evaluation. To be effective, capacity evaluations need to be connected in some way to real-time planning, budgeting, and decision-making. Lack of follow-up and follow-through of the results of the evaluation can give the process a bad name.

- A confirmation of the scope, structure, history, and dynamics of the human system being evaluated, including those likely to be reached by the intervention.[8] Some capacity evaluations lose direction and relevance at the beginning by focusing on the wrong configuration. CAS can be helpful on this aspect.

- A focus on the contextual factors—a situational analysis—that will likely influence the changes in behaviors and capacity. Political, social, cultural, security, and many other factors would be included here. It may be necessary to pick a certain number of key variables or influences that affect change and each other. Part of the challenge of evaluating capacity development is to try to disentangle (to the extent possible) this soup of factors that contribute to capacity development. CA can contribute here.

- An explanation of the theory or logic(s) of capacity development including the basic strategic assumptions that guided the intervention. The theory-based approach (TBA) can be used here. This might include frameworks such as outcome sequence charts, strategic assumptions, and other such tools that may or may not have proved useful. It is important to remember that more than one theory or logic (whose theory?) may have been at work at different times for different reasons. And the assumptions may have changed during the course of the work to date. What was meant to be done and what was actually done?

- The identification, assessment, and documentation of the behavioral changes, both intended and unforeseen. By behavioral changes, I am referring to attitudes, knowledge, relationships, behaviors, perceptions, and decisions. Both OC and MSC come with techniques to do this. An attention to unintended consequences might appear at this stage.[9]

- The tracking of the changing pattern of competencies, capabilities and capacity. A wide range of organizational assessments are available that can help to some degree (e.g., Lipson & Hunt, 2007). Some focus directly on capabilities. Two issues that have received little attention in most of the current discussion are those of un-learning and capacity destruction—that is, the abandoning of ideas, images, structures, and behaviors that have long been successful but are no longer.

- The tracking of the changing nature of the performance and results as the program proceeds. Much was said on this subject in the opening presentation of the workshop.

- The tracking of the process of implementation matters. We need to understand how capacity outcomes came about and when and why.

And we need to be able to distinguish between a strategic failure and an implementation failure.

- The tracking of time and timing issues. All capacity evaluations must make some judgments on what progress can reasonably be expected over what period of time.

I have not included here the growing list of tools and frameworks that are in various states of use in capacity evaluations. Such things as citizen score cards, report cards, focus groups, semi-structured questionnaires, culture audits, and so on.

CAPACITY EVALUATION MEASURES

I am not a fan of having a generic set of capacity measures that can be pulled off the shelf and stuck on to various capacity development interventions.[10] A number of IDAs over the years have set up (v) indicator factories to produce prefab measures but in the end had little to show for the effort in terms of improved understanding and operational effectiveness. Measurement itself must be assessed in its ability to contribute to learning, understanding, and adaptation. It should help to reduce uncertainty. It should be measurement for capacity development as well as capacity development.

So I set out in this section some principles for thinking about the issue of indicators.

- There is a debate about the value of even having predetermined indicators and measures (Sigsgaard, 2004). From this perspective, indicators are a mixed blessing. They emerge, provide some insight, and prove useful to promote discussion. But they can also act as a distraction and lose relevance over time.
- Multiple measures, both qualitative and quantitative, will be needed. Also some sort of triangulation of analysis.
- The suitability and relevance of indicators varies according to time, stage of the organizational life cycle, contextual influences, stakeholder preferences, type of system, type of capacity issue, and many other factors. Excessive measurement to a young organization is as much a problem as no measurement is to a more mature formalized structure.
- Capacity indicators *by themselves* can provide only modest gains in meaning. They are like operational "can openers" that raise questions such as "so what?" For example, increased awareness (a good thing) can lead participants to give more negative readings to indicators (supposedly a bad thing). "Results" can go down as

real capacity development interventions address difficult issues of change and resistance.

- Many indicators by themselves increase reductionism and fragmentation of the system behavior they purport to measure. They are attached to only a small piece or element and tell us nothing about relationships to other aspects. To improve their contribution to a deeper understanding of capacity, they have to reflect patterns of systems change and emergence.

- Indicators are used much more to assess the tangible "what" and "when" as opposed to the intangible "how" and "why." Few programs, for example, assess learning objectives. In practice, there are usually whole areas of human behavior, such as identity, commitment, confidence, tenacity, legitimacy, that are crucial for evaluating capacity but that receive little attention from outside evaluators.

- Measurement and indicators are used in many instances to exert control. Effective evaluations address this issue by working to build some sort of consensus on a range of indicators. Indicators lose their utility when they are seen as an imposed, standardized, specialist activity.

- The use of storytelling to help people reconstruct or re-author their own or the organization's life story can be a useful form of measurement.

- Indicators in many capacity development interventions lose traction if their sole purpose is to determine if something is going "according to plan." Capacity "plans" these days are more likely to have a strategic intent that gets elaborated as implementation proceeds. A changing cast of indicators can be useful in tracking the course of implementation.

CHALLENGES IN CAPACITY EVALUATION

A discussion of the ten challenges facing the poor souls tasked with producing effective capacity evaluations are listed below in no particular order. Many other issues could also make the list, and I have included a list of barriers to capacity development in Appendix C.

Deciding on the Strategic Importance of the Capacity Development Issue in the Work of the Agency

One way or the other, all IDAs make some sort of determination, tacitly or explicitly, on two issues to do with the strategic importance of the capacity issue as an element of their overall mix of evaluation activities. First, they come to some sort of view about the types of capacity and capacity interventions (see Appendix D for a rough typology) they think they should make. And second, they decide about the degree to which they will build their own capabilities to support capacity development (see Appendix E for another simple typology). The challenge for IDAs lies in aligning agency capabilities with the implications of their strategic choice about the capacity issue. And one of those capabilities is that of designing and managing capacity evaluations. IDAs that are only interested in the capacity "basics," for example, are not likely to make the investments in serious evaluations.

Most IDAs, in my experience, choose to fudge and muddle. Given the incentives and pressures in the aid business and the ease of creating appearances around the capacity issue, the temptation is to symbolically claim a lofty option ("capacity development is a core function") while tacitly avoiding the difficult operational decisions needed to support it. My sense is that the fudging and muddling option catches up with IDAs at the operational level in terms of weak capacity development (CD) strategies and, for our purposes, ineffective evaluations. In many cases, funds are available for only one-shot, conventional evaluations with limited chances to come up with a comprehensive analysis given the constraints.[11]

Building a Corporate Capability for Capacity Evaluation

Most IDAs encourage their country partners to make efforts to develop their capabilities. And then flinch a bit when they have to confront many of the same issues in their own organization. The question is not just how to carry out a capacity evaluation, but also "what kind of evaluations do we really want?" "What will be the mix of purposes for such evaluations?" "Who are the real audiences?" And "How should an IDA develop its own capacity for supporting effective capacity evaluations?" My own list of corporate capability would include corporate commitment and values, tested methodologies, varied approaches, staff skills and incentives, country ownership, intellectual mastery of the ideas, organizational culture, traditions of effectiveness, and tolerance for risk and failure.

Designing Different Kinds of Capacity Evaluations

The wide range of capacity situations requires a wide range of evaluation types. Some are summative and oriented to an overall judgment. Some are formative and aimed at improvements. Some are comprehensive, rigorous and detailed. Others are close to being "quick and dirty" or at least rapid and "good enough" to meet bureaucratic purposes. The challenge facing IDAs is to match up the right evaluation choice and strategy to the particular demands of an individual situation. As in most things, "one size fits all" no longer works in capacity evaluation.

Addressing the Substantive Capacity Issues

For reasons I won't go into in this chapter, the field of capacity as a body of theory and practice still has not come up with convincing answers to a range of questions. For example:

- What exactly is capacity or even a capability? What constitutes these conditions under a range of different circumstances and configurations? What do they look like? How do we know that capacity exists given its inherent condition as a potential state?
- How do capacity and capabilities come about? What are the processes and strategies of personal, organizational, institutional and systems change that lead to their formation or emergence?
- What does it mean for an individual to be capacitated? How do people develop that combination of faith, tenacity and confidence?

Most IDAs still have only rudimentary answers to these questions. Most evaluations thus start from scratch with the evaluators and some of the participants coming up with a variety of formulations, some of which may be limited or contradictory. But IDAs and their country partners need to be able to exert some sort of substantive guidance on these types of issues.

Country Participation and Ownership

As mentioned earlier, the evaluation of capacity is not an exercise that lends itself to objective, third-party extraction. Country participants need full involvement for a variety of reasons.[12]

- The vital, tacit information that is needed to help make serious judgments about capacity is usually locked up in the heads of the country participants. Any capacity evaluation that cannot tap into country learning and communication systems, especially those that are hidden and informal, is not going to come up with much in the way of useful insights. Demand-side approaches to capacity development, for example, are based on the assumption that citizens as "customers" are best placed to assess the capacity and performance of service providers.

- Inevitably, capacity evaluations need to address the multiple perspectives at the country level of capacity itself and of the conduct and purpose of the evaluation. That effort is needed to help give the evaluation the legitimacy and the audience in the country that will help to make it useful.
- Country staff at the middle levels of formal organizations are frequently asked to provide support for external evaluations. Most do not have the interest, incentives, time, or resources to do so. Some earlier involvement and support can help with this issue.
- Improving country competencies and capabilities to carry out evaluations should be a key objective of any capacity evaluation.[13] A number of countries such as Ghana are now designing and managing their own evaluations of external programs.
- Country participation forces IDAs to be clearer about the objectives and the agendas being served by the evaluation. And to decide whose reality finally counts in terms of evaluating success and failure, For example, not so much "what worked?" but rather "what worked for whom in what ways and from what perspectives?"
- Country involvement can mean more than just the inclusion of country people on evaluation teams. In some instances, it can refer to engaging the public in the discussion by disseminating key evaluation findings. In Haiti, for example, World Bank Institute findings on corruption became a subject of debate in the media. In South Africa, citizen report cards were combined with GIS and Google Mapping to give the public a pattern of good and bad municipal performance.

We need to be realistic about the potential and possibilities of country participation in capacity evaluation. Many country participants still see their involvement as part of the costs of doing business with IDAs. They remain to be convinced about whose views count in evaluations and who ultimately benefits. And many simply do not have the time given the pervasive shortage of competent people, most of whom are being courted by other IDAs to participate in their evaluations.

In addition, we know that in many instances, a whole host of ethical, security, and political economy issues arise that can be unsettling at the country level. The provision of information can be difficult particularly if it leads to questioning the power and legitimacy of existing leaders. Research results can destabilize a tacit consensus at the country or organizational level that can, in turn, lead to tension and conflict. And participation in an evaluation can put country researchers in professional or physical danger.

The Selection and Contribution of Capacity Assessment Tools

A constant refrain in the capacity world revolves around the need for more and better analytical tools despite (or because of) the fact that many of the existing ones produce little of value in terms of capacity analysis. Part of the explanation has to do with tacit country rejection of being constantly assessed and evaluated using generic, imported frameworks supplied by external funding groups. Such frameworks usually pay little attention to country patterns of thinking and learning. What appears to be needed are ways of thinking and learning that individual programs (and evaluations) evolve and create and legitimize over time.[14] The use of development evaluation allows that process to happen in a way that can better surface country opinion and generate discussion.

Capacity Evaluations as Exercises in Integration

All capacity evaluations face a major challenge of integration. To produce findings that are relevant and legitimate, they must bring together insights on the technical (e.g., environmental protection), the capacity (e.g., issues to do with in organizational and institutional change), the contextual (e.g., the influence of political pressures), the historical (e.g., the constraints facing the evolution of the capacity intervention over time), the methodological (e.g., data analysis), the managerial (e.g., lessons for operational staff), and the participatory (e.g., the views of diverse stakeholders in the country). Part of the issue facing IDAs is deciding on how best to achieve this kind of integration and the degree to which it is feasible. My own experience is that most capacity evaluations that come at the end of a program have only a limited chance to master the dynamics of the integration and synthesis that is needed to produce real insight.

Capacity Evaluation Should Be Part of a Broader Learning Process both Within the Overall Intervention and Within the Participating Governments and Funding Agencies

The utility of capacity evaluations, in my experience, can be greater if they can contribute to, and draw energy from, a broader culture and practice of learning and adaptation both in the IDA and in the country. All of us are aware of the barrier to learning in most development situations, but participants can do things to encourage the learning aspects.

- The tensions in capacity evaluations between learning and accountability can be diffused by having different types of evaluations support these objectives separately. Development evaluation is more learning-focused. Summative ones can contribute more to accountability.
- A developmental evaluation can be supported at the field level by action learning and research on specific issues such as those to do with political economy. Capacity as an issue usually gets less direct research attention outside the process of an evaluation.
- An IDA intervention can try to create a community of learning by supplying the incentives, discussion spaces, financial resources, and staff time.
- IDAs in particular can try to understand country thinking, learning, and communication styles and make some effort to tailor the evaluation process to fit within some of those processes. Huge amounts of country knowledge are usually trapped in pockets and bureaucratic caves in countries but with effort, it can still be harnessed for productive gain.
- IDAs can rethink the reporting procedures on a program to induce more country interest and involvement.[15]

Addressing the Simple, the Complicated and the Complex[16]

Many of the current conventional methodologies in development analysis—log frames, logic models, results-based management, planned change, linear cause and effect, optimal solutions, predetermined objectives and milestones, deliverables, targeting, strategic planning—are implicitly based on the assumption of capacity situations being relatively closed and simple, stable and predictable. But more and more capacity development interventions have now shifted into the complicated and complex categories as they move from "micro" to "macro" and from the technical to the political.

At the very least, IDAs now need a variety of mindsets and methodologies that can help country participants to address the full spectrum of capacity challenges, particularly those that involve greater uncertainty, conflict, and multi-stakeholder diversity.[17] The most obvious sign of this trend is the growing use of complex adaptive systems thinking, which is designed to help participants address complexity and "wicked" problems in which neither ends nor means are clear at the outset. This applies to capacity evaluations as well (see, e.g., Williams & Imam, 2007).

Failure, Success, Ethics, and Honesty

A sense of unreality pervades some of the discussion on capacity development in low-income countries. Part of this unreality has to do with the famous "hiding hand" theory articulated by Albert Hirschman (1967) many years ago, namely that if outsiders were actually clear on what they were getting into when trying to help low-income countries, they would never agree to get involved in the first place. Given their inherent difficulty and constraints, most CD interventions in international development fail to achieve their intended objectives. And yet the mindset and survival strategies of the international development industry are based on the likelihood of success and effectiveness. Failure is seen as an aberration which casts in doubt the overall value of development cooperation. That view creates the constant need for IDAs to persuade domestic constituencies of the symbolic value of taxpayer-supported interventions in post-conflict states. And that impulse, in turn, can lead to a pervasive set of incentives on all sides for fudging, lack of transparency, gaming, and limiting learning that exposes failure and underachievement.[18]

Three issues to do with risk and failure.

- First, we need to put this high potential rate of failure in perspective. The brutal fact is that most efforts at organizational and institutional change fail *everywhere* most of the time—*especially the first time*—including in the private sector in high-income countries. The idea that capacity development in low-income countries, arguably the most difficult institutional challenge imaginable, can expect (and sometimes claim) a higher rate of success is a bit far-fetched. Rescuing banks in America or reforming the European Union looks fairly simple compared to the challenge of helping to turn such countries into functioning Weberian states. Capacity development usually takes place in conditions of uncertainty, conflict, and complexity. The contextual factors are not well understood. Western models of planned institutional change, in particular, do badly in these types of situations. Knowledge amongst all the participants is limited. Most efforts are going to fail. Period. The challenge here is in balancing excusing and tolerating poor outcomes with the recognition of the need for greater realism in assessing and judging efforts and outcomes.
- Second, the basic line of argument in the private sector seems worth considering in capacity development, namely that initial failure is frequently a precondition of later success, that a solid failure should be so recognized, that losing efforts should be stripped of their insights and left behind, that the failure of most interventions is

the price of doing the business of capacity development, and that finally, the few successes will more than compensate for the many failures. Could this line of reasoning have any chance of influencing judgments about the overall effectiveness of CD in low-income states? Can it be done without the support of public and political opinion in IDA countries? Could IDAs be more open about publicly addressing the risks that lie in wait for any effort at capacity development? Or are IDAs condemned to promise levels of success in capacity development that are simply unattainable? Put another way, can we design and carry out capacity evaluations that can tell us when the results have been "good enough" (see Meharg, 2009)?

- Third, judgments of success and failure are rarely yes-or-no choices. Most capacity evaluations turn out to be complex mixtures of achievement, hope, and disappointment. Looked at from one perspective by one group, the outcomes are disappointing. Looked at from another by a quite different set of observers, the reverse can be true.

FINAL POINT

Capacity evaluation remains a work in progress to put it mildly, and yet its development is of real importance. Capacity is not simply a logistical means to larger development ends. It is rather an end in itself in the sense of people in low-income countries equipping themselves with the skills and abilities to make a life for themselves. IDA support of evaluation approaches that can give greater clarity and energy to the exercise is an important contribution to development.

APPENDIX A: DEFINITIONS OF CAPACITY

Not surprisingly, there are a range of definitions for capacity that reflect different perspectives on the idea and the interests of different organizations.[23] The following are typical.

- The Development Assistance Committee of the OECD defines capacity as "the ability of people, organizations and society as a whole to manage their affairs successfully."
- The UNDP views capacity as "the ability of individuals, organizations and societies to perform functions, solve problems, and set and achieve objectives in a sustainable manner."[24]
- The International Development Research Center defines capacity as "the ability of an individual, group, network, organization or society to identify and analyze situation, and to have the ability to perform critical tasks that enables it to solve development challenges over time and in a sustainable manner."
- A definition by Alan Fowler (independent consultant) states that capacity is "the capability of an organization as being able to achieve effectively what it sets out to do."
- The Pathways for Women's Empowerment at the Institute for Development Studies in Sussex understands capacity building as "facilitating adaptive learning processes through which individuals and institutions become better able to pursue collective goals."
- The Merriam-Webster online dictionary defines capacity as "the facility or power to produce, perform or deploy."
- An NGO (CDRA) in South Africa defines it as "the ability to function as a resilient, strategic and autonomous entity."[25]
- A systems view sees capacity as "that emergent combination of individual competencies and collective capabilities which enables a human system to create public value."

There is both difference and convergence in these definitions. Some are narrower and focus more on problem solving, carrying out technical functions and performance. Some are broader and are more concerned about country systems being able to survive, grow, and create value. But all have at their core a common idea that focuses on the ability or willingness, power, and skill to do something. From an aid perspective, capacity thus has to do with the collective ability of people to generate some sort of positive developmental gain over time. Such ability can be at the level of individuals (in the form of skills or competencies), groups, organizations, and systems (in the form of collective skills and capabilities). Such capabilities can be located in public sector organizations, in NGOs or in private firms. Capacity development can thus refer to the processes and interventions that enable such abilities to emerge over time.

Capacity as a condition then is a condition or state made up of individual competencies and collective abilities that combine and emerge into some form of system that allows performance to take place. Capacity development is the process that contributes the resources, the strategies, the motivations, the ideas and so on to encourage that emergence.

APPENDIX B: EVALUATION METHODOLOGIES

Most Significant Change (MSC)[19]

This is a methodology developed in the 1990s to get beyond the dysfunctional effects of the log frame. Its characteristics can be summed up as follows:

- Tries to identify significant changes, both foreseen and unforeseen, in system behavior
- Within certain domains of action
- Also positive and negative changes
- Does not rely on predetermined indicators or outcomes
- Tries to be as participatory as possible both internally and externally
- Can be used for capacity or performance
- Relies on the collection of stories and participant accounts
- Uses some form of purposive sampling
- Can be supplemented by additional conventional analysis

Development Evaluation (Gamble, 2008)

- Focused on adapting to the emergent uncertainties of social innovations in complex environments[20]
- Works better at early stages
- Compared to formative and summative evaluations[21]
- Focused on early stages of org development
- Ongoing process of continuous improvement
- Tries to balance rigor of evaluation with role of organizational development coaching
- Design of evaluation co-evolves with the program system
- Involves longer-term partnering relationships
- Combination of monitoring and conventional evaluation, of critical and creative thinking
- Designed to support experimentation, exploration and reaction to unforeseen events
- Focused on learning
- Based on emergence and complexity
- Is simultaneously engaged and reflective, diagnostic more than prescriptive
- May involve constant redesign and changing array of tools and frameworks
- Tries to track capacity patterns over time
- Capacity as a possible scenario result not a predicted outcome
- Instrument of transformative change especially at the earlier stages of innovation and experimentation.

- Part of the system by designing, implementing feedback loops
- Should be simple and self-documenting
- Each loop is a potential focus for observation, learning, measurement, assessment

Results-Based (Kusek & Rist, 2004)

- Based on ideas of strategic planning and logic models
- Differentiates between implementation monitoring and results monitoring
- Useful for simplifying and summarizing the rationale and components
- Useful in situations where the means and ends are relatively clear
- Emphasizes clarity and control over adaptation
- Best suited to projects and quantitative indicators
- More reassuring to provide upward development accounting and accountability
- Assumes the single-actor model
- Not oriented towards capturing the unforeseen and unexpected. Focuses on a narrow range of expected results.
- Assumes that a pre-implementation consensus of the participants is necessary and possible
- Pays little attention to the influence of contextual factors
- Offers few insights on how change happens. No process orientation. Mainly unidirectional causality.
- Assumes a cause and effect and attribution that is not usually relevant
- Usually combined with RBM techniques

Contribution Analysis[22]

- Works more on basis of plausible association
- Tries to paint a credible picture about the attribution of an intervention
- Based on the assumption that a number of other factors are influencing capacity development and performance
- Explores and discusses plausible alternatives
- Uses outside expert opinion
- Can use multiple lines of evidence

Theory-Based

- Based on a set of assumptions—the program theory—about causal relationships.
- Tries to disentangle various stages of the causal chain
- Focused on understanding not just what works but why

- Used to identify intermediate outcomes that might lead to longer-term impacts
- Identify the contextual factors

Outcome Mapping (Earl, Carden, & Smutylo, 2001)

- Boundary partners
- Spread of possible outcomes
- Behavioral change
- Moving to complexity and systems
- Not product-focused
- Focused on incremental changes
- Focused on immediate sphere of influence
- More on the context

Complex Adaptive Systems (CAS)

- Based on idea of a complex human system in a continuous state of change
- Complexity from large number of variables and number of system agents
- Change is mainly emergent and unpredictable and not amenable to cause and effect reasoning.
- No pattern remains for long and no single intervention has a predictable result
- Nonlinear change driven by behavior of agents interacting with each other and the environment
- System is self-organizing
- An "end-point evaluation only" will not work
- System recognizes no boundaries in time
- Needs to focus on both long-term and short-term
- Needs to incorporate multiple strategies, cycle times, time horizons, dimensions, and informants
- The evaluation process itself becomes an actor in the complex emergent behavior in a CAS
- Need to capture emerging patterns over time
- Complex systems are shaped by "attractors" that are governed by simple rules
- The use of an evaluation as a transformative feedback loop

APPENDIX C: SOME BARRIERS TO EFFECTIVE CAPACITY EVALUATION

Capacity evaluations underachieve for many reasons. Here is my own list of the usual suspects.

- Capacity development (CD) is seen by many as a general human development activity that everybody understands (more or less), everybody does, and anybody can do. It is not a particular body of knowledge. Hence anybody can also evaluate it without much in the way of specific knowledge about capacity issues. Both the UNDP and FAO, for example, have carried out evaluations of their CD work using a CD "adviser" on the team. It's hard to imagine a similar arrangement for an evaluation of economic or environmental policy or performance. To make matters worse, many evaluators also have no particular skills on evaluation.
- There is frequently a double "dead space" at the heart of most capacity evaluations. There is almost always no clear understanding of what a particular capability would look like, how it would be configured in an organization or system, or what its elements would be. If, for example, we think that the capability to adapt is crucial to the Ministry of Finance, what would that mean specifically? How would it be assessed and measured? We also are unclear about the complex change issues. Evaluators find it hard to disentangle the particular intervention being evaluated from other efforts and trends under way. The result is frequently a muddled analysis at the heart of the evaluation.
- Donors tend to avoid including their own behavior and contribution in the scope of the evaluation. And yet a capacity evaluation is, in practice, two complex systems banging into each other. Donor actions frequently have a major impact on the capacity outcomes. In retaliation, country participants can tacitly decide to retaliate by buffering their own systems from serious evaluative scrutiny.
- Evaluations are carried out in an effort to determine program extensions or increases/decreases to future funding. Invariably, participants at all levels come under pressure to play the game and contribute to an outcome that is at the least good enough to lead to more funding. Serious learning takes a back seat.
- There is a disagreement about the basic rules of the evaluation. Evaluators, many times with the tacit agreement of the donor, decide that success or failure will be judged against the preselected RBM objectives put in place at the beginning of the program. No documentation is available on how and why these objectives were

changed or adapted. Any consensus within the program about its potential value and fairness breaks down.

- Country managers can be unenthusiastic about evaluating capacity. They don't really get the concept, and to the extent that they do, they regard it as another donor fixation designed to complicate their lives. External evaluators with no clue about such things as political or tribal pressures will make lofty judgments about what can and should be done—and will go around the organization asking staff about the effectiveness of leadership.

- The evaluation does not end up with the data it needs to make serious judgments. People are uncertain about how to map capacity at the outset. Baselines were not or could not be collected for a variety of reasons including lack of trust. Some of the data relate to issues that are personally and politically sensitive. No real effort is made over time to collect much in the way of quantitative or qualitative information. The donor, for example, has not been prepared to pay costs involved. Middle-level staff has no incentive to do so. Simply put, the prior investment in data gathering and background analysis needed to help make the capacity puzzle emerge is not made by any of the participants.

- Evaluation can become a major barrier to innovation and experimentation. Demands for demonstrable results, accountability, and cost effectiveness as evidenced through evaluation can shut down the process of evaluation. Funding is sought only for those safer interventions that can fit within the confines of the conventional, narrowly focused, results-based logic model that comforts IDAs. Over time, a marriage of convenience emerges with donors providing the money and implementers providing the "proof" that enables the system to keep going at a steady but ineffective level.

- Too many capacity evaluations misjudge the boundaries of the system they are evaluating. They evaluate an organization for example, without realizing that the organization is simply one part of a larger, more complex informal network that has many elements and actors that shape the behavior and performance of the individual organization.

- The evaluation makes a mismatch between the stage of capacity development of the system to be evaluated and the nature and methodology of the evaluation. It assumes a system in, say, Stage 4 of its development and looks for capacity characteristics typical of that stage. But in practice, it is dealing with a system at a much earlier stage of development. Issues to do with time and pace of development are misjudged, leading to negative ratings on a system that is actually progressing well.

- Many capacity evaluations fail to make much contribution to accountability. They seem to be formulaic exercises that, in the words of one analyst, "guess at what will satisfy the demand for accountability without actually internalizing what it means to be accountable." Accountability upwards to donors frequently adds little. And accountability downwards to country citizens/clients/customers bumps up against IDA systems and procedures that are not designed to support this aspect.
- The whole capacity development process is fractured. People present at the beginning of a program in both the country and the IDA are often long gone by the end. Initial dilemmas and interpretations are lost. "Design" is done in one context, data collected in another and explained in yet another

APPENDIX D: TYPES OF CAPACITY DEVELOPMENT INTERVENTIONS

Level 1

- Focused on improvement to technical capabilities and functions
- Focused on knowledge as the main improvement
- Focused on addressing technical gaps and weaknesses
- Focused mainly on individuals and organizations

Level 2

- Focused on broader capacity improvements at the organizational level including the structural and the logistical
- Assumes that technical improvements need to be at least complemented and supplemented by systems upgrades

Level 3

- Intervening to address more complex multi-actor systems at the sector, network, regional, national or global levels

Level 4

- Intervening to address the so-called "softer" aspects of capacity including leadership, motivation, incentives, values, identity, culture, values

Level 5

- Intervening to address complex issues of institutional, organizational, political and social change such as legitimacy,
- Sees the creation or enhancement of country capacity in all its various forms as the key contribution.

APPENDIX E: POSITIONING AND CAPABILITIES OF THE IDA

Level 1: The Basics

- Capacity development (CD) is seen as an implementation means to larger policy ends.
- CD is seen as an individual "process" component of a larger "product" program.
- The donor needs no particular in-house expertise on capacity issues.
- It has no tested tools or frameworks that it uses on a regular basis.
- CD not seen as a key contribution of the donor in terms of "core function."
- It has no particular corporate CD strategy.
- Sees capacity as mainly an activity at the individual or organizational level.
- Senior managers have little direct interest in CD issues.
- It has no particular approach to CD evaluation.

Level 2: The Mid-Range

- Has a corporate CD strategy that tries to capture broader lessons
- The agency has some in-house expertise on the subject
- Has developed a range of tools and frameworks

Level 3: CD as a Genuine Priority

- Has mastered various analytical approaches to CD
- Sees CD as a developmental end in itself against which other objectives can be traded off
- Staff have individual competencies in analyzing and designing CD interventions
- Organization has a body of knowledge about capacity issues that can be used to support capacity evaluations
- CD is a key part of the contribution that legitimizes the organization

NOTES

1. To simplify the discussion, I have used the acronym IDAs to cover the range of external development agencies including NGOs.
2. An old theme. See Patton (2008).
3. "The monitoring and evaluation of capacity building is as much a challenge now as it was two decades ago" Nigel Simister (2009), p. 1
4. For example, a major workshop took place in Holland in May 20–21, 2010 on using complexity theory in evaluations.
5. Take for example, macro-capacities. See *The Atlantic Century: Bench Marking EU and US Innovation and Competitiveness,* February 2009, European-American Business Council.
6. There is a literature on evaluating empowerment in development. See, for example, Oakley (2001) and also Narayan (2005). This latter book defines empowerment as "the expansion of assets and capabilities of poor people to participate in, negotiate with, influence, control and hold accountable institutions that affect their lives."
7. Patton (2010) offers an introduction to this topic.
8. This accords with the idea of "boundary partners" in Outcome Mapping.
9. Outcome Mapping uses the technique of participants using outcome journals to capture the unforeseen (Earl, Carden, & Smutylo, 2001; p. 95)
10. Kusek and Rist (2004, p. 72) outline the debate about predesigned indicators. See also Morgan (2004).
11. A book that I have not read but which comes highly recommended is Michael J. Bamberger, Jim Rugh, and Linda Mabry's (2011) *RealWorld Evaluation: Working Under Budget, Time, Data and Political Constraints.*
12. For a full discussion, see Salmen and Kane (2007) and Bakewell, Adams, and Pratt (2004).
13. Kusec and Rist (2004, p. 40) have a useful section on doing a 'readiness' assessment to gauge the ability and willingness of country participants to develop an M&E system.
14. For a framework that emphasizes self-assessment and the customization for country needs, see Lusthaus, Adrien, Anderson, and Carden (1999).
15. For the analysis of an IDA attempting to do this, see Chapman, David, and Mancini (2004).
16. For an analysis of all three categories, see Westley, Zimmerman, and Patton (2007), p. 9.
17. One issue of interest: "Uncertainty" as a condition can frequently be addressed by the provision of more information and knowledge. "Ambiguity" and "paradox," in contrast, cannot be resolved in the same way.
18. For an analysis of the same pattern in the American education sector, see Ravitch (2010).
19. A manual on using MSC by Rick Davies and Jessica Dart can be located on the web (www.mande.co.uk/docs/MSCGuide.pdf).
20. Testing the theory behind the intervention in particular contexts and examining the role of other influencing factors to build a reasonably credible case about the difference an intervention made or is making.

21. Gamble (2008, p. 62) provides a comparison of "traditional" and "developmental evaluation."
22. For more analysis of this concept, see Mayne (1999).
23. For the most complete list of all the various definitions, see the IDS supplementary papers for the 2007 Capacity Collective Workshop, Table 1.
24. The UNDP uses the idea of 'functional capacities' in its Capacity Assessment Framework.
25. Alan Caplan, *The Development of Capacity*, 2003

REFERENCES

Bakewell, O., Adams, J., & Pratt, B. (2004). *Sharpening the development process: A practical guide to monitoring and evaluation.* Oxford, UK: INTRAC.

Bamberger, M. J., Rugh, J., & Mabry, L. (2011). *RealWorld evaluation: Working under budget, time, data and political constraints.* Thousand Oaks, CA: Sage.

Chapman, J. David, R., & Mancini, A. (2004). Transforming practice in ActionAid: Experiences and challenges in rethinking learning, monitoring and accountability systems. In L. Earle (Ed.), *Creativity and Constraint: Grassroots Monitoring and Evaluation and the International Aid Arena.* Oxford, UK: INTRAC.

Denning, S. (2004). *Squirrel Inc.: A fable of leadership through story telling.* San Francisco, CA: Jossey-Bass.

Earl, S., Carden, F., & Smutylo, T. (2001). *Outcome mapping: Building learning and reflection into development programs.* International Development Research Centre.

Gamble, J. A. A. (2008). *A developmental evaluation primer.* Montreal, Quebec: The J.W. McConnell Family Foundation.

Hirschman, A. (1967). *Development projects observed.* Washington, DC: Brookings Institution Press.

James, R. (2008). *Dealing with the dilemmas in monitoring and evaluating capacity building.* M&E Paper #2. Oxford, UK: INTRAC

Kelly, L. (2009). *Management and monitoring of capacity development. Guidance for AusAID program staff.* AusAID Report.

Kusek, J., & Rist, R. (2004). *Ten steps to a results-based monitoring and evaluation system.* Washington, DC: The World Bank.

Lipson, B., & Hunt, M. (2007). *Capacity building framework: A values-based programming guide.* Oxford, UK: INTRAC.

Lusthaus, C., Adrien, M.-H., Anderson, G., & Carden, F. (1999). *Enhancing organizational performance: A toolbox for self-assessment.* Ottowa, ON: IDRC Books.

Mayne, J. (June 1999). *Addressing attribution through contribution analysis: Using performance measures sensibly.* Paper by Office of the Auditor General of Canada.

Meharg, S. J. (2009). *Measuring effectiveness in complex operations: What is good enough?* Paper prepared for Canadian Defense and Foreign Affairs Institute.

Morgan, G. (1986). *Images of organization.* Thousand Oaks, CA: Sage.

Morgan, P. (2004). Measuring the development of capacity: Is this still a good idea? In L. Earle (Ed.), *Creativity and constraint: Grassroots monitoring and evaluation and the international aid arena* (pp. 47–62). Oxford, UK: INTRAC.

Narayan, D. (Ed.). (2005). *Measuring empowerment: Cross-disciplinary perspectives.* Washington, DC: The World Bank.

Oakley, P. (Ed.). (2001). *Evaluating empowerment: Reviewing the concept and practice.* Oxford, UK: INTRAC.

Patton, M. Q. (2008). *Utilization-focused evaluation.* Thousand Oaks, CA: Sage.

Patton, M. Q. (2009). *State of the art in measuring development assistance.* Retrieved from www.worldbank.org/ieg/conference/results/patton.pdf

Patton, M. Q. (2010). *Developmental evaluation: Applying complexity concepts to enhance innovation and use.* New York, NY: Guilford.

Ravitch, D. (2010). *The death and life of the great American school system.* New York, NY: Basic Books.

Salmen, L., & Kane, E. (2007), *Bridging diversity: Participatory learning for responsive development.* Washington, DC: The World Bank.

Simister, N. (2009). *Monitoring and evaluating capacity building: Is it really that difficult?*

Sigsgaard, P. (2004). Doing away with predetermined indicators: Monitoring using the most significant changes approach. In L. Earle, (Ed.), *Creativity and constraint: Grassroots monitoring and evaluation and the international aid arena* (pp. 125–136). UK: INTRAC.

Westley, F., Zimmerman, B., & Patton, M. Q. (2007). *Getting to maybe: How the world has changed.*

Williams, B., & Imam, I. (Eds.). (2007). *Systems concepts in evaluation: An anthology.* Los Angeles, CA: Edge Press.

ADDITIONAL RESOURCES

Bevan, P. (n.d.). *Evaluation methodologies for aid-financed development interventions: Some approaches to complexity,* PowerPoint presentation for Mokoro Ltd.

Ebrahim, A. (2003). *NGOs and organizational change: Discourse, reporting and learning,* Cambridge, UK: Cambridge University Press.

Hailey, J., James, R., & Wrigley, R. (2005). *Rising to the challenges: Assessing the impact of organizational capacity building. Praxis Paper #2* (pp. 137–153). Oxford, UK: INTRAC.

Light, P. (2004). *Sustaining nonprofit performance: The case for capacity building and the evidence to support it.* Washington, DC: Brookings Institute Press.

Morton, J. (2010). *A political economy of aid effectiveness.* Retrieved from www.jfmorton.co.uk

Sigsgaard, P. (2009). *Developing M&E systems for complex organizations: A methodology.* M&E Paper #3. Oxford, UK: INTRAC.

White, H. (2009). *Some reflections on current debates in impact evaluation.* International Initiative on Impact Evaluation (3ie) Working Paper 1.

CHAPTER 5

EVALUATING POLICY INFLUENCE

Fred Carden and Colleen Duggan

POLICY INFLUENCE

For a long time researchers have been struggling with the question of how their research can have an influence on public policy. While some research-ers focus exclusively on the research and leave the influence to others, there have always been some researchers who want to know that what they do is relevant and is used. So they struggle to figure out how, and that struggle has been going on for a very long time. Ideas on this were originally sim-plistic, even naive: good knowledge will be used, period. All we had to do was fund good, solid research and it would find its way into the policy arena and result in better quality of life for communities. However, researchers (and research funders) could not understand why their findings were not used: Why did policymakers ignore their findings? Why couldn't the policy-makers see what had to be done? Researchers slowly began to realize that policymakers were not waiting for evidence in order to act. They were in fact responding to many different factors at the same time. Knowledge was only one input. Very often—even usually—ideology and politics played a more important role—and still does today.

Emerging Practices in International Development Evaluation, pages 105–122
Copyright © 2013 by Information Age Publishing
105

Carol Weiss, in her seminal research on this topic in the 1970s and 1980s (Weiss 1977, 1982), found that research did have an influence, but that it was often incremental and took an extended period of time. She termed this phenomenon *enlightenment use through accretion*: the slow, consistent, and percolating process that research and evaluation findings undergo within policy debates and eventual influence on the policy decision process.

Weiss's insights help us understand the definition of policy influence, because we do not simply mean contributing to policy change. Sometimes that happens directly, but more often the influence is indirect. When we speak about policy influence, we also mean *expanding policy capacities*—both for researchers and decision makers. This involves increasing the capacity of researchers to think about the policy process in relation to their research as well as increasing the capacities of decision makers to make use of knowledge, especially knowledge that might not fit their preconceived notions of what is correct and what is politically feasible. Even though these efforts may not lead to immediate policy changes, over time we have a stronger policy environment that views research as a valuable asset. Expanding policy capacities also means broadening policy horizons, or opening up the understanding of both researchers and policymakers to the myriad influences inside and outside their scope of work that affect the decisions they have to make.[1]

We should not forget that research has to contend with politics, power, and position. Knowledge is not sufficient for change; there has to be a fit with the needs, expectations, and sociopolitical systems in place. In many situations, researchers have to bide their time until the conditions are in place for effective use of their findings.

THE EVALUATION

The International Development Research Centre (IDRC) is a public corporation supported by the Parliament of Canada. IDRC has a mandate to support research on development problems that face developing regions of the world and to build capacity for research in those regions. The focus on development suggests that some of the research IDRC supports should have an influence on public policy, but the Centre had never looked directly at this question. The evaluation unit led a study to define what the Centre means by policy influence, to identify where influence was evident and to map out the key factors that support or inhibit policy influence. This effort resulted in a study comprising 23 cases that cut across the regions and subject areas in which the IDRC provides active support. The cross-cutting nature of the cases was important to building a cross-center understanding of the nature and potential of policy influence. The cases were initially analyzed regionally in workshops where researchers, program staff, and evaluators presented their perspectives on policy influence and identified key factors. An analysis of the discussions at the four workshops (one each in Africa, Asia, and Latin America, as well as one at IDRC's head office in Ottawa) was used to carry out a more detailed analysis of the cases. This analysis led to the findings that will be outlined below.

THE LONG VIEW

When we were setting up this study to explore some of the research IDRC had supported to find out if and how it had an influence on public policy, Carol Weiss reminded us to take the long view. She reminded us that from the time the British Navy discovered the cause of scurvy, a disease that killed many sailors, until the time they enacted policy to deal with the problem was 150 years (fortunately the sailors did not wait for policy to take action!). So, we did take the long view by identifying projects with a long history and projects that were initiated in some cases 18 years before the start of this study. We wanted to find out where research had an influence with a view to identifying factors that could inform future research support (Box 5.1).

THE CASE OF THE ASIAN FISHERIES
SOCIAL SCIENCES RESEARCH NETWORK

An illustration of the long time involved is one of our cases, the Asian Fisheries Social Sciences Research Network (the network). The network was set up in 1983 when a small group realized that the fishery in South East Asia—which is the main resource of the poorest of the poor—was being managed only as a biological resource when its economic impact was so great. So they started the network, modestly at first, to bring a social science research perspective to the fishery. That started with training in economics and the economics of natural resources.

Once a number of people were trained, the network began to support research on fisheries economics and at the same time it continued to train more social scientists. So it was **expanding**. Research skills continued to develop in this period of **consolidation**.

Some policy research was tentatively initiated in the late 1980s. There was a significant group of researchers—14 teams, 80 researchers, from Thailand, Indonesia, Philippines, and Malaysia. Publication started and funding for research on the capture fishery and other topics began to emerge.

In the mid-1990s, some fifteen years after the network was first conceptualized, Vietnam joined. In this period, policy research began to take on a central function in the network. The network also took on **a life of its own** as the members recognized its value to their work. So the members began

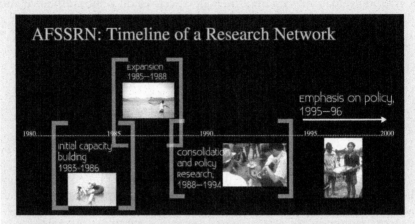

Figure 5.1 The case of the Asian Fisheries Social Sciences Research Network.

to build the other skills they would need to keep the network alive as an independent group. They continued to publish research, to meet, to build skills and to influence policy. The members were now in charge of research centers, senior players in ministries of fisheries and natural resources in their countries and in a position to influence decisions about management of the fishery.

Funding from the Centre ended in 1997, but the network did not fold at that point. The members found value in the group and they continue to meet and share knowledge and ideas and to influence fisheries policy.

THE FINDINGS

Perhaps one of the most interesting findings from this study is that findings are related to context, both the general context as well as the decision context. Context is messy and uncertain, difficult to define and capture how it influences how we act. The environment plays an enormously powerful role; we often put down success or failure to context without a very thorough understanding of what that means. It is a bit of a black box, but one that this study illuminated in some useful ways.

What emerged from the 23 cases was a set of five contingencies, or general factors in the context and five decision contexts within which research took place. How researchers acted in each of those contexts was necessarily different if they were going to be successful. The nature of their relationships varied, how they communicated was affected, and where they placed their effort changed. Maximizing opportunities for influence calls for researchers to have an understanding of the environments in which they work—and to adjust as the context changes over time.

EXPLOITING CONTINGENCIES: THE GENERAL CONTEXT

In our case studies we identified five system contingencies, or system context factors, that deserve attention because they played such a key role. These are not factors researchers can control but are variables that they need to consider in thinking through an influence strategy—if you are going to wend your way through the confusion, a strategy is helpful. The strategy needs to be emergent and accepted as a living strategy that will be affected by changes over time. As such it should address things that are fixed in a system as well as things that are changing. It considers power differentials; it includes choices that societies make; and it represents symbiosis in that all the different actors work together in a chaotic but ultimately successful enterprise, at least where a society is largely functional. These notions are represented in the five contingencies outlined below:

Capacity of Policymakers to Apply Research

Weak government capacity can limit the use of research findings. Some of the cases we looked at worked to overcome this problem by working with decision makers as well as researchers. In Senegal, where public advocacy and critique of government are not encouraged, the leader of a poverty research project spent much time over a number of years informally advising government officials, creating opportunities for exchange of ideas and dialogue to strengthen the capacities of government officials to work with the research findings. When the poverty needs research emerged, the policymakers had a ready understanding of what research could provide to meet their new need and had developed a trusting relationship with the researcher. In other projects such as the Latin American Trade Network, researchers found themselves spending a good deal more time than they expected educating policymakers on the use of research.

Stability of Decision Making Institutions

Because of the importance of relationships in policy influence, the nature of decision-making institutions must be taken into account. Where there is rapid turnover at the senior levels, it is extremely difficult for researchers to establish strong and trusting relationships. Shifts of power from the legislative to executive branches of government, as in the Guatemala case, left the researchers completely unprepared. In the Ukraine, researchers coped with institutional instabilities by focusing at two levels—the general public and the presidency—a highly stable part of a generally unstable system.

The Latin American Trade Network coped with rapid changes at the senior levels due to high turnover in government systems in the region by focusing on the third level down in the bureaucracy where relative stability prevailed and where the revolving bureaucrats at the top had to turn for policy advice. Mapping the characteristics of the system you operate within is key.

Nature of Governance: Decentralization or Tight Government Control

The influence of research is not solely in the purview of democratic systems of government, nor is it the purview of centralized or decentralized systems. What matters is *alignment* of the influence plan with the real-world structure of decision making. Whatever the governance system, knowledge can have an influence. In the Philippines when the poverty monitoring system was highly effective in helping with the policy process in Palawan province, there was a desire to expand the approach to other provinces. The decentralized system meant a more intensive effort to mobilize implementation. In Vietnam, economic analysis was avidly consumed by a highly centralized system of government as it made the transition to a market-based economy.[2]

Countries in Transition

The last example of economic transition in Vietnam highlights another important contingency. Countries in transition offer special opportunities for influence. Where a major change is under way, policymakers are much more willing to innovate and consider unorthodox thought. They are often more willing to admit a lack of knowledge and to seek external inputs. These are not easy settings in which to work, and major advances and major setbacks come quickly and often from unexpected directions.

Economic Conditions

Economic crisis is the final contingency. In most cases where government receptivity to research was highest, government leaders were responding to an economic imperative. In Vietnam, for example, policymakers were open because they were responding to an imperative to modernize and reform the economic system. In Senegal, leaders sought out research because of demands for reform put forward in the poverty alleviation process advocated by the World Bank and the International Monetary Fund.

These contingencies change over time in any setting. They may merge, new demands and crises take hold, and researchers need to be attentive to these changes if they are to continue to succeed in their quests for policy influence.

THE DECISION CONTEXT

The second element of context is the decision context. This describes the willingness of decision makers to make decisions. Clearly this plays a central role in the use of knowledge because even good data that do not fit into the decisions makers' framework will be far less likely to be used. Advocates can influence the decision context in a variety of ways once they understand it. They can influence it directly by advocating for findings through communities, the media, or through parallel research. In our case studies, we identified five decision contexts that were at play that affected the influence research was able to have.

The first decision context emerges when there is *clear government demand* for knowledge. Some may see this as the best of all possible worlds, and indeed it does mean that findings get used. At the same time, it requires two things of researchers or those doing analytical work: (1) they must have trusting relationships built on a reputation for solid research, and (2) they must have anticipated the demand in advance because there is nothing worse than having a policymaker come for advice and saying "give me a year to do the research." With these two provisos, the potential for influence is highest in this context. We also saw this most often in new policy contexts, where major transitions were underway in a government or where a new and unknown field emerged. For example, the explosion of internet and wireless communications put enormous demands on national regulatory systems. Governments did not have a history of dealing with these new systems and so were more willing to turn to research for help than in traditional fields such as health care or education. In this decision context, clear and cogent arguments are central.

The second decision context occurs when there is *government interest in the problem but leadership is absent.* The issue is well known, and as a result, there is no institutional structure to deal with the issue. In this context, researchers have to exercise a leadership role, building relationships and focusing attention on the institutional needs as well as on the research itself. In other words, beyond the findings themselves, an implementation plan is essential. This leadership role is not comfortable to all researchers. Of course, clear and cogent arguments remain central; policy briefs and related products become more important in moving the ideas higher on the decision agenda.

The third decision context is when there is *government interest in a salient policy problem, but there is a resources gap*. The implementation challenge here is different. Not only are institutional structures missing, but the priority of the issue must be increased so that resources are diverted to address it. Again, researchers are not used to operating in these spaces. The strength of argument becomes more important because there is some persuasion and even advocacy needed—not so much on the importance of the issue itself, but to assist decision makers in shifting resources from another priority.

The fourth, and most common, decision context is when there is *strong researcher interest in the problem, but policymakers are uninterested or even unaware*. It is not surprising this is the most common. Research is often at the forefront, and researchers are often ahead of the curve in defining issues. Because of a lack of interest from policymakers, it is also the most challenging position from which to create policy influence, but some succeed. In these success examples we see many relationship-building activities—relationships with decision makers, with the community, with the press. We see remarkable persistence and patience during the relationship-building process. We see strong communication skills, strong advocacy skills, and an ability to mobilize public opinion. Sometimes these efforts succeed, and sometimes they do not.

The fifth and final decision context is when there is *researcher/analyst interest in an issue, but there is disinterest or hostility from government*. This often represents the failure of efforts to influence policy and requires persistence and careful nurturing of research findings over a long period of time to seize any window of opportunity that might emerge to reintroduce the issue. As in science, policy conditions change over time, and analysts armed with good data can seize those moments to move an issue up the policy agenda. Researchers need to show great patience and persistence, to fight another day to bring their research to the policy table.

These five decision contexts were found across the cases. Together with the general context elements, they provide a framework for determining what environment you are working in and what your potential for success is. They also signal what you need to work on in order to achieve success.

HAVING INFLUENCE: WHAT YOU CAN DO

So far we have discussed context and knowing how to move in a chaotic, uncertain, and very real system. But there are also common elements that are under the control of the researchers that can be used to influence policy over time:

- Communications
- Relationship building

- Networks of influence
- Institution building

Over time and during different policy readiness contexts, the importance of these four activities (communications, relationship building, networks of influence, and institution building) can change and evolve. For example, in times when policymakers demand advice, *how* you communicate that advice is less important: a glossy brochure is simply not needed. But when you have to persuade, cajole, convince, or involve interested publics, communication involves more than transmitting a cogent message; it also involves the creation of both personal and well-prepared briefs, seeking support of advocates.

At all levels and all stages, relationship building is central. When decision makers seek advice, they are going to seek it most likely from people they know and trust (either personally or by reputation). So you have to have a working relationship that will allow them to talk to you and seek your advice when they are ready to listen.

Networks of influence are also needed at different times during the influence process. Key members in a network may become critical in different decisional contexts. If a policymaker is interested in understanding how a particular stakeholder group will respond to a change in policy that is research-based, then researchers should be able to utilize their network to answer this question. They may even go further and make sure that key stakeholder groups are represented in the network and are willing to endorse the research findings.

Institution building is an interesting issue because there is often a leadership gap in the decision-making process. The researcher must consider the implications of the findings for either the rules of the game (changing institutions) or implementation of the rules (changing organizations). How will the policy be implemented, by whom and in what setting, and in what department? As the process moves up the decision chain to towards open policy windows these issues becomes more important until the decision is taken.

In these contexts, researchers have to build a range of skills beyond their research function. They cannot content themselves with simply doing good research but must find ways to think about how it will be implemented and what their role will be. However, they don't need to do this all alone. Rather, they need to build teams and work with others to create a setting in which all these skills are present and are part of the process of using research— knowledge and ideas—to influence the policy process. We frequently heard from researchers that they could not do all these things, that they could do good research but that it was up to others to figure out how to use the findings. In our cases, research did have an influence when there was evidence of the abilities and characteristics outlined above. In some cases, we saw the characteristics embodied in a single researcher. More often than not, we saw teams and we saw researchers who could make use of other groups such as the media and special interest groups to advance their agendas.

WHAT DOES ALL THIS MEAN FOR EVALUATING POLICY INFLUENCE?

The goal of this chapter is to present a framework for evaluating policy influence. Given the central importance of context, it was important to situate this approach in the findings that gave rise to it. Below is a suggested framework for evaluation that is based in the findings of the case studies and that builds on the realist evaluation approach advocated by Pawson and Tilley (1997; Pawson 2006).[3] It is one of the few frameworks that directly integrates context into its evaluation approach rather than treating context as an external problem or an independent variable. "In the realist model, the primary ambition of research synthesis is explanation building.... [T]he overall intention is to create an abstract model of how and why programs work, which can then be used to provide advice on the implementation and targeting of any novel incarnation of the intervention" (Pawson, 2006, p. 74).

It is important to remember that influence is not an end in itself. Rather, in development contexts, we are seeking policy change that will be implemented and that will contribute to social betterment. As Mario Morino, Chairman of Venture Philanthropy Partners, discusses in his blog entry (Morino, 2010), what is critical is sorting out the real outcomes we are striving to achieve and measure our progress against those goals. Too often we focus on the intermediate steps that are easier to measure and lose sight of the end we are striving to achieve.

A second important aspect of evaluating policy influence is recognizing that contexts vary over time. It is therefore impossible to conceive of a singular approach, a silver bullet on how to make policy change that will contribute to development, because often it is an iterative process. What we are seeking is a better understanding of the patterns and relationships among key actors and their contexts. We are, as Lindblom noted in the follow-up work to his well-known disjointed incrementalism (or "muddling through") approach to planning, "still muddling, not yet through" (Lindblom, 1979). As such, realist synthesis is particularly relevant because it pushes for a focus on *why*, *when*, and *how* change happens, not on the more easily measured question of whether or not change has happened. In that framing, there is only good practice, there is no "best practice" in evaluating policy influence. As Pascale and Sternin (2005, p. 3) note, "Best practices are a foreign import. No surprise, then, that they suffer a dismal replication rate" (quoted in Amato & Armstrong, 2010, p. 2). This chapter presents one good practice. Other approaches should also be considered (for example, the Research and Policy in Development Program at the Overseas Development Institute).

One of the biggest challenges in evaluating policy influence is the lack of transparency in the policy process. How decisions are made is not always obvious, and there is not always willingness to give credit to evidence—nor is there always willingness to accept evidence. Finding evidence of change is therefore difficult. A thoughtful focus on the theory of change behind research intended to influence policy is a critical element in looking at the value of such research. It must not only be validated against whether or not clear and direct linkages can be attributed but rather against whether or not the theory of change proposed warrants inferences as to the influence of the research findings (Funnell & Rogers, 2010).

Finally, seeing the link between research and policy or advocacy and policy can be difficult because it takes place over extended periods of time. The enlightenment approach described earlier is an important dimension of bringing knowledge to policy. Tracing the linkages can be attempted as to identify the role research played (Tussie, 2009). Three methodological points are important in design of any evaluation of policy influence.

Comparison is the hallmark of good evaluation—some even call it the platinum standard (Khagram & Thomas, 2010). A strong approach to ensuring comparison where you cannot identify a counterfactual is a comparative case approach. In many situations we are examining attempts at policy influence after they are undertaken. In this situation a counterfactual cannot be identified because it has not been designed in the evaluation. In other cases, there are ethical or practical reasons why a counterfactual is neither desirable nor possible in a policy intervention. In other words, there is no viable way to have a controlled comparison (George & Bennett, 2005, especially Chapters 8 & 10).

In these situations, alternative ways should be used to achieve comparison. Brady and Collier (2004) present a number of alternatives in addition to those presented by George and Bennett (2005). In the study discussed above, we completed 23 rich case studies as the basis for our work. A common interview device was designed for the case studies, and because they were in a wide range of geographic settings, authors in almost all cases were identified from the country or region in which the case study was carried out based on the assumption that these authors would have a higher likelihood of being able to situate the study within key sociopolitical, geographic, and economic contextual factors.

The cases were also selected to cover the geographic and subject area interests of IDRC. This meant including case studies from Africa, Asia, Latin America, as well as the Middle East and North Africa. It meant cases in information and communication technologies, education, health systems, trade, financial reform, agriculture, and environment. So the comparison we had was deep and relevant. The issues around case studies in evaluation are covered in more depth in the technical notes in the book as well as in articles on the subject (Carden, 2004, 2009a, 2009b, 2009c). Case studies offer insights on complicated and complex questions because they look at events or activities with a common lens; they integrate context into the story of what happened; and they highlight the range of factors taken into account by looking across a variety of events.

User engagement is an important element to any evaluation of policy influence. In the study discussed above, users were engaged in the definition of the problem to be investigated, in the definition of the sample, in the preliminary analysis, and in exploring the findings. It is important to note that while users are engaged, the evaluation team should retain decision making and be responsible for the final analysis. But engagement of the users significantly enriches the analysis and—most importantly—use of the findings.

A *positive sample* was used and should be considered carefully. Success can serve as a useful starting point for analysis if we want to consider replication of approaches. Various approaches to positive samples have been developed, such as the success case method (Brinkerhoff, 2003), or positive deviance (Amato & Armstrong, 2010; Saïd Business School, 2010).

A FRAMEWORK FOR EVALUATING POLICY INFLUENCE

Figure 5.2 graphically illustrates the key components of an evaluation. It does not prescribe the precise details of each element because these are built incrementally in design.

Research as Intervention

This framework builds on the assumption that the research being evaluated is oriented to change. In terms of the elements noted in Figure 5.1, the research would be of high quality, would be communicated with and through the networks that could make change happen, would be focused on real problems, and would be conveyed using tools for knowledge translation and communication. It is not intended as a framework to assess research in and of itself but rather in terms of how and whether that research does support change and is addressing a development problem of some sort. Four key points should be noted:

1. *The research should be of good quality.* The meaning of this statement is a subject of considerable debate in the development evaluation com-

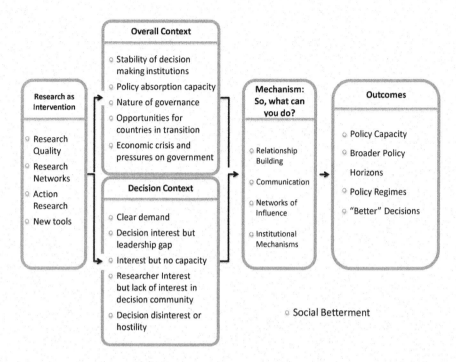

Figure 5.2 A realist framework for evaluation policy influence.

munity at the moment. Peer review has always been a key element of assessing research quality: If the research is acceptable to peers as demonstrated by publication in peer-reviewed journals, then this is the traditional access point for quality. Then one looks at citations and whether or not anyone has cited the work. But research that is designed for use in the decision process may or may not be published or publishable. That in itself does not render its quality inferior. The challenge for evaluation at this stage is to consider multiple definitions of quality that are based on ensuring the validity of the work undertaken. External validity is particularly important to decision makers because it relates to questions of relevance of the research beyond the confines the particular subjects and location of the original study. Going to scale requires that decision makers give careful consideration to the external validity of research. This is not to minimize internal validity or construct validity when one is assessing an evaluation, but to highlight an area of critical importance for decision makers who are often concerned with whether and how they can take an initiative to scale. External validity would cause one to probe:

– The unit of analysis (Who was involved and are they representative at scale?)

- The location of the work (where were the findings generated—urban/rural for example—and is that geography representative at scale?)
- The influence of context (How did the sociopolitical/environmental condition affect the outcome and how relevant is that in going to scale?)
- The nature of variation in implementation (What other changes were introduced and how variable were these other changes?)
- The relationship to outcomes (Did the change or the intervention contribute to the main outcome being sought—prolong life or improve quality of life, for example?)

Any evaluation of research that is meant to influence policy should take these points into consideration.

2. *Research networks are usually important.* Seldom is a research-to-policy process direct. As outlined in the study findings, in a few cases decision makers engage researchers for direct input on a planned policy change. More often, researchers identify knowledge before decision makers are ready to use it. Communications strategies and advocacy work, engagement with the media, engagement with interested publics, among other strategies, are often needed to move the findings to use. Here, one is concerned with how the research is to be disseminated and communicated.

3. *Action research is not the same* as other kinds of research. It assumes relevance to a problem and a desire for action. While criteria of research quality apply, the assessment of quality relates to utility in addition to validity of the data gathering and analysis. Here, one asks questions about utility, relevance to the problem, and appropriateness of method selection.

4. *New tools are often needed to move findings to application.* Often, intervention calls for new tools for researchers, especially in the area of knowledge translation. Much work is being done in this domain and one should examine whether or not the work is developing, modifying or adopting existing tools designed for enhancing the utility of research to decision makers. One would expect to see knowledge translation or communication tools as a central part of any research intended to influence policy.

The review of the first category in Figure 5.2, "research as intervention" should give a clear picture of the theory of the program or activity under study, what value it intends to add and how is expects to function.

OVERALL CONTEXT AND DECISION CONTEXT

Context was found to be central in policy influence. This suggests that any assessment of the relevance of research should include a careful review of the context as part of understanding why a particular initiative was successful or not. First, we have to think about context in two different dimensions:

1. The overall context: What was referred to as contingencies which capture the factors within a context that will drive the ability to negotiate policy influence.
2. The decision context is different: It represents the level of receptivity to knowledge at any given point in time.

Both dimensions change over time and space, so there is no singular analysis but rather an iterative process of context mapping and awareness. Overall context is influenced by both capacity building and changes in socioeconomic condition. Decision context is affected by sociopolitical conditions.

MECHANISMS

The mechanisms reflect the domains where the individual can have an influence. Each mechanism needs to be broken down and treated within its multiple dimensions. Relationships that affect policy process are not only with decision makers, but may also be with communities, media, interest groups, and legal entities. Communications may equally be important with these groups and may be broadcast or narrowcast. In both cases, links between purpose and approach are critical to understanding and assessing the theory of change.

Relationships are built over time. Trust is a key factor in influence. Researchers and research centers cannot expect to have influence based on great work alone. Rather, they need to foster relationships with a range of actors in the decision space: decision makers themselves, policy staff who support decision makers, the media, interested publics, other researchers.

Communication of ideas is almost as important as the ideas themselves. Ideas have to be communicated to audiences in ways they will understand. How has the research been communicated in language that decision makers can use? How have the ideas been communicated in ways the media can use? How have ideas been communicated in ways that will engage the public? How have the researchers overcome the public's fear to support the findings?

Networks of influence are an important mechanism in the spread of ideas. Have the research teams thought about the social networks they want to influence? Have they thought about networks that link decision makers, the public and the media that they could effectively exploit in fostering the uptake of ideas?

Finally, *institutional mechanisms* emerged as central. When decision makers are not fully open, they sometimes need help to think through the institutional and organizational changes needed to deal with the research findings. How findings can affect policy and practice is not always completely obvious, and if researchers are prepared to delve into these issue, then they will have a stronger appreciation of the factors that affect uptake and be able to put forward some alternatives. The evaluation should examine whether and how the research has attempted to bring these factors into the influence process.

Finally, short-term outcomes such as improving policy capacity have to be considered in the context of their contribution to social betterment, not in their own right. Is the success of the intervention actually leading to improved conditions, or has it replaced one problem with a different one? This means looking for unexpected side effects of a change, being open to a range of effects, and deliberately seeking out surprise.

This breakdown of the elements of a framework for assessing the influence of research on policy is not a simple recipe. It requires considerable effort on the part of the evaluator and the client to define each of the elements as they relate to their particular problem. It takes an emergent view of both the intervention and its evaluation, acknowledging that we cannot know all in advance. It recognizes the need to make a number of course corrections in design as the evaluation proceeds. It recognizes the importance of deepening understanding of each contextual element as well as the implementation—and interaction—of the mechanisms. As understanding deepens, further modifications to design and investigation will follow.

CONCLUSION

As Maureen O'Neil (2009) notes in her preface to *Knowledge to Policy*, research makes a major contribution to good governance in any society. It opens space for debate and inquiry; it empowers people with knowledge to hold governments to account; and it enlarges the array of policy options. Development is crucially about change. It is about improving the lives of people in communities through the effective and positive use of knowledge. Development researchers are themselves change agents, and this evaluative approach is about helping them improve their capacities in this regard by opening up the black box of the public policy decision process to broader scrutiny so that opportunities for influence are enhanced.

NOTES

1. This framework was first developed by Evert Lindquist in background work for this study and is presented in a paper called *Discerning Policy Influence* in 2001.
2. This is not to judge the relative merits of different systems of governance, but rather to note the importance of understanding the nature of governance as part of developing an influence strategy on the ground.
3. I would like to thank Sanjeev Sridharan for discussions that led to the elaboration of this framework.

REFERENCES

Amato, R., & Armstrong, J. (2010). *Exploring positive deviance further.* Unpublished paper. Saïd Business School, Oxford University.

Brady, H. E., & Collier, D. (2004). *Rethinking social inquiry: Diverse tools, shared standards.* Oxford, UK: Rowman and Littlefield Publishers, Inc.

Brinkerhoff, R. O. (2003). *The success case method.* San Francisco CA: Berrett-Koehler.

Carden, F. (2004). Issues in assessing the policy influence of research. *International Social Science Journal, 179: 56,* 135–151.

Carden, F. (2009a). *Knowledge to policy: Making the most of development research.* Thousand Oaks, CA: Sage & IDRC.

Carden, F. (2009b). Using Comparative Data: A systems approach to a multiple case study. In D. Byrne & C. C. Ragin (Eds.),_*The Sage handbook of case-based methods* (pp. 331–344). Thousand Oaks, CA: Sage.

Carden, F. (2009c). Understanding influence: The episode studies approach. In D. Tussie (Ed.),. *The politics of trade: The role of research in trade policy and negotiation* (pp. 273–298). Dordrecht, NL: Brill/Ottawa, ON: IDRC. Online at: http://www.idrc.ca/booktique/ev-113402-201-1-DO_TOPIC.html

Funnell, S., & Rogers, P. (2010). *Purposeful program theory.* Hoboken, NJ: Wiley.

George, A. L., & Bennett, A. (2005). *Case studies and their development in the social sciences.* Cambridge, MA: MIT Press.

Khagram, S., & Thomas, C. (2010). Toward a platinum standard for evidence-based assessment by 2020. *In Public Administration Review, 70,* s100–s106.

Lindblom, C. E. (1979). Still muddling not yet through. *Public Administration Review, 39,* 517–525.

Morino, M. (2010). Hitting reset on "Outcomes." Retrieved from http://www.ssireview.org/opinion/entry/1629/

O'Neil, M. (2009). Preface. In F. Carden, *Knowledge to policy: Making the most of development research.* Delhi & Ottawa: Sage & IDRC.

Pascale, R. T., & Sternin, J. (2005). Your company's secret change agents. *Harvard Business Review,* May, 1–11.

Pawson, R. (2006). *Evidence-based policy: A realist perspective.* Thousand Oaks, CA: Sage.

Pawson, R., & Tilley, N. (1997). *Realistic evaluation.* London: Sage.

Saïd Business School. (2010, May). *Exploring positive deviance: New frontiers in collaborative change.* Report from a practical research workshop, Oxford University.

Tilley, N. (2000, September). *Realist evaluation: An overview.* Conference Presentation at Danish Evaluation Society, Copenhagen.

Tussie, D. (Ed.). (2009). *The politics of trade.* Dordrecht, The Netherlands: Republic of Letters.

Weiss, C. H. (1977). *Using social research in public policy making.* Lexington MA: Lexington Books, DC Heath.

Weiss, C. H. (1982). Knowledge utilization in decision making: Reflections on the terms of the discussion. *Research in Sociology of Education and Socialization, 3,* 21–27.

CHAPTER 6

EVALUATING NETWORKS AND PARTNERSHIPS[1]

Heather Creech

INTRODUCTION

Since its beginnings in 1990, the International Institute for Sustainable Development (IISD) has been an active user of the internet and other electronic technologies. IISD's first Board of Directors took the decision that 50% of the institute undertakings would focus on communications. IISD would be more than just another think tank. As we were based solely in Winnipeg, Canada at the time, this decision moved us into electronic communications as the principal medium for reaching our audiences. We were not well situated for regular personal engagement with national and international decision makers, and we did not wish to compete with the established print cultures of other institutes and government agencies. So right from the start we worked with electronic mailing lists and the old store and forward email systems; we set up online databases and we began to publish and distribute information diskettes, moving to web communications in early 1994.

In 1996, we were challenged by the International Development Research Centre (IDRC) to examine the possibility of using web technology to fast track sustainable development research and action. We established a net-

Emerging Practices in International Development Evaluation, pages 123–150
Copyright © 2013 by Information Age Publishing
123

work of sustainable development institutes, built our mutual capacity in on-line communications through experimentation, and created one of the first online platforms for a network, the "Sustainable Development Gateway,"[2] that brought together the knowledge bases of some of the world's leading research institutes working on sustainable development policy and action. From that point on, our colleagues in other programs began to establish networks, including the Trade Knowledge Network (active), the Climate Change Knowledge Network (ended), the Sustainable Development Communications Network (ended), the Sustainable Coffee Partnership (active), the Canadian Sustainability Indicators Network (active), the Ookpik community of young northerners (active), SD Plan-net Asia (active), and so forth.

IISD's communications culture has evolved into a culture of networks and partnerships. Today, like many similar research and advocacy organizations, there is no single project that we undertake without another organization working with us; each of those partnerships, networks, alliances, and communities is grounded in good use of electronic tools for collaboration and external communications. IISD has developed considerable experience in building networks, fostering partnerships and influencing policy at the highest levels. In short, our ability to manage relationships at many levels has afforded us the opportunity to advance the issues we care most about.

Based on that reputation, in early 2000 other organizations began to call upon IISD for advice in planning, managing, and evaluating the performance of networks and partnerships. The author (Heather Creech) and her colleague, Terri Willard, began a series of consultancies to other organizations, and published the manual "Strategic Intentions: Managing Knowledge Networks for Sustainable Development" (Creech & Willard, 2001). The following chapter is an overview of lessons learned to date, noting in particular gaps and challenges in this evaluation practice area.

DEFINITIONS: UNTANGLING TERMINOLOGY AND TYPOLOGY

At the heart of collaborative undertakings are people and institutions choosing to work together for a greater good. However, these processes do not occur flawlessly, and so we have taken on the challenge of learning about assessing collaboration and improving performance in order to help partnerships partner, alliances ally, and networks work (Creech, Laurie, Paas, & Parry, 2012).

First, we need simplicity and clarity in recognizing the entity or process that is being assessed. This task is made difficult because there are so many different terms being used to describe types of collaborative efforts, such as alliances, knowledge networks, learning networks, partnerships, communities of interest, communities of practice, and so forth. We have learned through our research and consulting activities (for a selected list of our consulting activities, see Appendix B) that discussions of fine distinctions between these terms are of limited value in determining how to improve performance and how to help organizers and participants to account for the time and resources invested in the collaboration. These widely ranging collaborative modalities, in the end, have many basic characteristics in common, and only a few key distinctions. Managers and evaluators should focus on key attributes that are critical to designing for and assessing performance.

Our first observation would be that the term "social networks" is emerging as an all-encompassing term, understood as the nodes of individuals and organizations and the related systems that tie them together, such as shared values and ideas, social contracts, trade, and many other aspects of human relationships. Social networks embrace both personal and professional relationships. As an umbrella term, "social networks" covers many forms of social organization, including social communities on the web, networking applications (e.g., Twitter, Facebook), interest groups, policy and knowledge networks, and communities of practice (Serrat, 2010).

Within this social complexity, we focus our interest on those forms of social organization that are knowledge-based, learning-focused, and purpose-driven. In that context, we suggest that there are three major types of collaboration.[3]

Networked Governance

Collaborative, horizontal decision-making processes are coming to be understood as "networked governance."

The intersection of technology and social organization is at the heart of current thinking about an emergence of "networked governance" or "collaborative governance": the shift from hierarchical management structures (the "silos" of government departments and intergovernmental agencies) to more horizontal, "flat" networks that cross departmental boundaries and bring in active participants from the private sector and civil society. The rapid increase in access to the Internet and convergence with mobile technologies, together with increasing ease of use of new social media tools and platforms, have enabled new approaches to governance in which stakeholders across sectors and jurisdictions are engaged in consensus building and implementation processes. The key distinction here from other forms of collaboration is the redistribution and sharing of the power and responsibilities of centralized agencies to a broader spectrum of institutions and individuals, in order to enable the steering of complex, multisectoral challenges (Huppé, Creech, & Knoblach, 2012). From the point of performance improvement, the central issues for review include determining:

- The complexity of the governance challenge
- The social capital developed among the stakeholders necessary for engagement and mutual trust
- The effectiveness of the governance, decision-making, and co-management processes put in place

Networks of Individuals

Networks of individuals are collaborations of individuals seeking knowledge and support for purposeful individual or collective action (also known as communities of practice (CoPs), knowledge networks, campaigns, and so forth).[4]

These networks of individuals come together for professional or purposeful reasons. In many cases, particularly in those CoPs and networks focused on improvement of professional knowledge and skills, the driver is self-interest on the part of the participant, and possibly his/her employer seeking to strengthen institutional capacity through professional development of staff. In other cases, the driver for the network is the mutual interest of participants to solve a problem through research and knowledge exchange, and possibly joint action as well. Performance improvement of these collaborations focuses on determining:

- Whether there is sufficient social capital for participants to exchange information, learn from each other, and work together
- Whether individual participants believe and can demonstrate that their knowledge and skills have benefitted from the time invested
- Whether there has been progress in advancing solutions towards a shared challenge.

Interorganizational Relationships (IORs)

Collaborations of institutions for research and implementation are best understood as "partnerships" or "alliances," and termed "interorganizational relationships" by Universalia (Universalia, IISD, n.d.).

What distinguishes interorganizational relationships (IORs) from collaboration among groups of individuals is that they are established through agreements at a management or corporate level that the institutions should align their interests and work together. IORs are often driven by shared objectives among the participating institutions and are characterized by "the formality of the relationships (level of endorsement [by] senior management of the institutions involved), resource flows [and] shared institutional risks and liabilities" (Creech and Laurie, in Asian Development Bank, 2011, p. ix). Structures connecting institutions come in many shapes and sizes. While there may be differences among them based on the number of institutional members involved, the formality of the relationship, and the value appropriation among the members,[5] these structures have much in common, and the frameworks we have used in our evaluation practice for assessing their performance tend to be fairly consistent. We would therefore agree with Universalia that the umbrella term "interorganizational relationship" (IOR) is the most generic, and it will be used throughout the balance of this chapter to describe the wide range of collaborative efforts that involve agreements among institutions to work together.

The unique points of assessment include determining:

- The external value or change that the IOR seeks to achieve as a collective effort
- The relevance of the collective effort, not only to external stakeholders, but to the mandates of each of the institutions involved in the IOR
- Whether the work to be carried out is better accomplished as a collective or not
- Whether risks and liabilities are shared among the member institutions, in addition to the sharing of benefits

Once these three distinctions are made (networked governance processes, networks of individuals, and interorganizational relationships), one can then address more clearly the activities, value creation, and outcomes of the collaboration, and whether these are consistent with good practice in other similar entities. It almost goes without saying, of course, that individuals within decision-making processes and interorganizational mechanisms do the work. Central to each of these modalities, therefore, is the need to understand how to build social capital among the various actors in the collaboration, and how to measure whether social capital has been built and is sufficient for the collaboration to advance its work (Huppé & Creech, 2012).

A CURRENT SHIFT IN INTEREST FROM IORS TO COMMUNITIES OF PRACTICE

We have observed that the emphasis on network and partnership practice is shifting from institutional relationship to individual relationships—groups of individuals connecting through communities of practice, networks, and other forms of collaboration. With the increasing power and pervasiveness of social media tools, everyone is building his or her own personal and expert networks. This raises an important question: If staff of an institution are already personally networked to do what they need to do for their work, what then is the value of institutional partnerships? Experts we have talked with in the preparation of this chapter suggest that people who know each other, like each other, and want to work together figure out a way to do that. Some suggest that the legitimacy of networks is now more dependent on the willingness, support, and hard work of many individuals rather than the existence of a partnership agreement between institutions. They note further that, with the advent of social media, networks around development challenges could be engaging with millions—and the potential of "crowd-sourcing" for knowledge and solutions becomes significant. In this environment, it is more difficult to wrap an institutional context around a network. Changemakers, for example, has deliberately designed their knowledge-sharing strategies to focus on the individual; as a networking hub or platform, they convene and facilitate interactions among change agents as individual actors rather than institutional representatives.

In the sustainable development community, we suggest that there is a shift taking place, with less attention being given to establishing IORs and more attention being given to fostering networks of individual experts and practitioners. There may be several drivers for this shift:

- Increased access to online tools for collaboration among individuals: It has simply become easier to connect, and so people do. With the increasing power and pervasiveness of social media and related tools, individuals are building their own expert networks to find ways to share knowledge and work together on common challenges.
- The complexity of IORs: Securing agreement among institutions to work together has proven to be time consuming, often with less than satisfactory outcomes, given the level of effort involved (Creech, Vetter, Matus, & Seymour, 2008).
- A more mature understanding in the field of collaboration that an IOR is not always needed to support knowledge sharing, capacity development, and joint action on the ground. The development of an IOR may be driven more by the need to mobilize formal resources and the need for a collective institutional mandate to scale up actions for wider spread outcomes and impact. But the more immediate needs for knowledge exchange and joint learning can be served through individual connections across institutions, without the need for institution-to-institution frameworks.

Nevertheless, institutions continue to recognize that there is value in joining efforts with other institutions in more strategic and formal ways. And so the driving questions remain: How do we join forces, and with whom, to solve these challenges? What is the added value in terms of knowledge, capacity, innovation and action in building relationships across organizations to work together? And how do we know whether that added value has been achieved? In the following sections, we will explore the challenges in evaluating IORs and provide our observations on key points of assessment.

PROBLEM STATEMENTS

With the proliferation of IORs, particularly those emerging from the emphasis on multistakeholder partnerships at the World Summit on Sustainable Development in 2002,[6] various stakeholders are now asking for these structures to be reviewed. In addition, most institutions now take into consideration the value of their "institutional partnerships" as part of their own organizational assessment processes.[7] There is a suspicion that some relationships are failing or underperforming; and there is concern that investments of time and funding have not led to the transformations promised through collaboration. Often there is a disconnect between those participating in the IOR and those who support it financially over the definition of what has constituted "success" in the IOR, and over expectations about what could reasonably be accomplished within a specific timeframe.

In our own IOR evaluation practice, we have observed the following:

- Terms of reference for evaluations set by the IOR's donor agency/ agencies increasingly are based on the Organisation for Economic Cooperation and Development (OECD) Development Assistance Committee (DAC) evaluation criteria of relevance, effectiveness, efficiency, impact, and sustainability (OECD DAC, n.d.).[8] However, the guidelines provide insufficient clarity on how these criteria should be applied to IORs and what the appropriate indicators of performance would be—nor do the terms of reference consider what lies outside the DAC criteria that would be pertinent to good IOR practice.
- The evaluation "lens" required by the donor is often unhelpful in advising IORs how to move forward, particularly when there are issues around lack of engagement and participation among members.
- IORs themselves do not have a culture of self-assessment and reporting. They do not know what to demand or expect or how to use the

results. There are few tools for self-monitoring and assessment for IORs: Outcome mapping[9] has been helpful to some; but burdensome to others.

The overarching impression is that there are no common, agreed-to standards of performance. In interviews that informed this chapter, a number of practitioners appear to be moving away from structured approaches (guidelines, performance indicators) to a much more laissez-faire approach, with little structure beyond agreeing to share ideas either in person or through electronic means, and with no requirements for verifiable outcomes. Within this context, there is a growing contingent that believes that performance monitoring in particular is counter-productive. A few indicative comments follow:

- Partnerships are improvised; and formal strategies have the same chance to succeed as do chaotic qualitative approaches.
- It is not possible to manufacture a successful network.
- It is not possible, and may even be counter-productive, to be prescriptive in how networks and partnerships should function.

Nevertheless, most expressed views that a measure of deliberate design and structure was inevitable in some cases, often present in early stages of development, and desirable in many cases. Most also agreed that while assessing performance was an ongoing challenge, it was nevertheless important, both in terms of accountability to donors for funds invested in these processes and in terms of understanding how to ensure that collaboration does lead to innovation and transformative change.

WHAT DO IORS WANT FROM AN EVALUATION?

Fundamentally, IORs are looking for practical guidelines for evaluation that will provide helpful advice to the IOR and are consistent with frameworks they already understand and may in many cases be mandated to use. The OECD DAC evaluation criteria are becoming the standard framework around which IOR evaluations are being structured. In the evaluations that we have conducted, we have considered a wide range of issues. Many of these questions can be mapped against the DAC criteria (see Table 6.1).

In our research for the Asian Development Bank (ADB) on preparing guidelines for "knowledge partnerships" (ADB, 2011), we sought to map more closely the characteristics and actions of IORs against the DAC criteria (see Appendix A for a summary of our approach). In doing so, we recog-

TABLE 6.1

Questions we have been asked to consider in an evaluation of an IOR	Mapped to the OECD DAC criteria
What is the need or demand for the IOR?	Relevance
What are the enabling conditions and incentives for the work of the IOR • External to the institutions involved? • Internal to the institutions involved?	Effectiveness
What are the barriers to success? • External to the institutions involved? • Internal to the institutions involved?	Effectiveness
Governance: • Who are the members in the IOR? Are the roles and responsibilities clearly stated and understood? • How are decisions made among the members? • Who are the stakeholders and beneficiaries of the work of the IOR, and do they have a say in the work of the IOR? • How are members held to account for their work, both to the other members in the IOR and to the stakeholders/beneficiaries of the IOR?	Effectiveness

Strategic plan for the IOR:
• What issues drive the members?
• What were the proposed streams of activities?
• What have the members in the IOR done together?
  – What are the major research questions they are exploring?
  – What are the joint activities?
  – What have members accomplished, together with an assessment of the quality of their work?
• How are resources mobilized and deployed in advancing the strategic plan?
	Effectiveness

Where is the energy within the IOR, and how has the location of that energy influenced IOR direction, influence and impact?	Effectiveness
What are the plans and tools used for communications • within the IOR • from each member to their own institutions • beyond the IOR, to stakeholders/beneficiaries and beyond?	Effectiveness
What is the coordination mechanism for the work of the IOR?	Effectiveness
What inputs are available to meet the need for the IOR? [people, information, resources, time]	Efficiency
What is the competition? [other sources of inputs to meet the need: other institutions, other processes, other IORs]	Efficiency
Has the IOR achieved change through its strategies?	Impact
What are the unexpected outcomes that have made a difference?	Impact
What are the phases and the timeframe for the IOR's work?	Sustainability
Is there monitoring and reporting on work, and is it adequate to the needs of the IOR?	Sustainability
What is the IOR's ability to adapt to change?	Sustainability
What is the viability of the IOR to continue into the future?	Sustainability

nized the limitations of the DAC criteria for assessment of collaborative processes: We did not find the logical frame of the criteria particularly sensitive to the adaptive approaches and innovation that emerges when institutions with different skills, perspectives, and capacities come together to pursue a shared objective. Nevertheless, the DAC criteria are the standard operating framework for evaluation of development-related activities, whether those activities are conducted by single institutions or groups of institutions working collaboratively. The challenge for evaluators lies in adhering to the criteria where relevant and appropriate; understanding what constitutes relevance, effectiveness, efficiency, impact, and sustainability in the context of IORs; and, most important, addressing the principal and often unique assessment points for IORs.

PRINCIPAL ASSESSMENT POINTS
FOR THE EVALUATION OF IORS

The Primary Assessment Point for Evaluation of IORs: External Value

In our discussions with Universalia, we have agreed that our overarching goal should be to improve interorganizational collaboration so that institutions are better able to adapt to and meet the challenges associated with sustainable development, given that sustainability challenges are greater than any one organization can handle. The purpose of the IOR is the mobilization of institutions around a common challenge. A starting point for the IOR must therefore be that the group defines what the particular challenge is that they are seeking to address together, and a primary assessment point is that:

- The challenge is in fact greater than any one member can address
- The challenge to be addressed is clear to the members
- The members share the goal to address that challenge.

Every evaluation of an IOR should therefore be considered an "empowerment evaluation": one that starts with an expectation that an external value is to be achieved beyond the individual organizations involved. We are not neutral about this. A common misconception of evaluators is to place primary value in the structure and management of the IOR: assessing it against criteria such as openness, democratic governance, power equalities, and so forth. But this value is misplaced; and the primary assessment should be on the change the IOR wants to achieve.

The Second Assessment Point: Deployment of the Appropriate Operating Model for the Collaboration

The evaluator needs to determine whether he or she is assessing a networked governance process, a network or community of individuals, or an IOR. As noted earlier in this chapter, the IOR is distinguished by the corporate or managerial level of commitment between the participating institutions and the formality of those relationships. Within IORs, there are a few operating models that are useful to understand. There can be a mismatch between the challenge the IOR seeks to address, and the operating model chosen for the collaboration—including whether any kind of IOR is in fact appropriate for the challenge.

We suggest that there are two main distinctions, between open and closed IORs, and additional distinctions within those based on whether the purpose is focused on making connections (connectivity), alignment of interests, and knowledge exchange, or whether it is focused on joint research, production, and implementation activities.

1. An "open" IOR, in which relationships are established among an expandable group of institutions. Criteria for membership may be set, but members who meet the criteria may be encouraged to join. A desirable feature of an open IOR is that the whole becomes greater than the sum of the parts, and that the collective gains recognition in addition to the recognition normally accorded to the individual members. There may be additional considerations for the evaluator, based on whether the IOR is an independent legal entity (such as the Renewable Energy and Energy Efficiency Partnership[10]) or a nonlegal entity, hosted by another institution (for example, the Asian Environmental Compliance and Enforcement Network, hosted by the Institute for Global Environmental Studies[11]) (Creech et al., 2008).

   In open IORs, two additional distinctions can be made:
   a. The interorganizational knowledge platform, supporting the exchange of knowledge and alignment of interests among member institutions (for example, the Global Donor Platform for Rural Development[12]). The evaluator should consider:
      - Whether there is interaction among the members based on the knowledge shared, that creates value for all members, and contributes to the achievement of goals shared by all members
   b. The partnership approach for research and implementation (for example, the Global Village Energy Partnership[13]). The evaluator should consider:

- Whether the defined program of work is shared among all
  members, with each member understanding its role and
  contributing actively towards the achievement of the goal
  shared by all members.

2. A "closed" IOR in which relationships are established between two
   or three institutions only. One institution may seek out another institution according to certain needs or interests, but not open up the
   relationship to others.

We have observed, at our own institution and elsewhere, the tendency for one institution to refer to a wide range of other institutions
as "partners," "collaborating institutions," "allies," and so forth, but
without any guidelines on what constitutes that relationship and how
that relationship is to be fostered and assessed over time. In addition to the primary assessment point, that the relationship should
exist to deliver external value, we would suggest that the evaluator
needs to explore the reciprocity of the relationship: Do each of the
institutions involved consider the other to be a "partner"? The evaluator should look even further beyond the high-level agreements to
whether more informal networks of staff have been built across the
institutions. We would suggest that a key difference between an open
and a closed IOR is that, in the latter, the whole does not become
greater than the sum of the parts, and that individual corporate
identity is retained and perhaps reinforced through the collaboration. The desires for protection of institutional reputation, brand
and intellectual property must be acknowledged and respected.

In closed IORs, we would again distinguish between those with an
emphasis on the sharing of knowledge and those designed for joint
research and implementation of activities.

a. Institutional cooperation, usually described through a Memo-
   randum of Understanding (MOU), with an emphasis on the
   exchange of knowledge and promotion of mutual interests (for
   example, the Asian Development Bank's MOU with UNICEF
   for cooperation in the Asia-Pacific region[14]). The evaluator
   should consider:
   - Whether the relationship is clearly connected to the cor-
     porate priorities of each of the institutions involved (the
     relationship must help each organization to deliver on its
     mandate)
   - Whether there is a phased approach to building the rela-
     tionship over time, with checkpoints to assess whether the
     relationship is changing over time as interests and priori-
     ties diverge

- Whether there is a defined process for the interaction between the institutions, with responsibilities assigned to specific staff persons for fostering the relationship over time
- Whether and how each of the institutions in the relationship represents that relationship to others.

b. Strategic collaborators (a strategic alliance), usually designed for more than institutional cooperation, to advance an agenda, combine resources, and conduct a joint program of work (for example, the collaboration launched in 2005 between IISD, the Stockholm Environment Institute and the International Institute for Environment and Development on a joint program of work on climate change adaptation[15]). In addition to the points noted under institutional cooperation, the evaluator should consider:

- Whether senior levels of the organizations are meeting regularly to review progress (demonstrating corporate ownership and responsibility for the success of the strategic relationship)
- Whether and how staff in each organization have been identified and supported in implementing the joint activities.

The Third Assessment Point: Presence and Fostering of Social Capital

We consider social capital to be the fabric of trust, shared values, and understanding that allows diverse participants to work together towards collective outcomes and common goals. Social capital has been shown to be related to the capacity of teams to process information, make sense of data and connect it to an empirical context (Huppé et al, 2012; Huppé & Creech, 2012). The successful outcome of a collaborative IOR endeavor is predicated, we suggest, on the nature and extent of social capital within that IOR.

The challenge for IORs is that social capital may vary across the organizational framework of the IOR. The senior representatives of the member organizations who have agreed to work together may have the mutual trust and understanding necessary to establish the IOR, but the individual staff assigned to represent their institutions in the actual work of the IOR may not (or vice versa: the individual staff may be very well connected with each other, but the more senior managers or corporate officers lack the shared values, understanding, and trust).

The evaluator will need to consider:

- whether social capital exists across the different levels of the IOR (corporate, program, administrative) and is sufficient for the IOR to move forward on its agenda, and
- if it does not exist, whether appropriate steps are being taken to build social capital.

The existence and development of that social capital may rest in the existence of other personal, social networks and ties within and beyond the group—as other researchers have noted, broader social networks that provide access to resources and support play a strategic role in building social capital (Franke, 2005). This poses a challenge to evaluators, with respect to setting boundaries for the assessment of IOR performance: How far can an evaluator explore the reach of the social networks of individuals in the IOR as a necessary consideration in determining the depth of social capital in a collaborative process (Creech et al., 2012)?

A more realistic assessment point on social capital might be to review the "animation" or facilitation of the interaction of members, starting with value exchange within the IOR: are the members giving as well as receiving value in the IOR? The evaluator should explore with each member what they have brought to the table and whether they know what the other members in turn are contributing. The dynamics of these relationships will need to be explored:

- Are there motivational differences among the members: What drives their interest in participating, and is that interest understood by the others?
- Have the roles and responsibilities of members been described and accepted?
- Is there clarity on leadership roles and coordination roles (or have the coordinators of the IOR become the de facto leaders, in the absence of broader ownership of the IOR among the members)?
- Do members understand and accept where authority to decide and to act rests?
- Do members consider that they themselves are accountable for the success of the IOR?

In assessing social capital, an evaluator will need to consider how the emergence of shared understanding of the purpose of the IOR and the expectations of all involved have been handled and whether the members have moved from competition to cooperation. The informal aspects of interaction in the IOR must also be considered. A group of people who like each other are more likely to stay in touch, share and work together more effectively over a longer period of time.

The Fourth Assessment Point: The Presence of Critical Success Factors

The presence of certain "success factors" can help an IOR achieve its goals. The presence, or absence, of these can form an important component of the evaluation process.

Capacity within the IOR to Manage the Purpose or Focus of the IOR as a Collective Undertaking
Bearing in mind the primary assessment point on external value, an evaluation should explore how the IOR is maintaining its focus in order to deliver that value. The evaluator should look not only for the existence of a strategic plan or work plan, but that it has been discussed with members, and whether members have a shared understanding of the goals, objectives, and stream of activities. Consideration should be given to the decision making and coordination mechanisms (boards, secretariats, coordinating units) and how those mechanisms have provided support for the implementation of work plans. The processes for working together across the co-ordination mechanisms and the membership as a whole on a regular basis can help to anticipate and resolve emergent problems and support shared decision making and ownership of outcomes.

How far the understanding of shared objectives has penetrated in each of the member institutions should also be explored. Are staff of member institutions (including the corporate level) aware of the IOR that their institution belongs to? Is there synergy between the individual institutional plans and the work of the collective? If there are disconnects, are they significant enough to impede the capacity of the IOR to manage its focus?

Understanding of Short- and Long-term Needs and Outcomes
The challenges that the IOR is seeking to address will usually be entrenched problems that require long-term commitments and "staying power" of the members. IORs may start with a long-term view, and may consider what the long-term benefits for the members and beyond will be, but short-term benefits also need to be identified that will keep members engaged. The evaluator should explore whether and how the IOR is identifying and celebrating incremental accomplishments and providing the members with some sense of progress.

Linked to the management of short- and long-term outcomes is the provision of incentives for participation. Incentives contribute to sustaining the participation of members through the short term progress of the IOR and build the base for longer term commitment. Self-interest on the part of each member can be a strong motivator for participation and should not be discounted or underestimated by the evaluator. The evaluator should explore whether the members believe they are gaining state of the art knowledge, access to experts and other persons of influence, using the IOR as a testing ground for ideas prior to broader dissemination or commercialization, and are building institutional profile and reputation through participation. The evaluator should also look for those incentives that empower participation beyond self-interest, including the value that comes from building a critical mass of voice and influence on entrenched problems and the creativity and innovation that can emerge through collaboration.

Presence of Knowledge Sharing and Communications Skills

Individual institutions typically have a communications and knowledge management function as an essential part of the structure of the organization, staffed with individuals with the appropriate skills and expertise. IORs, however, often do not, even though one of the main activities of the IOR may be the mobilization and exchange of knowledge among the members and communications beyond the membership. If a coordination unit exists to support the membership, it is usually small, and staffed with substantive experts and administrative support rather than with those who bring professional expertise in knowledge management and communications. The individuals in the IOR representing their institutions are also usually substantive experts, but are expected to share knowledge without having the necessary skills and experience in how to do that effectively across the IOR. The IOR as a whole may lack the expertise to communicate the work of the IOR more broadly. The presence of knowledge sharing and communications skills is a precondition for the success of an IOR, and an evaluator should look particularly closely at the existing skills, capacities, and methods available to strengthen those.

Monitoring Performance and Adaptive Capacity

In our evaluation practice, we have observed that IORs tend not to have mechanisms in place for the monitoring of performance, including whether internal and external risks to success have been identified, with capacity to adapt in response. Common risks affecting all IORs include:

- Financial resources fall short of what is desired or needed
- The individual who is the champion or key driving force behind the IOR leaves

- Individual experts representing their organizations in the IOR leave their organizations (and therefore leave that member unrepresented in the IOR)
- Member organizations shift interests and priorities and reduce their participation accordingly

Whether any of these events has occurred may not, in and of itself, be subject to critical comment; rather, the evaluator should consider how the IOR has recognized the risk, put mechanisms in place to manage the risk, and subsequently followed those plans as needed.

How an IOR performs and adapts will vary as well according to the phase of development or life cycle of the IOR. These entities do go through cycles of growth and evolution, from development to maturity to crisis and creative reinvention (Cabaj, 2011). New IORs must achieve a balance between building social capital and getting something done. Older IORs must demonstrate adaptability to changing circumstances and contexts, particularly with respect to reinvigorating leadership and maintaining relevance of their work (Willard, 2009). The evaluator will need to take into consideration what phase the IOR is in, what to expect in that phase, and how to advise the IOR how best to move into the next phase of existence.

WHAT TO WATCH FOR WHEN FOLLOWING
THE OECD DAC CRITERIA

With the specific points of assessment in place, the evaluator should revisit the OECD DAC criteria and take into consideration a few specific interpretations of the criteria when applied to an assessment of an IOR.

Relevance

The evaluator should review not only whether the development intervention to be undertaken by an IOR is relevant to the field, but also whether the work of the IOR is relevant to each of the member organizations. As we noted for our work with the ADB, the purpose of the IOR should serve to address one or more sustainable development challenges, *and* that purpose should be suited to the priorities and policies of the member institutions (see Appendix A). If the IOR is not relevant to the members, its performance will be limited (ADB, 2011).

Performance Metrics for Assessing Effectiveness

From our research and consulting work (see Appendix B), it would appear that there is simply not much done and shared on performance metrics for IORs. There is some use of web analytics to monitor collaboration sites, but in general, we believe that performance metrics would be the next significant issue to be addressed in IOR evaluation. We would suggest that this is a particular issue in the determination of "effectiveness." The effectiveness of an IOR and, in particular, the effectiveness of group participation in contributing to the goals of the IOR needs to be considered in terms other than frequency of interactions or numbers of members that have joined the IOR.

Some experts interviewed for our research were not in favor of performance measures and assessment, suggesting that performance frameworks satisfy a bureaucratic need for accountability but do not in fact lead to improved performance. Others, however, were willing to suggest what they felt to be simple, practical indicators that relationships among institutions are performing as planned:

- Organizations get together in the same room and start to talk with each other
- Organizations contribute what they have agreed to share (either financial resources, or in-kind support, or knowledge)
- The organizations actually accomplish something together that has had value, combined with the counterfactual, that without the collaboration, there would be no such outcome
- Individuals who participate on behalf of their organizations believe that they have gained something (contacts, knowledge, skills) from the collaboration.
- Organizations keep in touch; conversations are ongoing after the end of the initiative that brought them together

What Constitutes Efficiency in Evaluating an IOR?

A common point of contention with donors and the IORs they support is that transactional costs seem to be high, with much invested in the costs of travel, meetings, and communications but without obvious progress towards an external outcome of the joint work. We agree with Universalia that transaction costs should be defined as the time and resources required for building the relationship, in the context of the long-term value and impact of that relationship (Universalia, IISD, n.d.). The costs should not be taken out of context and compared to the cost of undertaking a project by a single institution (with the corresponding reduction or elimination of costs for meetings, travel, communications, and so forth).

It is, however, very much an efficiency issue if the work could have been done as effectively by a single institution without the challenge of building an IOR, and the evaluator should not avoid investigating this consideration.

Understanding Impact in the Context of IORs

The DAC criteria assume a more or less logical progression from activities to outcomes, recognizing the attribution challenge in linking those outcomes to impact of the development intervention. With IORs, however, the unexpected plays a much more direct role. Indeed, it would be unusual if the IOR did not in some way modify, change, or adapt its objectives and program of work. Members bring new capacities, new ideas, and innovation to the IOR that can change the IOR's original direction and planning. What an IOR started out to achieve is not necessarily what the IOR ultimately is able to influence and change. The challenge for the IOR managers is to keep donors and members informed and engaged in the change, and for the evaluator to assess whether there is shared understanding of the change in direction and whether that change leads to external value.

As with relevance, the evaluator should also look at the impact of the IOR on each of the individual member organizations. What has changed with respect to levels of knowledge, capacity, and influence for each of the member institutions as a result of participation in the IOR?

Understanding Sustainability in the Context of IORs

Sustainability, as defined by the DAC criteria, refers to the sustainability of the development intervention. In assessing an IOR, it is our experience that evaluators tend to be asked to consider only the sustainability of the IOR itself: whether and how it can continue its work, usually in the context of diminishing resources and declining participation of members. What the evaluator should not overlook, however, is whether the work of the IOR— the external value it achieves—can be sustained independent of ongoing attention and intervention of the IOR. This exploration should include the sustainability of those outcomes within each of the member organizations as well. Have members gained knowledge, expertise, and capacity that can be sustained within each of the organizations?

With respect to the sustainability of the IOR itself, our earlier work with IDRC on the sustainability of networks established four assessment points (Willard & Creech, 2006):

- Relevance: whether the purpose of the IOR is still relevant
- Relationships: whether the members are still active
- Resources: whether resources are available
- Time: whether the IOR has given itself sufficient time to achieve its purpose or if continuation is necessary

In reviewing the data on these points, the evaluator will need to determine whether to advise that the IOR can continue and sustain its work, or whether it has run its course.

SHOULD AN EVALUATOR RECOMMEND THAT AN IOR HAS RUN ITS COURSE?

How can an evaluator suggest that an IOR should be disbanded? Few informants in our research tackled the issue of winding down interorganizational relationships, and there is little in the way of documented good practice in winding down. For some, who focus more on the impacts of knowledge processes on the individuals working in an IOR, this is almost an irrelevant discussion: the relationships have been built, and may continue, or they may not. People come into and out of knowledge sharing activities as a matter of course. For others, there is a recognition that we should be frank when institutions have either achieved the objectives of the IOR, or when circumstances have changed and the IOR is no longer needed, or when the institutions simply do not fit together anymore.

As we advised the ADB, the risk is that wind-down may take place too soon: knowledge generation and sharing must be placed on a much longer time scale (beyond two to three years), as it can take that length of time to clarify purpose and focus, identify partners, encourage the building of shared understanding, develop capacities, create an environment in which trust can be built, and see some initial progress (ADB, 2011).

When wind-down is a valid consideration, the evaluator should be prepared to guide the IOR through an effective and empowering wind-down process, noting with the members what lessons learned should be documented and shared, and celebrating what has been accomplished. Without such a process, too often the value gained is lost—websites vanish, papers and reports become scattered, and future institutional relationships can be affected by a poor experience of collaboration. In our view, there are too many non-performing IORs on every organization's list of relationships, and we would like to see improved practices for appropriate and timely closure of IORs that have run their course.

FINAL THOUGHTS

When assessing a collaboration of institutions, the evaluator should consider what the purpose is of those organizations coming together, the mechanics of interaction, and the desired outcomes from their interaction. Are the desired outcomes benefiting the organizational members and achieving a common purpose or a greater good beyond the collaborators?

This chapter suggests that different forms of collaboration are often overlapping, and this has made assessment confusing. However, rather than getting tangled in the terminology, we suggest the first point to address is whether the collaboration is:

- A multistakeholder, multisectoral, networked governance process,
- A collaboration of individuals, or
- An interorganizational relationship: collaboration among two or more organizations

After this distinction is made, and it is determined that the entity being assessed is an IOR, one should explore carefully the external value being created or provided by the group, the structure of the collaboration, the social capital developed, and the presence of critical success factors. If the OECD DAC criteria must be applied, consideration should be given in particular to how relevance, effectiveness, efficiency, impact, and sustainability are defined and measured in IORs.

NOTES

1. This chapter is based on work conducted by Heather Creech, Director, Global Connectivity, IISD and Terri Willard, IISD Associate, including outcomes of a working session in 2009 with Universalia (universalia.com) on the evaluation of inter-organizational relationships, and subsequent interviews with practitioners in knowledge management and collaboration. We advanced this work through an assignment with the Asian Development Bank (ADB) to design guidelines for knowledge partnerships. Michelle Laurie contributed to this latter assignment. In particular, we would like to acknowledge the guidance of Olivier Serrat, Head, Knowledge Management Centre, Regional and Sustainable Development Department, ADB, in the exploration of the Organisation for Economic Development and Cooperation (OECD) Development Assistance Committee (DAC) criteria for evaluation and their application to partnerships (see Appendix 1). IISD's body of work on the management and assessment of networks and partnerships can be found at www.iisd.org/networks.
2. Core components of the SD Gateway and the SD Communications Network have been archived at http://www.iisd.org/sd/ and www.iisd.org/sdcn/, respectively.

3. We have promoted these definitions in a series of presentations and papers, the most recent articulation being Creech, et al. (2012): Performance improvement and assessment of collaboration: starting points for networks and communities of practice (forthcoming, IISD).

4. For further insights into performance improvement and assessment of collaboration among individuals, we would direct the reader to Creech, et al. (2012): Performance improvement and assessment of collaboration: starting points for networks and communities of practice (forthcoming, IISD).

5. We consider "value appropriation" to be what the members contribute and receive from each other in the relationship.

6. For more information on the WSSD partnerships agenda, consult http://www.un.org/events/wssd/.

7. See, for example, IISD's own review of its partnership practice: IISD Partnership Review: Selected Observations (Willard & Creech, 2011), available at www.iisd.org/pdf/2012/iisd_partnership_review.pdf.

8. The criteria are available at www.oecd.org/dac/evaluationofdevelopment-programmes/daccriteriaforevaluatingdevelopmentassistance.htm

9. For more information on outcome mapping, see www.outcomemapping.ca.

10. www.reeep.org

11. www.aecen.org/

12. www.donorplatform.org/

13. www.gvepinternational.org/

14. www.adb.org/news/speeches/signing-mou-unicef

15. www.iisd.org/climate/unfccc/cop_dadays.asp

APPENDIX A: SUMMARY OF GUIDELINES FOR THE EVALUATION OF IORS USING THE OECD DAC CRITERIA, PREPARED FOR THE ASIAN DEVELOPMENT BANK

RELEVANCE

DAC: The extent to which the aid activity is suited to the priorities and policies of the target group, recipient and donor.

- In the context of interorganizational relationships (IORs), relevance relates to whether or not the purpose of the IOR serves to address one or more sustainable development challenges, and
- That the purpose is suited to the priorities and policies of:
  - The member institutions and
  - Those that the members wish to influence

In evaluating an IOR for *relevance*, it is useful to consider the following questions:

1. Does the IOR have a clear, shared purpose that meets defined needs?
2. Will the IOR help each organization to achieve more than they could on their own?
3. Will the IOR help each partner to define their own areas of influence more clearly?

EFFECTIVENESS

DAC: A measure of the extent to which the aid activity attains its objectives.

- In the context of IORs, effectiveness refers to the extent to which the IORS attains its purpose.

In evaluating an IOR for *effectiveness*, it is useful to consider the following questions:

1. Does the IOR have a clear outcome identified?
2. Are there processes, infrastructure, and resources with sufficient flexibility in place for:
   - Quality exchange of knowledge and experience
   - Regular communications and meetings
   - Communicating beyond the IOR?
3. Have the members mutually agreed upon a framework for monitoring their work over time?
4. Have the members examined and disclosed other IORs that they are committed to (do they belong to other similar networks, partnerships)?

EFFICIENCY

DAC: Efficiency measures the outputs—qualitative and quantitative—in relation to the inputs. It is an economic term that signifies that the aid uses the least costly resources possible in order to achieve the desired results. This generally requires comparing alternative approaches to achieving the same outputs, to see whether the most efficient process has been adopted.

- In the context of IORs, efficiency measures the outputs—qualitative and in relation to the inputs. Attention should be given to:
  - Alternative approaches to achieve the same outputs.
  - The extent to which the IOR made optimal use of all the resources available to it.

When evaluating an IOR for *efficiency*, it is useful to consider the following questions:

1. Has the IOR explored alternative models to achieving the desired outcomes (open/closed membership; use of crowd sourcing approaches; contracting out), including whether an IOR is the best approach?
2. Are the necessary resources (staff, time, funds) available, properly allocated, and well matched for planned activities?
3. Is there scope for adjustment of processes, activities and resources during the lifespan of the IOR?
4. Is there clarity on management of the assets of the IOR, including funds, intellectual property and brand?

IMPACT

DAC: The positive and negative changes produced by a development intervention, directly or indirectly, intended or unintended. This involves the main impacts and effects resulting from the activity on the local social, economic, environmental and other development indicators. The examination should be concerned with both intended and unintended results and must also include the positive and negative impact of external factors, such as changes in terms of trade and financial conditions.

- In the context of IORs, impact refers to the positive and negative changes produced by the IORs sustainable development interventions, directly or indirectly, intended or unintended. The impact should be examined at two levels:
  - The contribution that the IOR as a whole makes to the resolution of sustainable development challenges
  - The improvement of each member's institutional capacity to have impact.

When evaluating an IOR's contribution to *impact*, it is useful to consider the following questions:

1. How will the IOR ascertain whether its outcomes will lead to impact?
2. How will the IOR ascertain whether people outside of the IOR are aware of its knowledge, actions, and influence, and, in turn, act upon them?
3. How will the IOR ascertain whether members' capacity increased as a result of the IOR?
4. Does the IOR have flexibility for the unexpected to emerge?

SUSTAINABILITY

DAC: Sustainability is concerned with measuring whether the benefits of an activity are likely to continue after donor funding has been withdrawn. Projects need to be environmentally as well as financially sustainable.

- In the context of IORs, examining sustainability has two components:
  - The likelihood that the achievements of the IOR will be sustained
  - The sustainability of the IOR itself

In examining the latter, four dimensions should be considered:

- Relevance: whether the purpose of the IOR is still relevant
- Relationships: whether the members are still active
- Resources: whether resources are available
- Time: whether the IOR has given itself sufficient time to achieve its purpose or if continuation is necessary.

When evaluating an IOR for sustainability, it is useful to consider the following questions:

1. How will the outcome of the IOR's work be sustained?
2. Should the IOR itself be sustained and if so, how?
3. Does the IOR know what motivates the members to join and continue participate?
4. Are there mechanisms in place to jointly reflect, learn and adapt, over the lifespan of the IOR?

APPENDIX B: TABLE OF SELECTED IISD PLANNING AND EVALUATION CONSULTANCIES RELATED TO PARTNERSHIPS AND NETWORKS

Organization	Project Description
Asian Environmental Compliance and Enforcement Network	Guidance on the evolution of the network
Association for Progressive Communications and the International Development Research Centre (IDRC)	Assessment of capacity building between two organizations
Asian Development Bank	Guidelines for the establishment and assessment of knowledge partnerships
Community of Practice on Ecosystem Health, Latin America and the Caribbean (COPEH-LAC), and IDRC	Evaluation of COPEH-LAC
Electronic Networking for Rural Development, Asia Pacific (ENRAP) (International Fund for Agricultural Development (IFAD) and IDRC)	Evaluation of IFAD's Asia and Pacific networking project
Federation of Canadian Municipalities	Evaluation of knowledge transfer actions across communities
Global Development Learning Network (World Bank Institute)	Governance processes
Global Knowledge Partnership (Swiss Agency for Development Cooperation [SDC])	Assessment of Strategy 2010
Global Village Energy Partnership (World Bank and others)	Communications and Knowledge Management strategies
FIDAfrique (IFAD)	Evaluation of IFAD's West and Central Africa network
International Forum for Rural Transport and Development	Capacity assessment of the network
International Union for the Conservation of Nature	Knowledge management study
Karianet (IFAD and IDRC)	Study supporting the devolution of the network
Mountain Partnership (FAO and others)	Evaluation of the Secretariat
SDC Mobility Mandate, including the Transnet network	Evaluation of the mandate, including the networks supported under that mandate
The SEED Initiative	Research into performance monitoring for small, micro and medium sized enterprises working in partnerships
Trade Knowledge Network (IISD and the International Centre for Trade and Sustainable Development)	Evaluation of phase 2
UNESCO	Evaluation of Community Multimedia Centres pilot program and network
United Nations Environment Program	Knowledge management study

REFERENCES

Asian Development Bank (ADB). (2011). *Guidelines for knowledge partnerships*. Mandaluyong City, Philippines: Author. Report prepared for ADB by H. Creech and M. Laurie. Retrieved from www.adb.org/publications/guidelines-knowledge-partnerships.

Cabaj, M. (2011, November). *Network death and renewal in the adaptive cycle*. Unpublished presentation at the Networks Leadership Symposium 2011, Royal Roads University, Victoria, BC.

Creech, H., Laurie, M., Paas, L., & Parry, J. E. (2012). *Performance improvement and assessment of collaboration: starting points for networks and communities of practice*. Winnipeg, ON: IISD. Forthcoming: www.iisd.org.

Creech, H., Vetter, T., Matus, K., & Seymour, I. (2008). *The governance of non-legal entities: An exploration into the challenges facing collaborative, multistakeholder enterprises that are hosted by institutions*. Winnipeg: IISD. Retrieved from http://www.iisd.org/publications/pub.aspx?pno=1044

Creech, H., & Willard, T. (2001). *Strategic intentions: Managing formal knowledge networks for sustainable development*. Winnipeg: IISD. Retrieved from http://www.iisd.org/pdf/2001/networks_strategic_intentions.pdf

Franke, S. (2005). *Measurement of social capital: Reference document for public policy research, development, and evaluation*. Ottawa, ON: Policy Research Initiative, Government of Canada. Retrieved from http://www.horizons.gc.ca/doclib/Measurement_E.pdf

Huppé, G. A., Creech, H., & Knoblach, D. (2012). *The frontiers of networked governance*. Winnipeg, IISD. Retrieved from www.iisd.org/pdf/2012/frontiers_networked_gov.pdf

Huppé, G. A., & Creech, H. (2012). *Developing social capital in networked governance initiatives: A lock-step approach*. Winnipeg: IISD. Available: http://www.iisd.org/pdf/2012/developing_social_capital_network_gov.pdf

OECD DAC. (n.d.). *DAC criteria for evaluating development assistance*. Retrieved from http://www.oecd.org/dac/evaluationofdevelopmentprogrammes/daccriteriaforevaluatingdevelopmentassistance.htm

Serrat, O. (2010). *Knowledge Solutions: Tools, methods and approaches to drive development forward and enhance its effects*. Asian Development Bank. Retrieved from http://www.adb.org/documents/books/knowledge-solutions-1-90/knowledge-solutions-1-90.pdf

Universalia, IISD. (n.d.). Unpublished minutes of a two-day closed workshop between Universalia and IISD evaluation staff.

Willard, T. (2009). *Assessing network health*. Winnipeg, ON: IISD. Retrieved from http://www.iisd.org/pdf/2012/assessing_network_health.pptx

Willard T., & Creech, H. (2006). *Sustainability of international development networks*. Ottawa, ON: IDRC. Available: http://www.iisd.org/pdf/2007/networks_sus_int_dev.pdf

Willard, T., & Creech, H. (2011). *IISD partnerships review: Selected observations*. Winnipeg, ON: IISD. Retrieved from http://www.iisd.org/pdf/2012/iisd_partnership_review.pdf

CHAPTER 7

EVALUATING COALITIONS

Jared Raynor

In every historian's description of a revolution, in every political biographer's descrip-
tion of the ascent of his subject, there is a more or less explicit account of the coalitions
and alliances which furthered the final outcome. Few areas exhibit less external uni-
formity. "Politics makes strange bed fellows" we say to express our bewilderment at some
new coalition which belies our expectations from past knowledge of the participants.

—William Gamson (1961, p. 373)

EVALUATING COALITIONS

Emerging out of the more generic networks and partnerships arena, coalitions are particularly prone to broad definitional liberty. There is an
emerging body of literature that looks at nuances between various forms
of group efforts, but the basic essence is a difference of formality and accountability. Tom Wolff (2003) articulates a typology of organizational
structures stemming from informal networks, through committees, coalitions, collaborations, strategic alliances, joint ventures and mergers, progressing from least formal and least accountable to most formal and most
accountable. In the end, coalitions are likely to be both more formal and
have more accountability than networks and less formal with less accountability than strategic alliances.

Emerging Practices in International Development Evaluation, pages 151–164
Copyright © 2013 by Information Age Publishing
All rights of reproduction in any form reserved.

Perhaps the most robust definition of a coalition comes from Mizrahi and Rosenthal (2001), who state that a coalition is formed when "an organization or organizations...commit to an agreed-on purpose and shared decision making to influence an external institution or target, while each member organization maintains its own autonomy." One reason this definition is appealing is that it accommodates many different types of entities labeled as coalitions. The phrase "to influence an external institution or target" is specific enough to reflect an external advocacy role, but broad enough to encompass a variety of advocacy targets such as national/local policy; the public at large; and judiciary, executive, school, or healthcare systems. As with any organization, coalitions are likely to progress through several stages from formation to growth.

At its simplest, a coalition is a unique entity of its own accord, comprised of other actors, institutional or otherwise, working together (see Figure 7.1). As such, it exhibits properties of a standard organization (leadership, management, adaptability, and technical skills)[1] as well as standard group dynamics.[2] At a more complex level, looking at a coalition means analyzing multiple sets of relationships and understanding how they function and operate in pursuit of specific goals. As seen in Figure 7.2, adding organizations to a coalition creates a set of relationships, as depicted by overlaps in the concentric circles. In all, there are six different potential relationships that emerge:

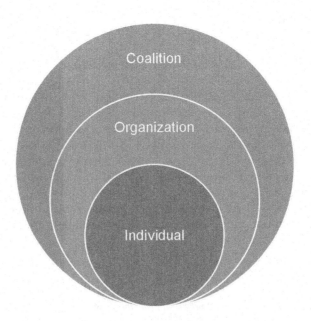

Figure 7.1 What is a coalition?

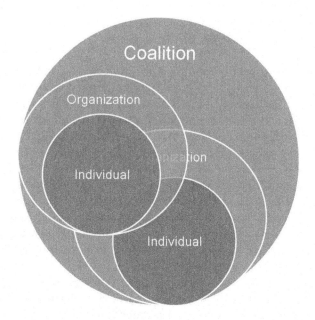

Figure 7.2 Coalitions: Creating relationship.

1. Coalition to the external world
2. Organization to coalition
3. Individual to coalition
4. Individual to individual
5. Individual to organization
6. Organization to organization

Each of these relationships could be evaluated as a way to understand coalitions and their effectiveness, and each has a separate body of literature associated with it. For example, some of the relationships that could be evaluated include:

- Coalition to External World: general advocacy evaluation techniques, brand identity
- Organization to Coalition: Equity analysis, power sharing, identity politics, matrix decision-making
- Individual to Coalition: Power dynamics, identity politics, group dynamics
- Individual to Individual: Interpersonal skills, social network analysis, knowledge exchange
- Individual to Organization: Power dynamics, identity politics, Brand identity, positive perception/attitude

- Organization to Organization: Network analysis, collaborations, systems theory, mergers and acquisitions

In almost all instances, building a coalition is not enough to influence outcomes; rather, the coalition must itself act, implementing advocacy strategies such as *issue analysis, organizing, raising public awareness,* and *lobbying.* Within the context of policy and advocacy work, coalitions take on a dual identity. In developing a generic logic model associated with doing policy and advocacy work, coalitions occupy the role of both a strategy to be used by advocates *or* as an agent of action, as depicted in Figure 7.3.[3]

Beyond this task of defining a coalition and its multiple components, the concept of evaluating coalitions allows for significant simplification of terms and concepts. While the differing perspectives on coalitions have discrete measures that allow for insight into coalition performance, they are generally impractical for evaluators working in development contexts. A more applicable model was developed by Lasker, Weiss, and Miller (2001), who offered a framework for looking at the various determinants of successful collaborations, which included: resources, partner characteristics, relationships among partners, and partnership characteristics. Butterfoss and Francisco (2004) made it even simpler, recommending three levels of evaluation indicators that capture a coalition's performance:

1. The presence of processes to sustain and renew coalition infrastructure and function
2. Programs intended to meet target activities or those that work directly toward the partnership's goals
3. Changes in community status around the targeted goals.

I propose minor modifications to Butterfoss' measures, adding an individual measure that examines the organizations' capacity to be good coalition members, which would preempt joining the coalition or its functioning, and conflating the elements of program activities (essentially output monitoring and short-term outcomes) with longer-term outcomes of changes in the target area (community, policy, etc.). While I agree that evaluating long-term changes helps keep a coalition focused, from a practical standpoint such long-term changes are seldom attributable to coalition activities, therefore there will be a premium on shorter-term indicators of progress (discussed more below). Summarized, I propose evaluating coalitions with measures in three areas:

- Capacity of organizations to be good coalition members
- Capacity of the coalition to carry out the needed activities
- Outcomes/impact of the coalition work

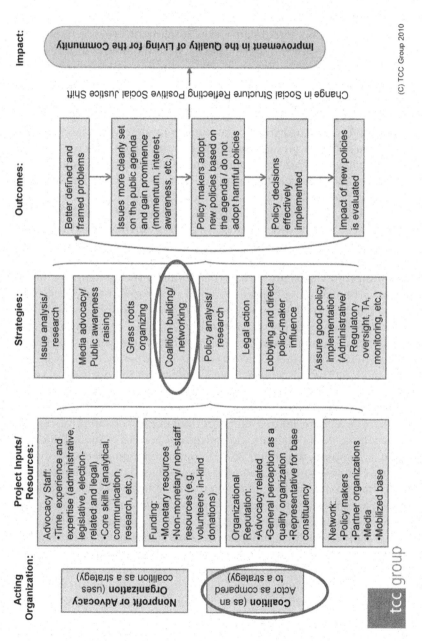

Figure 7.3 Logic model: Advocacy initiatives.

CAPACITY OF ORGANIZATIONS
TO BE GOOD COALITION MEMBERS

If a coalition's value lies in either a sum of its parts (to reach economies of influence/scale) or some synergistic added value stemming from the sum of individual parts (see Lasker et al., 2001), then it stands to reason that the value of the individual parts contain deterministic factors that limit the bounds of the overall coalition. As such, evaluating the (potential) coalition membership, *ex parte*, can provide insight into the value of the coalition.

In considering the capacity of organizations numerous models exist (see Peter Morgan's chapter on capacity building in this book). When it comes to the specific capacity of advocacy organizations, the literature is more scant. Raynor, York, and Sim (2009) recently developed a comprehensive model of advocacy capacity after a review of relevant literature and several original evaluations. Using a "core capacity model" developed by Connolly, York, and TCC Group (2003), the advocacy model organized and developed a quantitative assessment tool, the Advocacy Core Capacity Assessment Tool (ACCAT), to assess capacities specific to advocacy organizations, acknowledging that general nonprofit capacities were also applicable. The Alliance for Justice developed a similar, though more technical skills-based model of advocacy capacity, including a self-assessment tool. Inherent in both these models are key indicators of collaborative capacity within any given organization.

I believe that holistic models of capacity are important to be able to contextualize specific capacities, which, as discussed earlier, were led by holistic capacity models. There is a more nuanced literature that focuses on capacity to collaborate that is at least tangentially relevant to coalition member capacity that is explored in a broader network literature that I won't discuss here. There is a more limited literature looking at collaborative capacity as it pertains to coalition work and advocacy. Foster-Fishman, Berkowitz, Lounsbury, Jacobson, and Allen (2001) conducted a qualitative analysis of 80 articles, chapters, and practitioners' guides focused on collaboration and coalition functioning and identified four critical levels of collaborative capacity that are needed within collaborative bodies to facilitate their success. They include member capacity, relational capacity, organizational capacity, and programmatic capacity. A partial list of member capacities (mixed with member capacities drawn from other sources) can be found in Box 7.1.

Several studies have examined the factors contributing the decision to join coalitions. For example, Hojnaki (1997) explored the factors that affect the likelihood of organized interests joining a coalition or working alone and found that interest groups will weigh the costs and benefits of joining a coalition and will use that to estimate whether joining will improve their chances of success. She also found that organizations will be more likely to join a coalition when organizations perceived to be "pivotal" to success are

---

BOX 7.1   CAPACITIES OF EFFECTIVE COALITION MEMBERS

☐ Skills/knowledge to work collaboratively
☐ Commit to the coalition in action as well as name
☐ Ability to articulate what you bring to the table (e.g., time, resources, access, relationships, reputation, expertise, etc.)
☐ Ability to articulate what you want from the table
☐ Ability to weigh the value of coalition membership against scarce resource expenditure
☐ Willingness to share resources
☐ Willingness to openly identify conflicts between the individual organization and the coalition
☐ Willingness to share power and credit
☐ Willingness to speak as one
☐ Willingness to dedicate staffing at a high enough level to make decisions
☐ Willingness to dedicate staffing to implement assigned tasks
☐ Strategic use of coalitions to fill critical gaps and leverage resources toward achieving your mission
☐ Willingness to commit to the coalition for an extended (relevant) period of time
☐ Understanding of how your issue fits into a broader network of issues

---

members of an alliance, when groups represent expressive interests, and when the organization perceives a strong organized opposition.

Butterfield, Reed, and Lemak (2004) used an inductive, interview-based methodology based in stakeholder theory and interorganizational collaboration to examine issues such as why stakeholder organizations form collaborative alliances and what outcomes result from the collaborative process, while Guo and Acar (2005) used survey data from 95 urban charitable organizations to examine the factors that influence the likelihood of formal versus informal collaborations among nonprofit organizations. The authors find that an organization is more likely to increase the degree of formality of its collaborative activities when it is older, has a larger budget size, receives government funding but relies on fewer government funding streams, has more board linkages with other nonprofit organizations, and is not operating in the education and research or social service industry.

CAPACITY OF THE COALITION

Coalitions exhibit all the classic elements of an organization—social arrangements in the pursuit of collective goals, control over its own performance, and boundaries separating it from its environment.[4] Here the role of organizational capacity becomes highly relevant as it relates to the overall functioning of the coalition. Given difficulties in assessing very long-term outcomes (e.g., a policy actually changed, homelessness statistically reduced), shorter-term indicators of progress are important from an evaluation perspective. While some of these potential short-term indicators of success are discussed below in the section on outcomes/impact of coalition work, capacity serves as a potentially powerful short-term proxy for likely long-term success by identifying the extent to which a coalition and its member organizations are prepared to exploit any relevant windows of opportunity that may arise.

The literature on coalitions and the factors that predict their success is relatively long and varied. In one of the earlier coalition studies, Butterfoss, Goodman, and Wandersman (1993) examined the current state of knowledge about coalitions and provided several advantages of using coalitions. The article then discussed characteristics of coalition functioning that relate to their effectiveness and outcomes. Kegler, Steckler, Herndon Malek, and McLeroy (1998) later sought to identify factors that facilitated or impeded coalition effectiveness in the implementation state of coalition development by studying 10 local coalitions. Levi and Murphy (2006) looked at a subset of the more than 200 organizations and groups that mobilized during the WTO meetings in Seattle in 1999. In looking at these groups, the authors attempted to identify the key factors that make or break organizational coalitions and how coalition members resolve interorganizational tensions and conflicts and realign themselves in crises. Mizrahi and Rosenthal (2001) used the results of three focus groups with 70 past and current coalition organizers and leaders to study coalition dynamics, operations, and outcomes. One of their key findings is that sophisticated and experienced leaders are needed to sustain and use coalitions for community improvement and social change.

Alexander et al. (2003) discussed five primary attributes/activities of sustainable partnerships including outcomes-based advocacy, vision–focus balance, systems orientation, infrastructure development, and community linkages. Wolff (2001) identified nine dimensions of coalition success: coalition readiness, intentionality, structure and organizational capacity, taking action, membership, leadership, dollars and resources, relationships, and technical assistance. Cramer, Atwood, and Stoner (2006) developed a conceptual model for measuring the internal effectiveness of coalitions. The conceptual model has seven hierarchical levels, including:

- Social vision
- Efficient practices
- Knowledge and training

- Relationships
- Participation
- Activities
- Resources

These seven factors typically build upon each other to form a strong coalition. The model considers that effective coalitions have two distinct features. First, they have a diverse community membership that works well together to achieve outcomes in each of the seven above areas. Second, they have leaders that facilitate a learning environment where members can achieve agreed-upon outcomes.

Perhaps the broadest academic review to date came from Zakocs and Edwards (2006). They reviewed published articles from 1980 to 2004 that empirically examined the relationships among coalition-building factors and indicators of coalition effectiveness. The literature review identified 55 coalition-building factors that were associated with coalition effectiveness. Six factors were found to be associated with indicators of effectiveness in five or more studies, and they included:

- Formalization of rules/procedures
- Leadership style
- Member participation
- Membership diversity
- Agency collaboration
- Group cohesion.

In reviewing all this literature, Raynor (2010) organized those areas where some overlap appeared regarding coalition capacity into a cohesive framework of coalition capacity utilizing a common nonprofit organizational capacity model (Table 7.1).

OUTCOMES/IMPACT OF THE COALITION WORK

Just like any direct service or advocacy work, coalition success includes a number of interim achievements such as network development, skill building, and incremental gains in policy development, as well as long-term goal attainment (e.g., reducing malnutrition, passing specific policy, etc.). As a result, coalitions need a continuum of measures and indicators for their outcome work. Clarifying goals from the start and measuring them on a regular basis allows for true lessons learned rather than retrospective justification. Since clarity of purpose is one capacity upon which there is widespread agreement, it seems like an appropriate place to search for evalu-

TABLE 7.1 Framework of Coalition Capacities

Leadership Capacities:
- Shared purpose and vision
  - Common goal destination
  - Clear value proposition
- Formalized set of rules/procedures
- A "core" leadership team
- A commitment to action
- Transparent decision-making processes
- Strategically developed and engaged membership

Adaptive Capacities:
- Ability to monitor the advocacy policy environment
- Effective and action-oriented planning
- Ongoing monitoring and evaluation
- Measures of goal destination
  - Measures of value proposition
  - Measures of "positive externalities"
- Membership assessment
- Procurement of resources (both in-kind and financial from coalition members and external sources)
- Foster inter-member non-coalition collaboration

Management Capacities:
- Frequent and productive communications
- Facilitate language differences (e.g., translation, definitions, etc.)
- Managing member participation
  - Deliver on reciprocity/ expectations
  - Clear task and goal assignments
  - Clarity around member and staff roles
  - Ability to manage conflict
  - Careful record-keeping

Technical Capacities:
- Appropriately diverse membership
- Coalition staffing (as strategically deemed appropriate)
- Communication skills
- Policy/advocacy expertise
- Tangible non-human resources (e.g., space, equipment, funding, etc.)
- Resource development skills

ation criteria. As coalitions and external stakeholders (including funders) evaluate coalitions, they might focus on the extent to which a coalition is making progress on goal destination (i.e., progress on an issue) and/or the coalition as the value proposition (coalition as the right vehicle), both discussed below. Table 7.2 summarizes some prominent indicators for evaluating coalitions in each area.

- On the *goal destination* side, there is nothing particularly unique to coalition goal destination outcomes as compared to others doing advocacy work. These include such things as the obvious visibility of the issue, policy win/block, and shorter-term "outputs" like media placements or testifying on an issue. Refer to *A User's Guide to Advocacy Evaluation Planning* for a more comprehensive list of advocacy related goal outcomes.[5] Measures of goal destination that seem particularly relevant to coalitions include increasing visibility/knowledge of the issue, better relationships (by virtue of having additional relationships to draw on), overcoming important "sticking points" (as described above—a particularly important role for coalitions in today's advocacy environment), and increasing public goodwill.

TABLE 7.2 Indicators for Evaluating Coalitions

Goal Destination	Value Proposition
• Policy adoption/Policy blocking • Increased visibility/knowledge of issue • Better relationships with policy-makers and allies and reduced enemies • Development of good research (increased data) • Writing/testifying on effective policy • Overcoming important "sticking" points in moving an agenda/policy • Activation of broader constituency • Increased public will	• Increased coalition capacity (e.g., clarity of vision; ability to manage/raise resources; better policy analysis; etc.) • Increased visibility of coalition • Increased membership • Increased quality/prestige/engagement of membership • Increased collaboration between coalition members outside the coalition • Merging/strategic relationship with other coalitions • More rapid and organized ability to respond • Number of different "faces" that the coalition could credibly put forward to advance the issue

- On the *value proposition* side, indicators are more specific with regard to the legitimacy and relevance of the coalition. These include increased capacity, visibility and membership, stronger external engagement, and ability to rapidly respond to opportunities/threats.

Apart from these specific coalition objectives, coalitions also serve as fertile ground for other positive developments. We use the economic term and refer to these as "positive externalities"—things that aren't central goals but are positive byproducts. These include better coordination of non-advocacy program work, reducing the sense of isolation that advocates might feel, the emergence of innovative ideas through cross-fertilization, and any other objectives the coalition might set for itself. See Table 7.3 for a list of common positive benefits of coalitions. For example, the members of one coalition we worked with reported that their participation in the coalition gave them renewed energy in their own organizations because they saw other people who were also dedicated to their issues even though they were working on different aspects of the problem.

TABLE 7.3 Coalition Positive Externalities

Better implementation/coordination of actual programs addressing the issue
Sustained networks/relationships
Reduced sense of isolation
Cross-fertilization and innovative ideas
Other specific project goals met

METHODS

As with most evaluations, mixed methods are generally the most appropriate for coalition evaluations, with the obvious caveat that the methods should be well suited to answer the evaluation question(s). I have discussed methods inherent in capacity evaluation, as well as outcomes-based evaluation. In addition, social network mapping has clear potential benefits in evaluating coalition reach and influence. A few key methodological principles related to evaluating coalition work include:

- With rare exceptions, methodologies should be able to provide rapid feedback that can be incorporated into ongoing activities.
- Quantitative methods, such as scaled surveys and trend data, should be encouraged, rather than discouraged. This is to push for evaluations to be more concrete and avoid the tendency to rely on anecdotal evidence.
- Measures and indicators should be developed *ex ante* to implementation. While clearly the evaluation should attempt to capture unforeseen challenges and outcomes, the evaluation methodology should push solid planning with clear anticipated causal pathways.

CHALLENGES

There are several challenges associated with evaluating coalitions in the context of development. Among these are:

- Extremely high levels of power differentials among coalition partners. Frequently, there are one or two organizations that have particularly high capacity within the development context geographic area, with many smaller, less powerful organizations. These power differentials can lead to distortions in data collection as well as coalition functionality. It can also make it hard to disaggregate the work of the coalition from the one or two strong partners.
- Difficulty in identifying "replicable" components from the evaluation. Given that local contexts vary significantly from place to place (and within a place over even short periods of time), the concept of replicability often associated with evaluation can be problematic. Even if evaluations are able to identify replicable aspects or "best practices," other localities or coalitions often have difficultly understanding how to abstractly apply the concepts to their own work.
- Competing demands of funders can distort the focus of the coalition and complicate data collection.

- In areas where democracies are still emerging and there is a more nascent civil society, the work of coalitions can be easily conflated with the political process itself.

NOTES

1. Connolly, Paul and Peter York, TCC Group (formerly The Conservation Company) (2003). "Building the Capacity of Capacity Builders: A study of Management Support and Field-Building Organizations in the Nonprofit Sector," a report produced with funding from the David and Lucile Packard Foundation, with additional assistance from The Alliance for Nonprofit Management and Grantmakers for Effective Organizations.
2. The broad field of game theory has developed a host of variables for exploring dynamics related to individual decision-making within a group setting, which may pit individual goals against group objectives. See, for example, Komorita (1978).
3. This generic advocacy logic model was first presented in Raynor, York, and Sim (2009).
4. Drawn from Wikipedia, March 17, 2010: http://en.wikipedia.org/wiki/Organization
5. See "A User's Guide to Advocacy Evaluation Planning" (2009) published by Harvard Family Research Project for a more comprehensive list of advocacy related goal outcomes that are as applicable to coalitions as individual advocacy organizations.

REFERENCES

Butterfield, K. D., Reed, R., & Lemak, D. J. (2004). An inductive model of collaboration from the stakeholder's perspective. *Business and Society, 43*(2), 162–195.

Butterfoss, F. D., Goodman, R. M., & Wandersman, A. (1993). Community coalitions for prevention and health promotion. *Health and Education Research, 8*(3), 315–330.

Connolly, P., York, P., & TCC Group (formerly The Conservation Company). (2003). *Building the capacity of capacity builders: A study of management support and field-building organizations in the nonprofit sector.* Report produced with funding from the David and Lucile Packard Foundation, with additional assistance from The Alliance for Nonprofit Management and Grantmakers for Effective Organizations.

Coffman, J. (2009). *A user's guide to advocacy evaluation planning.* Cambridge, MA: Harvard Family Research Project

Cramer, M. E., Atwood, J. R., & Stoner, J. A. (2006). A conceptual model for understanding effective coalitions involved in health promotion programming. *Public Health Nursing, 23*(1), 67–73.

Foster-Fishman, P. G., Berkowitz, S. L., Lounsbury, D. W., Jacobson, S., & Allen, N. A. (2001). Building collaborative capacity in community coalitions: A review and integrative framework. *American Journal of Community Psychology, 29*(2).

Hojnacki, M. (1997). Interest groups' decisions to join alliances or work alone. *American Journal of Political Science, 41*(1), 61–87.

Kegler, M. C., Steckler, A., Herndon Malek, S., & McLeroy, K. (1998). A multiple case study of implementation in 10 local Project ASSIST coalitions in North Carolina. *Health Education Research, 13*(2), 225–338.

Komorita, S. (1978). Evaluating coalition theories, some indices. *Journal of Conflict Resolution, 22*(4),

Lasker, R. D., Weiss, E. S., & Miller, R. (2001). Partnership synergy: A practical framework for studying and strengthening the collaborative advantage. *Milbank Quarterly, 79*(2), 179–205.

Levi, M., & Murphy, G. H. (2006). Coalitions of contention: The case of the WTO protests in Seattle. *Political Studies 54*, 651–670.

Mintrom, M., & Vergari, S. (1996). Advocacy coalitions, policy entrepreneurs, and policy change. *Policy Studies Journal, 24*(3), 420–434.

Mizrahi, T., & Rosenthal, B. B. (2001). Complexities of coalition building: Leaders' successes, strategies, struggles, and solutions. *Social Work, 46*(1), 63–78.

Raynor, J., York, P., & Sim, S-C. (2009). *What makes an effective advocacy organization.* Los Angeles, CA: The California Endowment.

Summit Health Institute for Research and Education, Inc. (SHIRE), with Out of Many, One (OMO). (2004). *Building coalitions among communities of color: A multicultural approach.* Manual prepared for the State Partnership Initiative of the U.S. Office of Minority Health, Department of Health and Human Services.

Wolff, T. (2001). A practitioner's guide to successful coalitions. *American Journal of Community Psychology, 29*(2), 173–191.

Wolff, T. (2003). A practical approach to evaluation of collaborations. In T. E. Backer (Ed.), *Evaluating community collaborations.* New York, NY: Springer.

Wood, C. J. (1989). Challenging the assumptions underlying the use of participatory decision-making strategies: A longitudinal case study. *Small Group Research, 20*(4), 428–448.

Zakocs, R. C., & Edwards, E. M. (2006). What explains community coalition effectiveness?: A review of the literature." *American Journal of Preventive Medicine, 30*(4), 351–361.

CHAPTER 8

EVALUATING SUSTAINABLE DEVELOPMENT

Steve Bass and Alastair Bradstock

INTRODUCTION

While most governments, local authorities, and some companies have made commitments to achieve sustainable development (SD) in the last few years, their policies, plans, and codes of practice are not matched by demonstrations of real progress towards sustainable development. This situation could be attributed to many reasons such as lack of clarity and priorities, weak measurement and evaluation (M&E) of outcomes, which leads to reductions in accountability. In practice, all of these reasons apply—and the M&E question remains central. Sustainable development is a *journey* rather than a destination, and good M&E is needed to identify where one is on that journey to help confirm or change direction on policies and practices.

Several characteristics make it difficult to assess net progress because sustainable development aims to integrate multiple objectives (e.g., economic, social, environmental, and institutional) and multiple time scales (e.g., intragenerational and intergenerational equity, as well as uncertain futures in complex systems) at several levels (from local to global, depending upon the system in question). This is the reason why many current SD evaluations focus on "enabling conditions" that attempt to capture some of the dispa-

Emerging Practices in International Development Evaluation, pages 165–197
Copyright © 2013 by Information Age Publishing
All rights of reproduction in any form reserved.

rate objectives. Evaluations can help to determine if enabling conditions have been established and ascertain whether they are being implemented, and it should be viewed as a way to strengthen existing conditions as well as proposing new alternatives that can support SD in the future.

Although the phrase *sustainable development* can be found on approximately 22 million web pages (by 2010), and the term is used in many institutions, organizations, development programmers, and countries, the most commonly used definition for SD is taken from the 1987 Brundtland Commission, which states "that development that meets the needs of the present without compromising the ability of future generations to meet their own needs" (World Commission on Environmental Development, 1987; p. 43) is ambiguous.

Reid (1995) argues that the term *sustainable development* came into the mainstream with the publication of the World Conservation Strategy (1980) that was written jointly by the International Union for the Conservation of Nature (IUCN), the World Wide Fund for Nature (WWF) and the United Nations Environmental Program (UNEP). The strategy identified sustainable development as maintaining essential ecological processes and life support systems, preserving genetic diversity, and ensuring the sustainable utilization of species and ecosystems.

Arguably the most influential event that preceded the World Conservation Strategy was the 1972 United Nations Conference on the Human Environment held in Stockholm. This was an important step in the evolution of sustainable development: It was the first major conference that discussed international environmental issues and marked a turning point in the development of international environmental politics. Although sustainable development was not referred to explicitly, there was agreement that both development and the environment should be managed in a mutually beneficial way.

Following Brundtland's attempt at capturing the meaning of SD, attempts have been made to clarify the definition—to be more precise about what was being sustained (for example, nature, life support systems, or community) and what was being developed (for example, people, economy, or society) as well as the relationship between them and the difficulties of defining a time period where something can be said to be developed in a sustainable manner (Bartelmus, 2003; Parris & Kates, 2003). The Rio and Johannesburg summits confirmed the "three pillars" framework for sustainable development: economic development, environmental protection, and social progress. Kates, Parris, and Leiserowitz (2005) argue that this attempt to include human development as an issue of equity and social justice addressed some of the concerns about the limitations of the Brundtland definition. A criticism of the three pillars is that they fail to include or make sufficiently explicit both the governance of SD and the mechanisms needed to hold people accountable for delivering it. While these issues are sometimes contained in the social pillar, an argument can be made for creating a fourth discrete pillar that addresses these important issues.

Following the Earth Summit of 1992, the concept was taken up by national governments, the UN system, multilateral donors, business, and civil society. For example, the United Nations Development Program started to promote "sustainable human development," the International Monetary Fund spoke of "sustainable economic growth," and the World Bank committed itself to "sustainable development and equitable development." Cities begin to strive for "sustainability." Business also began adopting the phrase, for example, a group of global mining companies including Anglo American, Rio Tinto, and BHP Billiton committed themselves to a set of 10 *sustainable development principles* following the Johannesburg summit (see, for example, http://www.icmm.com/our-work/sustainable-development-framework). Local government made perhaps some of the clearest commitments in the form of plans for cities and districts.

The concept of sustainable development has not been a communications triumph, yet it remains conceptually compelling. As Jonathan Porritt (2001), ex-chair of the UK Sustainable Development Commission, has expressed: "Sustainable development is the only intellectually coherent, sufficiently inclusive, potentially mind-changing concept that gets even half-way close to capturing the true nature and urgency of the challenge that now confronts the world. There really is no alternative."

As outlined above, the Brundtland definition has remained largely intact despite much buffeting and some tweaking over the last 20 years or more. But it remains somewhat conceptual. In practice, all of the international summitry on SD has driven the development of an impressive sustainable development toolkit, nine key components of which are listed below. These are primarily enabling conditions, which are more apparent on the ground than improvements in the three pillars. This suggests that evaluations will still be looking at "enabling conditions" rather than SD factors on the ground (or they might be looking for changes in disabling conditions). The tension between process monitoring and impact monitoring bedevils SD evaluation.

BOX 8.1: SUSTAINABLE DEVELOPMENT—MORE PROGRESS IS EVIDENT IN OUTCOMES (ENABLING CONDITIONS) THAN IMPACTS (SUSTAINABILITY ON THE GROUND)[1]

It is 20 years since the World Commission on Environment and Development—the Brundtland Commission—released its influential report. Since then, sustainable development has become the declared intention of most governments, many international organizations, and an increasingly large number of major companies and civil society groups. Behind the high-profile governmental summitry and intentions, a bewildering array of sustainable development plans, tools, and business models has also mushroomed:

1. **The "three pillars" concept of integrating environmental, economic, and social objectives.** This idea has been adopted by many governments in sustainability appraisal of new policies, and businesses in "triple bottom line" planning. The public is increasingly aware of how the issues are interconnected—for example, "sustainable consumption."

2. **Legal principles.** Among the more impressive developments is the articulation and use of legal principles such as "polluter pays," precaution, and prior informed consent to balance the three pillars. Brundtland's report identified 22 such principles. Many are now widely used in multilateral environmental agreements and national laws. Along with the three pillars concept, they offer an international *lingua franca* for sustainable development.

3. **International agreements.** The Rio Declaration expresses global aspirations, while the three UN conventions on biodiversity, desertification, and climate change offer shared objectives for global public goods—even if they lack adequate teeth to be effective.

4. **Many plans and strategies.** International plans such as Agenda 21 and the Johannesburg Plan of Implementation were vague, as they had to accommodate various national positions. But they have inspired progressive responses from many governments. There are many national sustainable development strategies, and sustainability components in development plans, but these tend to be idealistic. They lack clear priorities, and have little influence on budgeting, investment, and public administration.

5. **Political councils.** From the UN Commission on Sustainable Development, through national councils for sustainable development, to local or sectoral initiatives, these serve mainly to identify and debate issues. Few have high status or are adequately linked to the key processes of legislation and government.

6. **Tools for sustainability assessment and for market, project, and fiscal intervention.** There has been considerable innovation in information, analytical, planning, management, and deliberative tools—particularly for internalizing environmental issues and for enabling stakeholders to express views. But approaches that enable the machinery of government and business to routinely address all three pillars of sustainable development, and especially to change priorities, are in short supply.

7. **Voluntary codes and standards.** Many resource-intensive sectors— notably food, forestry, energy, and latterly mining—have been driven to develop these codes for varied reasons of reputation, cost, and

resource security. So far, they have tended to mark out existing good players rather than transform whole sectors.

8. **"Triad" partnerships.** After initial excessive faith that governments would lead the way to sustainable development, the notion of the "sustainable development triad" of government, civil society, and business actors has taken root. Some partnerships have led to "soft policy" change in several sectors—for example, the Forest and Marine Stewardship Councils were deliberately articulated around sustainable development principles.

9. **Considerable debate and research.** The discourse has been wide, reflecting many academic and professional perspectives—from the technical (rooted in ecology, economics, and sociology) to the applied (management and planning) and the political (assertions and criticism of values and structures). This pluralistic approach is critical. While strides have been made in multi-stakeholder debate and policy processes, setting impressive precedents, we do *not* yet have truly integrated research approaches—"sustainability science" for today's complex problems.

These nine components are very much the product of the formal sustainable development "industry," which is based largely in the West and a few international institutions. But they rarely appear as a complete, coherent set, deeply rooted either in multilateral organizations or in any one nation. They also lack clear values and norms connected to basic ideas such as the "quality of life." Perhaps most critically, smaller and poorer countries, communities, and businesses have not been able to access, use, or contribute to many of these elements.

But these have *not* triggered the pace, scale, scope, and depth of institutional and behavioral change that is needed to make development sustainable. Two other components are needed, and better evaluation may itself be a tool to put them in place.

We could identify a potential 10th component that includes other approaches to sustainable development much more closely associated with local, traditional and non-Western institutions. Many such institutions have evolved precisely to integrate changing social, environmental, and economic objectives in people's daily lives, to make clear trade-offs where integration is not possible, and to foster equity within and between generations—in other words, sustainable development. But we need to ask the kinds of evaluation questions that will unearth them.

We could also identify an 11th component—improved criteria, incentives and accountability mechanisms for SD. Only when these are securely in place are the prospects for SD good. This component would derive from better evaluation, and would improve evaluation: again, evaluation itself is needed as a core contribution to sustainable development.

CHALLENGES IN EVALUATING SUSTAINABLE DEVELOPMENT

Before exploring the measures, methods, frameworks, and how to make SD evaluations useful, it is worth describing some of the challenges that make evaluating SD so difficult. These include (1) data inadequacies, (2) the multiple spatial and temporal levels of SD, (3) institutional resistance to evaluating SD, (4) the real difficulties of keeping track of and measuring the spill-over effects that are inherent to SD, and (5) the lack of formal SD evaluation frameworks.

1. *SD represents a considerable paradigm shift that has not yet occurred in operational terms.* Thus there are rarely strong baseline information, monitoring systems, and accountability mechanisms in place to inform any SD evaluation.
2. *Evaluation itself is needed as a core contribution to the sustainable development journey, yet it has not been strong to date.* As the concluding paragraphs of Box 8.1 suggest, evaluation is a necessary component on the journey to SD.
3. *SD is a hugely comprehensive, long-term agenda with multiple spatial levels that present many evaluation problems.* It covers a wide range of environmental, social, economic, and political dimensions—in each of which, and in relation to the interaction of all of which, there are multiple forces at play. "Socially blind" conservation work can show some SD gains but also create poverty by pushing people off their land; "environmentally blind" poverty reduction can raid nature by asset-stripping forests even though it shows income gains. When evaluating at the micro level there is a real danger that the scope of the evaluation is set too narrowly and these spillover effects are missed. Much corporate CSR consists of little more than companies bragging about the things they like to do, which may be easier to do—and not about the tough choices they choose to ignore. Evaluation needs to assess these cross-objective as well as cross-temporal trade-offs.
4. *There are short-term as well as vested interests that do not support a full evaluation of SD.* Even if information were available, it is difficult to find the entry points into mainstream decision-making that would encourage and enable fruitful SD evaluation. Where this does exist, it often prefers a partial approach—only evaluating the few factors on which progress has been relatively easy. A long-term, comprehensive approach is both intrinsically difficult and avoided by many authorities.
5. *SD trade-offs can be pushed upwards or downwards from global to local.* Thus, whatever level you are evaluating (local SD business, national plan, global public goods provision), you need to consider other levels. A global carbon sequestration financing mechanism might be good at

a global level of analysis, but not if it causes local suffering of poor people or degradation of national biodiversity assets. On the other hand, a farming project might use local resources and engage local stakeholders sustainably but depend upon importing inputs (such as fertilizers) that have been produced unsustainably elsewhere.

6. *SD trade-offs can be pushed 'sideways' to other spatial units.* This also means the need to evaluate 'footprints' elsewhere. The UK's forests can be almost entirely preserved for recreation and biodiversity as we import most of our wood from other countries; but with what sustainability effect on those countries?

7. *Frameworks other than SD have often taken precedent,* consequently never allowing a baseline and time series of SD data to be prepared. For example, in developing countries, UN bodies and donors favor the Millennium Development Goals and their targets (which cover some, but not all, of the SD indicators relevant to a country).

8. *Thus it is not surprising that there is rarely a single, recognized SD evaluation framework in place in any jurisdiction.* Consequently, SD evaluation will involve clarifying the links between, and possibly rationalizing, the existing major measurement and evaluation (M&E) approaches:
   - Development planning M&E and its 60 Millennium Development Goals indicators
   - Public expenditure review M&E, which engages in analytical work around the budget and, if you are lucky, has some links to the above
   - Household surveys, censuses, and poverty monitoring
   - Environmental assessments—which are often under-resourced and/or focused on international commitments rather than things that matter locally.

MEASURES OF SUSTAINABLE DEVELOPMENT: ASSESSING BOTH PROCESS AND IMPACTS

Three measurement approaches are commonly used in SD evaluations: (1) indicator-based assessments at the outcome and impact level, (2) reference frameworks at the input/process level, and (3) narrative approaches as a way to describe changes and make the most of limited information.

Indicator-Based Assessments at the Outcome and Impact Level

Following the Rio conference in 1992, Chapter 40 of *Agenda 21* urged countries to more accurately measure progress being made towards reaching

SD either by using existing data sets more effectively or by collecting new data if a clear need was identified. The focus was on sets of social, environmental, economic, and sometimes institutional (or governance) indicators and the establishment of baselines to reveal later changes. There was, however, an acknowledgement of the difficulties facing some countries in terms of the capacity to collect, analyze, and present a range of appropriate data not only to support decision making on environment and development but also to inform the public about progress made towards achieving SD.

Since then, considerable effort has been made to develop indicator data sets that help to measure progress towards SD. Following the 1992 Rio Earth Summit, the United Nations established the Commission on Sustainable Development (CSD) under the auspices of the Economic and Social Council that was tasked with developing SD indicators. The first phase of the commission's work generated 134 SD indicators, and these have since been reduced to 58 that cover the key social, environmental, economic, and institutional aspects of SD. The UN (2007) argues that CSD's indicators are widely applicable and can be used by national governments to assess the progress of their national sustainable development strategies (NSDS). Bartelmus (2008) noted that in 2004 there were approximately 600 ongoing initiatives, and in 2006 the International Institute for Sustainable Development (IISD) had a global compendium of nearly 700.[2] Bell and Morse (2003), while acknowledging the numerous efforts in this area, put great emphasis on allowing flexibility at the local level and not being too prescriptive when developing (or calling for) indicators. This freedom to devise appropriate indicators that accurately reflect the intended outcomes and impact of SD initiatives is highly relevant to ensuring that programs are accurately evaluated. In each case, the appropriate social/economic/environmental interactions, triggers and priorities will be highly context-specific.

One of the problems of having an abundance of indicators is that it is difficult to get a holistic view of what actual progress is being made towards achieving SD. Aggregation is one obvious option. The danger of aggregation, however, is that it can lead to general statements about progress that do not provide insights about the performance of individual variables as well as giving a nuanced picture of progress. Newman (1998) suggests that framing indicators that demonstrate nonsustainability rather than sustainability may be more effective as they are often easier to measure and more noticeable. SD is not alone in being a complex issue to evaluate, but this emphasizes the importance of clearly framing evaluation questions and choosing the appropriate measures in order to answer evaluation questions accurately.

However, SD is rightly considered a "journey" as much as a "destination"; thus, its evaluation should involve process as well as outcome and impact indicators. If an initiative is being evaluated for its SD achievement, in practice the most meaningful part of the "results chain" to evaluate is the initiative's role in creating *enabling conditions* for better SD impacts on the ground and in people's lives. This is because there are usually too many factors, apart from the initiative in question, that have an influence at "impact level."

Most countries have developed sustainable development indicator (SDI) sets to help them measure progress towards sustainable development, some as part of their NSDS process, others independently. There are numerous existing indicator frameworks and sets, varying in their sophistication and coverage. Some set hard and quantitative targets, while others are more general goals. Some of the more commonly used frameworks include:

- Pressure-state-response (PSR), limited mostly to environmental issues (see, for example, Bell & Morse, 2003, p. 32 for an overview)
- Linked human/ecosystem well-being frameworks (see for example Bossel, 1999, p. 12 for a discussion) and the Millennium Ecosystem Assessment (see http://www.millenniumassessment.org/en/index.aspx)
- Wealth or capital-accounting based frameworks used at national level. These cover changes in manufactured capital (infrastructure), natural capital (natural resources), human capital (health, well-being, and productive potential of individuals). and social capital (see, for example, UN, 2007, for more details).

However, many of these frameworks are experimental, applied only as pilot exercises, or are supplanted by other frameworks. For example, the UN Millennium Development Goals framework (with its associated targets and indicators, some of which cover SD) is promoted in developing countries more than the UNCSD's framework, leading to inconsistent recording and incomplete time series. Other international indicator sets and initiatives include the UN System of Integrated Environmental and Economic Accounts.

The IISD has been a leader in developing and assessing SD indicators and their frameworks for some time. Pintér, Hardi, and Bartelmus (2005) at IISD identified several emerging trends:

- Continuing interest in the development of aggregate indices (e.g., human development index, barometer of sustainability, genuine progress indicator)
- Interest in core sets of "headline indicators" (e.g., a dozen or so, as used in the UK, Austria, and Australia, and by the European Environment Agency)

- Emergence of goal-oriented or target indicators (e.g., MDG indicators, Norway)
- Measurement of sustainability by capital ("green") accounting systems
- Making better use of indicators in performance assessment (of organizations)

BOX 8.2: ADVANTAGES AND CHALLENGES OF INDICATOR-BASED MONITORING

Advantages

Source: Dalal-Clayton & Bass, 2006

- Based on the concept of SD as a cross-sectoral, cyclical process, sustainable development indicators (SDIs) can play an integral role in several phases of the cycle: from the identification of strategic priorities, through planning and implementation of specific policy interventions, monitoring progress and learning from successes and failures. It is important, therefore, to couple indicator and NSDS development so they are mutually supportive. An NSDS provides an institutional framework for realizing the full potential of SDIs.
- SDIs can help the design of strategies and specific interventions so that they address real priorities, take interactions between sustainability issues into account, and identify weaknesses.
- Although SDIs can be a political challenge, as they point to issues about which groups are really concerned, they help to improve accountability both in terms of specific sustainability initiatives and the success of an overall NSDS.

Challenges

Source: Pintér et al., 2005

- Often, SDIs are developed with a rigorous review of national statistical data collection systems, leading inevitably to major *data gaps and data quality issues.* There is often a *lack of long-term, consistent monitoring mechanisms* to supply data with adequate temporal and spatial resolution. Data collection can be *costly.*
- Key challenge is to ensure that SDIs are *integrated into mainstream policy mechanisms,* instead of being an environmental "add-on" to existing and used statistical, measurement, and reporting systems.
- SDIs are still often assigned to environmental agencies without sufficient mandate, capacity, and influence to ensure indicators are brought to *bear on key policy decisions* such as the development of government budgets, sectoral policy frameworks, or long-term and sustainable development strategies.

- There remain uncertainties and debates about what and how to measure and how to link specific indicators to *time-bound targets and thresholds.*
- *Comparability* of indicator system continues to be limited by the use of different sets and frameworks that often adhere minimally to standards of how the same variables should be measured.
- *Aggregate indices* are attractive for communication but require high-quality data for consistent, comparable, and complete indicator sets, plus a political consensus on indicator weights that is difficult to achieve at international, national, or subnational scales.

Reference Frameworks for Evaluating SD Processes: At the Input/Process Level

The Organization for Economic Co-operation and Development–Development Assistance Committee (OECD-DAC, 2001) has identified a set of principles for good practice in developing and implementing national strategies for sustainable development (NSDS) or similar processes.[3] Indicators can be developed from these principles to help in process evaluation:

BOX 8.3: THE OECD-DAC PRINCIPLES FOR SUSTAINABLE DEVELOPMENT STRATEGIES

1. People-centered
2. Consensus on long-term vision
3. Comprehensive and integrated—across economic, social and environmental objectives, and over time periods
4. Targeted with clear budgetary priorities
5. Based on comprehensive and reliable analysis
6. Incorporate monitoring, learning and improvement
7. Country-led and -owned
8. High-level government commitment and influential lead institutions
9. Building on existing mechanism and strategies
10. Effective participation
11. Link national and local levels—in an iterative way
12. Develop and build on existing capacity

To the above list of principles endorsed by the OECD-DAC (2001) could be added:

Principle 13: Incorporate effective conflict and negotiation management systems

Source: Dalal-Clayton & Bass (2002)

Narrative Approaches—Stories of Success or Failure

Where it is difficult to single out individual factors, narratives can offer real benefit by postulating how, in a given (and well-described) context, changes actually occurred and the various combinations of factors and drivers that contributed to the change. They also have benefits beyond evaluation: because they can offer confidence to others that change is possible.

The challenge facing SD evaluators is to identify those indicators that generate the right mix of data that succinctly summarizes SD's "direction of travel" while also providing decision makers with the information they need to make informed decisions about how best to support efforts contributing towards delivering the SD agenda. An appraisal of contextual factors should help in the identification of the right suite of indicators.

METHODS—BEST AVAILABLE FOR EVALUATING SUSTAINABLE DEVELOPMENT

The UNCSD categorizes its SD indicators under four headings: social, environment, economic and institutional. There is considerable diversity across these indicators and the majority has been framed in such a way that quantitative methods are best suited to determine change. While this approach works if there are sufficient resources to collect and analyze the data, where the data cannot be collected, qualitative techniques can often offer a cost effective and complementary way in which to assess a country's performance towards achieving SD. A description of seven participatory processes that have been used in evaluating progress in SD processes and at the impact level is given below.

- Learning groups
- Peer reviews
- External auditing
- Watchdogs
- Public expenditure reviews
- Outlook studies
- Public engagement

Learning Groups

A useful way to evaluate progress towards SD can be to establish a "learning group" (of national SD "champions," key leaders, and decision-makers notably from development, environment, and finance). Such a group can work informally to, for example, examine what SD means in the country context; take stock of relevant plans and targets; identify where SD is beginning to be achieved in the country at the level of impact; postulate which initiatives led to such improvements; identify the drivers and antagonists of this; and assess their effectiveness, efficiency, sustainability, and prospects. This approach has recently been used by the International Institute for Environment and Development (IIED) with some success in relation to the issue of environmental mainstreaming (one key SD component) in Tanzania, Zambia, Vietnam, Philippines, and Malawi.

BOX 8.4: TANZANIA—ENVIRONMENTAL MAINSTREAMING LEARNING GROUP: FINDINGS

An IIED-facilitated learning group of environment and development experts met in 2006, co-hosted by the vice president's office and WWF-Tanzania. It evaluated the ways in which the national development and poverty reduction plan (MKUKUTA) had included environmental issues. The group concluded that a *'planning gap'* had been bridged, notably through:

- The *joint mandate* of the vice president's office for both poverty reduction and environment
- *Outcome-based* development planning processes (as opposed to "priority sectors"). This allowed environmental interests to show what they can contribute to *all* outcomes
- A special environmental expenditure review being included in *public expenditure reviews*—asking questions of how environmental assets and hazards are being managed—which was a critical turning point in greatly improving the government budget for environment
- An effective *donor coordination group* on environment, which worked well in government

The learning group moved on to recommend ways in which to tackle *investment, capacity, and decentralisation gaps* to ensure that environment was acted on in development:

For report, see Assey et al. (2007).

Peer Reviews of SD Strategies, Plans and Other Processes[4]

Peer review presents a powerful approach to monitoring that is increasingly being employed. It involves inviting other countries (peers) to review SD strategy progress. For example, the African Peer Review Mechanism was launched by the African Union in 2003 as a voluntary self-monitoring approach—now being undertaken by 22 countries. A good example of the application of peer review to NSDSs was undertaken in 2004–2005 by the French government. This set out to develop and test a simple, relatively quick, replicable, voluntary, nonjudgmental, and cost-effective methodology for peer review of NSDSs, using the French NSDS (Ministry of Sustainable Development, 2003) as a pilot case. The French process involved:

- A technical meeting to develop a methodology for testing
- Interviews and preparation of a background report
- A workshop involving representatives from peer countries
- Preparation of a final report and proposal for an improved methodology.

The workshop was attended by peers—two representatives (one from government, one from civil society) from each of four peer countries (Ghana, Mauritius, Belgium, and the UK). The workshop involved French participants providing answers and commentary related to a set of key questions with the peer countries sharing their own experiences. The questions were set by the peers, grouped under four strategy components: process, content, outcomes, and monitoring and indicators. The peers then agreed on 44 recommendations structured in the same way and grouped under "headline" recommendations

External Auditing[5]

A good example is Canada's external audits of departmental SD strategies (there is no national-level or federal SD strategy). These are carried out, as a statutory requirement, by the Commissioner of the Environment and Sustainable Development (CESD), located within the Office of the Auditor General (OAG). The CESD is mandated to provide parliamentarians with objective, independent analysis and recommendations on the federal government's efforts to protect the environment and foster sustainable development. The CESD submits an annual report on audit findings and associated recommendations to parliament in the autumn. Given the comprehensive nature of SD, a focal issue approach is taken. Specific commitment(s) to be audited that year are selected, and a detailed questionnaire is developed, tailored to the commitment.

The questions cover issues such as: the planning undertaken to support implementation of the commitment, the action taken on it, how monitoring and assessment has been carried out, outcomes achieved, factors that have assisted or limited progress, and whether and how progress has been reported to Parliament and/or other stakeholders.

Other topics covered through the CESD's audit work and studies can generally be grouped into three categories:

- *quality of the strategies* themselves (the documents)—form and structure, overall strategic quality, meaningfulness of commitments
- *foundations for implementation of the strategies*—management systems put in place, accountability, performance measurement, horizontal management (coordination with other departments)
- *performance measurement and reporting*—measurability of targets; links between objectives, targets, activities, and performance measures; quality and level of detail in self-reporting.

BOX 8.5: ADVANTAGES AND CHALLENGES OF THE CANADIAN CESD AUDIT APPROACH

Advantages

- broad powers of access to the information required to undertake thorough fact-finding
- subject to clear requirements and procedures to maintain independence, objectivity, and rigor
- independence also applies to selection of audit topics according to significance and risk
- mandated to enable the elected Parliament to keep government accountable for its sustainable development commitments
- audit process also engages senior levels of management within departments.

Challenges: Some challenges arise from the audit being conducted by a national audit office:

- A strict statutory approach, not adaptive and collaborative
- relies on Parliamentary interest and engagement
- demands a level of evidentiary rigor that sometimes makes it difficult to express important generalizations or intuitive connections
- must steer clear of policy critiques (i.e., it must focus on how well a policy is implemented, not on how good policy is)
- audit process can only help to the extent that departmental senior managers are committed to SD Strategies—this varies.

Further challenges for the CESD's audit work arise from the decentralized, disaggregated, department-by-department approach to SD strategy development in Canada:

- Lower profile and impact, with reduced appeal for ongoing stakeholder involvement;
- Difficult to address collective significance of departmental SDSs, (i.e., even if all were fully implemented, would federal government be clearly and forceful on the road to SD?)
- Difficult to link action on SDSs and their commitments to actual improvements in state of environment/SD?
- Difficult to engage and support innovation in public service
- Difficult to ensure integration of SDSs with other business planning

Watchdogs

The long time needed to complete major societal changes towards SD, the extent of vested interests, and the multiple institutional accountabilities, may suggest a "watchdog" approach. This can be an NGO or, as in the UK, quasi-governmental—the SD Commission aims to act as a "critical friend" of the government. In addition, several parliaments (e.g., UK, Netherlands, and Germany) maintain parliamentary committees on SD to examine the effectiveness, efficiency, and coherence of government work towards SD.

BOX 8.6: WATCHDOG TASKS OF THE UK SUSTAINABLE DEVELOPMENT COMMISSION

- Monitoring the effectiveness of the Accountability Framework (the combined scrutiny activity of all organization involved in SD assessment/monitoring)
- Monitoring SD policy-making and proofing (risk impact assessments, public service agreements, spending reviews, budget and pre-budget reports, etc.)
- Departmental scrutiny (SD action plans)
- Thematic in-depth reviews
- On-going, cross-governmental performance appraisal (indicators, Framework for SD on the Government Estate, sustainable procurement, etc.)
- State of the nation progress reports

Public Expenditure Reviews

When societies cannot make decisions easily, it is almost invariably at the budget stage when *de facto* decisions are actually made. The standard government public expenditure review (PER) process is, therefore, a key entry point for assessing SD in practice, and the process of reviewing government expenditure can also open up avenues for improving the sustainability of investments. For example, Tanzania's PER is an important part of the national planning and budgeting mechanism (Assey et al., 2007). It aims to ensure the allocation and effective utilization of financial resources from local and external sources to meet Vision 2025 and the National Strategy for Growth and Reduction of Poverty. Though the government had recognized the importance of environment as a cross-cutting issue in its previous poverty reduction strategy and had developed a program to integrate environment into the strategy, environment was not defined as a "priority sector" and received no extra investment. By making the revised national strategy focus on outcomes (rather than assuming priority sectors) and asking all sectors to show what they could offer to achieve such outcomes, the door was open for improved environmental investment. To put some hard figures behind this potential, the Ministry of Finance called for a special environment sector public expenditure review as part of the overall PER. This (1) established the levels, trends and distribution of environment expenditure by government and (2) assessed the level of environmental expenditure required to meet the national strategy.

The process involved assessing:

- The contribution of the environmental resources to national income over several years
- The pricing of environmental products in relation to replacement cost
- Environmental budgetary allocations and expenditures of central and local government, and key sectors for two financial years
- Government expenditure on capacity building for environmental management and proposing elements for capacity building
- The proportion of expenditure on environment from aid flows in relation to requirements for the implementation of multilateral/bilateral environment agreements
- Reviewing sector program/strategies and planning/budget guidelines to identify strengths, weaknesses and gaps in capturing environmental issues

Although the review was hampered by limited access and availability of data on environmental revenue and expenditure, its findings have directly informed the national strategy for growth and reduction of poverty. They have led to increased environmental allocations by over 400% within the government budget and more routine environmental indicators in the routine PER process.

Outlook Studies

In some countries, periodic reports are prepared which review the state of progress towards sustainability, rather than the process issues associated with the relevant SD plan. An early example is the sustainability outlook produced by the Netherlands Environmental Assessment Agency (from 2004 onwards). These are important sources of information for public debate on SD. The Netherlands reports cover:

- Four different "world views" (scenarios) on structuring the sustainability issue, and a survey of Dutch opinions on these world views
- Sustainability indicators
- Future trends on mobility, energy, and food supply
- Changes in key factors for sustainable development (technology, behavior, population growth, and governance)

UNEP's work in supporting developing countries to prepare "state of the environment" (SoE) reports is increasingly adopting this more futures-oriented "outlook" approach, often taking a focal theme of high political significance, in contrast to the more encyclopedic SoE approach.

Public Engagement

Interest is growing in the use of websites, often managed by NGOs, to chart the performance of authorities (and especially local authorities) towards SD. For example, COS Netherlands (a network of regional centers for international co-operation) manages the "Local Sustainability Meter" (available at www.duurzaamheidsmeter.nl). This participative instrument provides a benchmark with information covering most Dutch municipalities in 12 provinces, providing up-to-date information on policy measures related to sustainable development. The indicators were developed with citizens groups, government officials, and researchers, based on best practices around the country.

There are four questionnaires:

- sustainable development
- climate and water policies
- social, poverty, and international cooperation policies
- local sustainable economic policies and nature and planning policies.

The questionnaires are brought to the attention of about 80 municipalities by local environmental and developmental groups that participate actively in interviewing their officials, invoking debate and publicity. In areas where no local group is involved in the survey, COS Netherlands approaches the municipality directly.

The questionnaires comprise lists with yes/no answers. With numerous questions such as "does the municipality employ an energy coordinator?" "did the municipality decide about concrete cut-backs in CO_2 emissions for its own building?" and "did the council decide that sustainable procurement is the way to go?" it was possible to get a good overall picture of the accomplishments of most Dutch municipalities.

For each positive answer, the municipality can earn points. More points are given for positive replies concerning pioneer activities, and fewer points for policies that are more or less mainstream or not obligatory (such as general policy statements). The total score provides an indication of the state of affairs in the particular municipality. The website provides policymakers and NGOs with a complete overview of all answers and the contacts of informers. A quantitative and qualitative analysis of the results has been made by COS Netherlands (Box 8.4).

BOX 8.7: SOME RESULTS OF LOCAL SUSTAINABILITY METRE SURVEY, THE NETHERLANDS

The general conclusion of the latest results is that out of the 432 municipalities, only 10% were able to get sufficient results, being able to answer over 54.5% of the answers positively. The cities of Tilburg (over 91% positive results), Delft (86%), and Alkmaar (82%) showed that policies can be developed in a successful way. Also smaller villages, such as Bolsward in the Northern Province Friesland (9,500 inhabitants), were able to get good results. The extensive research, done with the cooperation of over 1,200 local officials and 600 volunteers from NGOs, showed also that it is difficult for the municipalities to maintain a long-term commitment. Water policies, extremely relevant to the Netherlands, have not yet reached the mainstream in two-thirds of the local communities, while climate change is putting increased pressure on the dangers of both flooding and drought. Climate policies, focusing on reducing emissions of carbon dioxide and reducing fossil energy use, are still weak and can only be developed with wide-scale support of the central government.

The benchmark exercise was expected to be repeated in full in 2009/2010, shortly before the next municipal elections.

Source: www.duurzaamheidsmeter.nl

Designs or Evaluation Frameworks—Best Practices for SD

Key Contexts for Evaluation

A simple overarching framework to use when undertaking SD evaluations is the three interlocking circles: economic, environmental, and social being contained in an institutional/governance box (see Figure 8.1 below). Such a framework can be used at the macro level to assess a country's progress towards meetings its SD targets as well as to carry out micro assessments on the performance of the three core areas or certain elements within them that are key to reaching SD aims. It might also be expressed in terms of the desired outcomes (officially agreed, or expressed by different stakeholders) that apply in a specific context (Box 8.8). Sometimes these will be expressed as targets or indicators.

The entry point—and/or potential demand—for evaluation is key. One option is to focus on the major SD initiatives such as national sustainable development strategies—where the need for public accountability is high and recognized, which could form a key entry point for evaluation. But care must be taken not to make the mistake of assuming that this initiative is actually significant for SD. Another option is to focus on the underlying problems that need to be addressed, making no assumption about which initiative to assess.

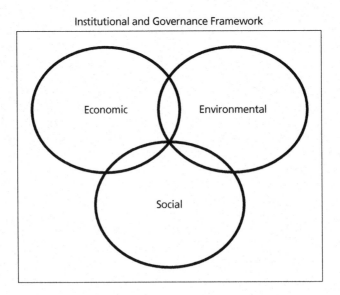

Figure 8.1 Interlocking circles of SD.

BOX 8.8: ILLUSTRATIVE 'SUSTAINABLE DEVELOPMENT' OUTCOMES

Economic Sphere

- Maximize human well-being
- Ensure efficient use of all resources, natural and otherwise, by maximizing rents
- Seek to identify and internalize environmental and social costs
- Maintain and enhance the conditions for viable enterprise

Social Sphere

- Ensure a fair distribution of the costs and benefits of development for all those alive today
- Respect and reinforce the fundamental rights of human beings, including civil and political liberties, cultural autonomy, and social and economic freedoms
- Seek to sustain improvements over time. Ensure that depletion of natural resources will not deprive future generations through replacement with other forms of capital
- Protect minority rights

Environmental Sphere

- Promote responsible stewardship of natural resources and the environment
- Minimize waste and environmental damage along the whole of the supply chain
- Exercise prudence where impacts are unknown or uncertain
- Operate within ecological limits and protect critical natural capital

Institutional/Governance Sphere

- Support representative democracy, including participatory decision-making
- Encourage free enterprise within a system of clear and fair rules
- Avoid excessive concentration of power through appropriate checks and balances
- Ensure transparency through providing all stakeholders with access to relevant and accurate information
- Ensure accountability for decisions and actions, which are based on comprehensive and reliable analysis
- Encourage cooperation in order to build trust and shared goals and values
- Adhere to the principle of subsidiarity, which recognizes that decisions should be decentralized and taken as close as possible to and with the people and communities most directly affected

Focus on Sustainable Development Strategies— A Key Context[6]

SD is both a journey and a comprehensive agenda involving many actors, and sustainable development strategies (SDS) have most often been the primary vehicle for pulling together associated plans, targets and roles. In the run up to the World Summit for Sustainable Development (WSSD) in 2002, many countries developed or revised national sustainable development strategies (NSDS), and additional strategies have been developed since then. For many developing countries since 2002, the focus shifted to preparing poverty reduction strategies (PRS), with donor support and/or to adding environmental dimensions to five-year plans or national development plans (NDPs). With PRSs and NDPs now undergoing revision and environmental and intergenerational dimensions increasingly being addressed, they are seen as providing a platform for evolution to effective NSDSs.

NSDSs have multiple objectives: social, economic, and environmental conditions will change over time, and so will strategy activities. This presents a considerable challenge for monitoring and evaluation, but one that must be met, since the premise of a strategic approach is to learn and adapt. Strategy monitoring therefore contributes to five basic strategic purposes:

1. Systematically *tracking changes* that support or hinder sustainable development
2. Supporting common *learning*
3. Providing strategy steering and *adaptation*
4. Enabling *accountability* of strategy stakeholders
5. Building *confidence* that effective change is possible

To serve these purposes, monitoring is required in relation to key strategy elements: (1) the strategy process, (2) strategy outputs, (3) SD outcomes, and (4) SD impacts. Some processes for doing this have been introduced; and typical requirements are laid out in Appendix A.

Focus on the Underlying Causes of Unsustainable Development

The reasons that we do not often see SD in practice are surprisingly common (Bass, 2007):

- Economic and finance authorities have tended to be more politically and financially powerful than environmental and social authorities.

- This is strongly linked to dominant economic growth models being considered inviolable, rather than people's rights and welfare, or environmental processes and limits.
- Environmental benefits and costs are externalized.
- Poor people are marginalized, and inequities entrenched.
- Governance regimes are not designed to internalize environmental factors, to iron out social inequities, or to develop better economic models.
- Therefore, unsustainable behavior has not been substantially challenged.
- Elites often like to keep things this way, with sustainability commitments and plans vague at best, with little attention to accountability and consequently weak investment in collecting SD-relevant data.

A strong case could be made for evaluating changes in these *disabling* conditions. Various organizing tools are available to aid discussion and debate, to focus attention on expected results, and to record conclusions. For example:

1. *Logical Framework Analysis:* The logical framework or logframe is a sixteen-box matrix that helps to clarify the goal, purpose, outputs, and activities of a project, program, or policy. There is a causal logic that describes the results chain and this runs in both directions (i.e., up and down the framework). The four columns in the framework describe a narrative description of the results chain, indicators of achievement, how to verify results, and the assumptions that underpin the logic. The logframe is widely used in international development as a tool to engage different stakeholders in program planning as well as being utilized to evaluate a program's approach, effectiveness, and success in reaching its objectives (World Bank, 2004).
2. *Theory Based Evaluation:* White (2009) outlines six key principles of a theory-based impact evaluation which are:
    a. Map out the causal chain (program theory)
    b. Understand context
    c. Anticipate heterogeneity
    d. Rigorous evaluation of impact using a credible counterfactual
    e. Rigorous factual analysis
    f. Use mixed methods

   While there are similarities between logframes and theory-based evaluation (TBE) as they both utilize causal logic, the main difference is that TBE describes the results chain and the assumptions that underpin the logic in greater detail and can accommodate more than one causal factor.

What both the logframe and TBE frameworks do is to distinguish between what program can be held accountable for delivering and to what outcomes they should contribute. Such a distinction can help evaluators to focus more on how effectively programs generate their outputs and manage their key assumptions rather than trying to estimate to what extent they might have contributed to outcomes or impacts. Of course, the effectiveness of an analysis of this kind depends upon, among other things, the ability of programs to collect the right data that documents a range of different processes.[7]

3. *Visual ranking tools*—for example:
   - *Traffic lights system* (as used in the UK to assess progress on major government targets, and the likelihood of successful delivery of major projects and programs; and in Sweden for systematic review)[8]
   - *Placement on a "change spectrum"*—to map state of play on particular issues, or the spread of results, for example, from mere awareness, through to improving specified enabling conditions, to changed behavior, and ultimately to impact on the pillars

It is worth noting that while on the one hand the development of SD indicators has been prolific to a degree that may appear excessive, on the other, the number of frameworks to evaluate SD has been low, and many of them are still in their experimental stages.

USE—DESIGNING SD EVALUATIONS SO THAT THEY ARE USEFUL

Useful for whom? This is an obvious but critical question for evaluators to ask before embarking upon an evaluation. An evaluation may produce important insights, but if it fails to resonate with end users or address the key issues with which they are preoccupied, it is unlikely to be an effective driver of change. Moreover, if evaluations do not accurately identify the incentives that will motivate professionals to change their behavior, working practices, and policies after an evaluation, they, too, are less likely to be useful.

An evaluation is likely to be considered useful if it makes a significant contribution to improving the profile of the initiative (and hence attention to its aims by stakeholders), improving the way in which the initiative is implemented (e.g., identifying those tools, tactics or methods that lead to higher participation rates), and confirming or rethinking of its fundamental premise (in this case, the desirability and practicability of approaches to SD).

SD is a complex process, and evaluations will be of use to decision makers where they provide an analysis of the extent to which the critical enabling conditions (outcomes) are being created as well as the state of disabling conditions and how this mix affects the manifestation of impacts in the three SD pillars.

One indicator of a useful evaluation is one that promotes internal learning from experience, a corollary of which is improved programmatic performance. If the evaluation is able to establish a process or processes that provide space and time for critical reflection, then staff may be more willing to consider and adopt new working practices. Such a process may be complicated and costly to establish in all cases especially where programs are spatially diverse, but for challenging programmatic areas such as SD where new solutions are required, this is a method that is worth exploring.

Evaluations should strive to hold program staff to account for the resources for which they are responsible. This is not always the case, and SD programs are no exception. Accountability arguments are well rehearsed but there is a need for officials to be held accountable for how they spend their budgets. Evaluations should try to review SD rigorously, thereby limiting it from being used as a fig leaf behind which inefficiencies can be hidden.

APPENDIX A: MONITORING REQUIREMENTS FOR SD STRATEGIES—A FRAMEWORK FOR GENERATING BETTER INFORMATION THAT CAN HELP IN EVALUATION

Monitoring is needed in relation to key strategy elements: (1) the strategy process, (2) products, (3) outcomes, (4) impacts, and (5) dissemination and use of monitoring information. However, monitoring everything is impossible. It is impossible in *theory* because we do not know enough about natural, social and economic systems to know all the aspects we could record—and new techniques and approaches are being developed all the time. It is impossible in *practice* because there will never be enough resources—time, money, equipment, expertise—to record everything. Therefore, monitoring is necessarily selective. Issues to consider are elaborated below, based on literature and IIED's observations.

(a) Monitoring SD Strategy Process (Inputs Applied, Stages Reached, Principles Adopted)

Monitoring purpose: A strategy is a complex management process that, at the same time, seeks to build on existing decision-making machinery. Monitoring is essential to keep the process on track, to ensure all stakeholders know what stage the process has reached so they can engage more effectively. Process quality also matters: stakeholders have usually committed to a strategy being carried out through certain principles.[9] It is also helpful if these principles (e.g., participation and building on existing initiatives) are monitored. Such monitoring offers transparency of information, mutual accountability and confidence building.

Issues to monitor include:

- *inputs applied*—financial, physical, and human resources against a timetable
- *stakeholder* involvement/interaction—numbers and types engaged at key stages
- *government machinery links*—strategy role in key formal plans and budgets, and vice versa
- *international, business and civil society links*—engagement of strategy process in key events or initiatives, and vice versa
- *principles applied*—how well the agreed strategy principles have been applied in practice

Key monitoring criteria include: *economy* (in procurement and expenditure), *equity* (in stakeholder engagement) and *efficiency* (in building on other initiatives).

How to monitor: A mix of internal program management accounting and reporting, with government administrative monitoring. Stakeholder opinion surveys will help with monitoring strategy process quality (principles). Frequency may range from monthly (finances) to quarterly (government links) to annual (principles)

(b) Monitoring SD Strategy Outputs (outputs generated to date and their contents)

Monitoring purpose: The strategy will produce a rich range of data, opinions, ideas, options for decision-makers, actual decisions and some institutional innovations such as sustainable development policy frameworks and information systems. Monitoring is necessary in part to keep track of them, but more especially to be able to identify how key social, environmental and economic issues have been covered, and how these relate to targets and commitments.

Issues to monitor include:

- *type of product:* database, survey, agreed policy, instrument, delivery system or other capacity
- *how it links to international commitments:* notably MDGs and Agenda 21/CSD
- *how it links to other national initiatives:* existing or new, government- or NGO-led

Key monitoring criteria include: degree of coverage of particular issues—for example, mention, analysis, or defined response to sanitation issues; direct or indirect link to key international or national targets; extent of budget/personnel applied to any new system/capacity; and how far strategy principles are applied.

How to monitor: Primarily through internal program management monitoring; but also government administrative monitoring, such as budget and spending round reviews.

(c) Monitoring SD Strategy Outcomes (use of products and changes in behavior)

Monitoring purpose: The strategy's direct outputs should start to influence the diverse plans, budgets and operations of wider government actors, as well as businesses and individuals.[10] Consequently, monitoring is needed to assess the use made by stakeholders of strategy outputs and their satisfaction with them; and, further, to identify whether behavioral changes are beginning to take place in areas recommended by the strategy (although attribution is not possible until the impact assessment stage). This may often be the most critical monitoring task, as outcomes are under the direct control of strategy actors, and therefore outcome information offers a basis for steering the strategy.

Issues to monitor include:

- *users of strategy products:* who has used strategy documents, databases and other resources—their numbers and stakeholder type; and what they say about the utility and quality of these resources
- *strategy citation:* direct citation of strategy by new analyses, innovations, policies and instruments (governmental or otherwise)
- *changed behavior in planning, budgeting and investment:* major qualitative and quantitative change in key areas, lined up against strategy recommendations.

Key monitoring criteria include:

- strategy product user numbers, types, and satisfaction
- percent of new policies, laws and initiatives citing the strategy
- percent of budgets directed at strategy recommendations (government, business and household levels)

How to monitor: Website statistics from strategy site, on-line user questionnaires, government departmental annual reporting, parliamentary reporting, industry and commerce annual reporting household surveys (routine as well as multi-topic special strategy surveys and public inquiries—the latter are also applicable at community level), independent research systems, and media monitoring. The use of many systems is considerably eased when monitoring calendars are consistent or coordinated. Whilst this is difficult in the short run, joint projects (e.g., poverty–environment mapping) can be used to link key monitoring agencies together. Frequency is likely to be annual—with one-off studies as and when required.

(d) Monitoring SD Strategy Impacts (changes to human and ecosystem well-being)

Monitoring purpose: The strategy's direct impacts are difficult to assess. Firstly, they may not be separable from the impacts of many outcomes (see section C above) that the strategy will have inspired—clearly it is not right to attribute all SD impacts to the strategy alone, or to other initiatives alone. Secondly, they may not be discernible in short time frames. This problem of attributing causation worries many people who have attempted strategy monitoring. The strategy's overall influence is best assessed when monitoring outcomes (see (c)). Here, the added value of monitoring is to assess wider changes to key aspects of human and ecosystem well-being, in order to inform *both* the strategy *and* all the various initiatives to which it is linked. Thus, it is helpful if the strategy includes putative *impact pathways* linking needs with policies or other products, with outcomes, and with likely impacts.

Monitoring information over subsequent years will then offer some fundamental insights into the *'theory of change'* that is built in to the strategy; it may help to test its *assumptions*; it will offer *lessons* on strategy effectiveness in encouraging action in general areas; it may suggest *course correction* in specific areas (national, local or development assistance); and it is certainly central to any formal *revision* of the strategy. Thus, it is helpful if impact monitoring relates to specific, meaningful indicators, triggers or targets rather than to a very comprehensive survey of the wider environment. Indeed, such monitoring should become a central function of a permanent SD information system.

Issues to monitor include:

- *key 'headline indicators':* perhaps a dozen dimensions of sustainable development which matter most to a variety of stakeholders (rather than a plethora which may have some academic purpose but little policy use). Also, it is important that indicators stay stable over time to facilitate monitoring;
- *key triggers:* whether environmental or social thresholds are being breached, or acceptable risk levels exceeded, which would signal the need for rapid responses;
- *progress towards major targets:* easier if the strategy is defined in terms of specific targets, e.g., a national articulation/reinterpretation of the MDGs.

Key monitoring criteria include: sustainability (e.g., quantitative or 'barometric' directions for each headline indicator, trigger or target); effectiveness (has the strategy been associated with any significant improvement in these indicators? and equity (distributional impacts, notably on poor/ disadvantaged groups and on other countries).

How to monitor: By its nature, monitoring strategy impacts is neither a one-off task nor one that can be accomplished with the kinds of limited budgets attached to strategy exercises. Indeed, it will often be considered a major area for capacity development. Ultimately a dedicated SD information system is required which will produce a continually changing picture of the nation's indicators, triggers and targets in order to inform a continuously-improving NSDS or its equivalent. In the meantime, there will usually be a construction/integration task to bring the capabilities together.

Ingredients will include:

- wiring together environmental assessment, demographic and economic information systems, and poverty monitoring with administrative reporting (e.g., health and agriculture departments);
- reconciling differing data periods, time lags and degrees of aggregation;
- agreeing frameworks (Millennium Ecosystem Assessment, livelihood capitals, Agenda 21 and MDGs all have advantages)
- developing specific official capabilities in key trade-off areas, notably green accounting (to trace state of environmental assets against other assets) and poverty mapping (to link poverty with spatial issues such as environmental deprivations);
- independent watchdogs to attest to the quality of the above, to fill gaps, and to follow specific issues;
- public opinion and behavior surveys (web-based);
- multi-stakeholder learning groups around specific issues;
- Involving communities and indigenous people – eg the report on the review of the *Monitoring Progress Towards a Sustainable New Zealand* (2003), indicates a need to better assess Maori interests in relation to indicator reporting (eg monitoring the government's Treaty obligations towards Maori people and their culture).

Frequency is likely to be every 3–5 years, as part of a process of formal strategy review, although some of the input data may be available on an annual basis.

(e) Feedback: Reporting and Disseminating Monitoring Results

Reporting and dissemination purpose: Given the fact that an NSDS is predicated upon strengthening the culture of dialogue, learning, and continuous improvement, it is axiomatic that monitoring results need to reach the multiple stakeholders and levels involved. Feeding back information from monitoring the four strategy elements above, (a)–(d), to key stakeholder groups enables them to 'track progress, distil and capture lessons, [steer processes], and signal when a change of direction is necessary (OECD DAC 2001). The periodicity of formal NSDS reviews will influence the approach taken.[11]

One of the key dilemmas will be linking process, input, output and outcome indicators. It is not always possible, for example, to relate input cost data to output figures, partly as they may be related to several periods or activities. Ideally, monitoring would be able show the value of output-based (if not outcome-based) planning and costing.

Target groups for reporting and dissemination include: parliament, key civil society (issue-based) groups, standing government committees, existing fora for local and national debate, international institutions and agreements, and donors.

Reporting and dissemination media include: websites and annual conferences/publications—focused on progress, learning and dynamic contexts. Annual parliamentary debates, review meetings in the country's treasury, and donor conferences have ensured results are linked to key decisions. A diversity of media both engages multiple stakeholders and minimise the possibility of political blockages.

NOTES

1. From Bass (2007).
2. See www.iisd.org/measure
3. A UN process also produced similar elements characterizing NSDSs (UNDESA (2001)
4. Much of this section draws from: Dalal-Clayton and Bass (2006).
5. Much of this section is drawn from: Dalal-Clayton and Bass (2006).
6. Much of this section from: Dalal-Clayton and Bass (2006).
7. IIED is currently sketching out its different "theories of change" across its five programs of work as part of its "results-based management" program.
8. Green: significant change, in direction of meeting the objective; Amber: no significant change; Red: significant change, in direction away from meeting the objective; White: insufficient/incomparable data.
9. People-centered, participation, consensus, comprehensive, integrated, targeted, based on reliable evidence, incorporating learning, country-led, high-level commitment, building on existing processes and capacity, linking local to national (OECD, 2001)
10. In some countries, there will be a fine line between strategy outputs and outcomes, as the strategy mandate may include direct intervention in specified policy arenas.
11. There is considerable variation in the periodicity of reviews. In the UK, Germany, Sweden, and Belgium, formal review terms are clearly set (5, 2, 4 and 4 years, respectively). PRSs are generally supposed to be reviewed every five years. For some strategies, an annual progress report is prepared (e.g., UK, for the 1999 strategy, and the annual PRS report is a key monitoring tool). Sometimes, a strategy has been revised without any review of the previous one, for example, Belgium's 2003 strategy (Niestroy, 2005). Other countries have no official review terms (e.g., Finland, Ireland), but produce various progress reports (e.g., for WSSD).

REFERENCES

Assey, P., Bass, S., Cheche, B., Howlett, D., Jambiya, G., Kikula. I., Likwelile, S., Manyama, A., Mugurusi, E., Muheto, R., & Rutasitara, L. (2007). *Environment at the heart of Tanzania's development: Lessons from Tanzania's national strategy for growth and reduction of poverty.* London, UK: IIED.

Bartelmus, P. (2003). Dematerialization and capital maintenance: Two sides of the sustainability coin. *Ecological Economics, 46,* 61–81.

Bartelmus, P. (2008). *Indicators of sustainable development.* Retrieved from http://www.eoearth.org/article/Indicators_of_sustainable_development

Bass, S. (2007). *A new era in sustainable development.* London, UK: IIED.

Bell, S., & Morse, S. (2003). *Measuring sustainability: Learning from doing.* London, UK: Earthscan.

Bossel, H. (1999). *Indicators for sustainable development: Theory, method, applications.* Winnipeg, ON: International Institute for Sustainable Development.

Dalal-Clayton, B., & Bass, S. (2002) *Sustainable development strategies: A resource book.* London, UK: OECD, UNDP and Earthscan

Dalal-Clayton, B., & Bass, S. (2006). *A review of monitoring mechanism for national sustainable development strategies.* London, UK: IIED, Report prepared for the OECD. Retrieved from http://www.nssd.net/otherdocuments/OECD_Review_final.pdf

IUCN (1980). *World Conservation Strategy.* Gland, Switzerland.

Kates, R., Parris, T., & Leiserowitz, A. (2005). What is sustainable development? Goals, indicators, values and practice. *Environment: Science and Policy for Sustainable Development, 47*(3), 8–21.

Ministry of Sustainable Development. (2003). *Stratégie nationale de développement durable.* Paris, France: Author.

Newman, P. (1998). *Can sustainability be measured?* Retrieved from http://www.renewableway.org.uk/sustain/concepts/measures.html

Niestroy, I. (2005). Sustaining Sustainability—A benchmark study on national strategies towards sustainable development and the impact of councils in nine EU member states. *EEAC series, Background study No.2* (p. 308). Lemma, Utrecht.

OECD-DAC. (2001). *Strategies for sustainable development: the DAC Guidelines.* Paris, France: Organisation for Economic Co-operation and Development.

Parris, T. M., & Kates, R. W. (2003). Characterizing and measuring sustainable development. *Annual Review of Environment and Resources, 28,* 559–586

Pintér, L., Hardi, P., & Bartelmus, P. (2005). *Sustainable development indicators: Proposals for a way forward.* Winnipeg, ON: International Institute for Sustainable Development.

Porritt, J. (2001). The only game in town. *green futures magazine.* London, UK. Retrieved from http://www.forumforthefuture.org/greenfutures/articles/only-game-town on

Reid, D. (1995). *Sustainable development: An introductory guide.* London, UK: Earthscan Publications.

United Nations. (2007). *Indicators of sustainable development: Guidelines and methodologies* (3rd ed.). New York, NY: Author.

United Nations (1992) *Earth Summit Agenda 21.* United Nations, USA

White, H. (2009). *Theory based impact evaluation: Principles and practice.* New Delhi, India: 3ie.

World Bank. (2004). *Monitoring and evaluation: Some tools, methods and approaches.* Washington, DC: Author.

World Commission on Environment and Development (1987). *Our Common Future.* Oxford University Press, UK.

CHAPTER 9

EVALUATING INNOVATION

Steve Rochlin and Sasha Radovich

INTRODUCTION

Innovation has long been understood as a driving force for economic, political, and social development. While innovation has been a staple of many successful approaches to inclusive economic growth, it has only recently begun to receive special attention as a strategy to improve the lives of poor people. This approach, which is labeled "innovation for development," is an effort to create a mix of incentives, investments, analytics, and tools to catalyze the creation of innovative solutions to major development challenges that transform the lives of poor people and improve the sustainability of ecosystems. Prominent examples include micro-finance, creative application of mobile telephony in rural villages, community cooperative approaches to basic service delivery such as water and sanitation (e.g., "play pumps"), breakthrough vaccines, and numerous others. Yet innovation for development (I4D) remains poorly understood. Few agree on a common definition. Anecdotal evidence suggests "innovation" is used loosely to dress existing development approaches in more appealing clothes. In other instances, investments are made in initiatives that possess high ambitions but little understanding of the complex, challenging, and risky methods necessary to innovate.

Emerging Practices in International Development Evaluation, pages 199–223
Copyright © 2013 by Information Age Publishing
All rights of reproduction in any form reserved.

This chapter provides background on Innovation for Development. It suggests useful definitions and summarizes lessons learned on the requirements for grant-makers pursuing Innovation for Development. We have also included an evaluation matrix for consideration as a framework toward evaluating Innovations for Development based on our research. The chapter has two objectives: (1) to identify findings and lessons from a wide range of evaluations of innovation for development in the field of philanthropy and development, and (2) based on these lessons to offer an evaluation framework to use in measuring results related to innovation and in structuring learning from grants that have innovation as a major objective. The findings in the chapter should be useful for grant-makers, grantees, and other philanthropic and development leaders in planning monitoring and evaluation and reporting on innovation.

INNOVATION AND DEVELOPMENT

Innovation is crucial for the development of every country. Leading economists agree that innovation is the key component to long-term growth and wealth, and a key component to putting countries on a path toward recovery and a more sustainable—and smarter—growth coming out of the current global recession. A recent UNESCO report declares, "Innovation offers the *only* sustainable route out of poverty for developing economies"[1] (emphasis added).

What Is Innovation and Innovation for Development?

A review of leaders in the field of innovation studies and Innovation for Development—such as Acumen Fund, ASHOKA, Doblin, the Economist Intelligence Unit, Harvard, MIT, Monitor, OECD, and numerous others reveal a diverse set of definitions for innovation. Some in the development field use the *Economist* definition of innovation: "new products, business processes or organic changes that create wealth or social welfare," or "the fresh thinking that creates value." Monitor's definition is based on innovation management and is "about creating and capturing new value in news ways—through new products, services, new processes, or business models, new technologies or applications." Many development organizations think about innovation in an entrepreneurial sense and refer explicitly to the value innovation provides for the poor or disenfranchised communities.[2] Both Acumen Fund and ASHOKA characterize innovative solutions as having the ability to tackle major social issues and offer new ideas for wide-scale change.

The key is that innovation for development—"*the process of making changes to something established by introducing something new*"[3] whether it is an idea, method, or device—is leveraged or harnessed to produce change that benefits the poor. Economists and political scientists often add the element of *scaled dissemination*, or, as it is termed, "diffusion," to the definition. A shorthand way to capture the idea is to suggest that an innovation is an invention that is applied and adopted at scale.[4]

What Constitutes an Innovation?

The OECD Oslo Manual for Measuring Innovation defines four types of innovation, as seen in Table 9.1. These four types of innovation can also be applied to Innovations for Development. However, the differential factor is that each type of innovation is applied to benefit poor and vulnerable populations.

Innovations for development create economic, political, social, or environmental transformations that seek to improve the health and well-being

TABLE 9.1

Type of Innovation	Description/Example
Product	This involves a good or service that is new or significantly improved. This includes significant improvements in technical specifications, components and materials, incorporated software, user friendliness or other functional characteristics. An example of a product innovation would be a new vaccine, or more specifically Proctor & Gamble's PUR water purification sachet targeted at extremely low-income populations.
Process	Involves a new or significantly improved production or delivery method. This includes significant changes in techniques, equipment and/or software. For example, crowdsourcing, innovation for development competitions such as those run by ASHOKA, and Positive Deviancy methods are process innovations.
Market	Involves a new marketing method involving significant changes in product design or packaging, product placement, product promotion or pricing. In education, this can for example be a new way of pricing the education service or a new admission strategy. A recent example includes effective new marketing strategies to encourage men to obtain circumcisions as a defense against HIV-AIDS.
Organizational	Involves introducing a new organizational method in the firm's business practices, workplace organization or external relations. Examples include new multi-sector collaborative arrangements such as the Global Alliance for Vaccines and Immunizations, the Amazon Fund, the Forest Stewardship Council, and the StopTB Partnership.

of poor people and ecosystems.[5] Innovations for development also seek to deliver inclusive economic growth outcomes more efficiently, with high levels of access, greater scale, with transformative effect, and in an enduring and sustainable manner.[6]

Experts interviewed agree that for innovations for development to achieve transformational change, a combination of the types of the four innovations must be present. For example, consider "micro-finance"[7] which can be described as a "product innovation." Micro-finance succeeds as an innovation only if it is coupled with process and market innovations that create new policies, distribution channels, and awareness-building mechanisms for micro-finance. Innovations also differentiate according to their scope defined in Table 9.2.

It is often, but not always, the case that large-scale impact comes from "breakthrough innovations." However, it is possible for incremental, additive, or complementary innovations to generate profound, lasting, and large-scale impacts that benefit poor and vulnerable populations. Figure 9.1 demonstrates the transformative impact of some different categories and types of innovation on the impact for development.

TABLE 9.2

Category[a]	Definition
Incremental Innovation	Doing more of the same things one has been doing with somewhat better results. For example, one sees incremental innovations in the microfinance arena, which adds creative modifications to credit scoring, lending mechanisms, business and demographic focus areas.
Additive Innovation	More fully exploiting already existing resources, such as product lines extensions. Kiva.org is an example of an "additive innovation" to the microfinance field. The online source provides new means to provide lending capital.
Complementary Innovation	Offers something new and changes the structure of the business/sector/development process/market, etc. Mobile banking is an example of a complimentary innovation that is changing how banking is handled in low-income communities (and potentially high-income as well).
Breakthrough Innovation	Changes the fundamentals of the way the business, sector, process or market has traditionally functioned and creates a new industry, product, process, market and new avenues for extensive usability and/or accessibility. A breakthrough innovation would include a vaccine for HIV-AIDS, or a scalable electric car.

[a] Peter F. Drucker (1993). *Managing for results.* New York: Harper Collins, pp. 204, 205.

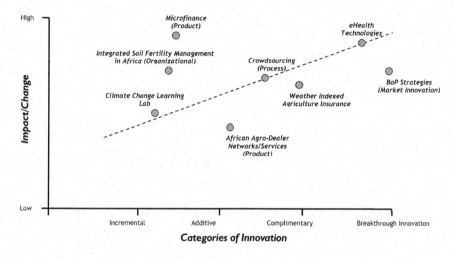

Figure 9.1 Innovation type and transformational change.

CHARACTERISTICS OF INNOVATIVE ORGANIZATIONS

The traditional approach to innovation was viewed as a pipeline, from the minds of brilliant scientists or inventors, to those building the innovation, distributing it, promoting it, and finally those using it. This model still dominates the imagination. It requires healthy spending on research and development and heroically brilliant individuals to succeed. However, its reliability and effectiveness is doubted. Research and development (R&D) spending is often a necessary, but not sufficient, factor in building an innovative organization. A Booz Allen (Jaruzelski, Dehoff, & Bordia, 2005) report found no significant relationship between R&D spending and business success. Sustained innovation success has more to do with orchestrating and coordinating the process, internally and externally, than investing dollars in research.

A wealth of recent studies and surveys—such as IBM's Global Innovation Outlook (2006); Boston Consulting Group's Most Innovative Companies survey (Borden et al., 2006); McKinsey reports (2006); as well as management articles from Davila (2005); Moss Kanter (1996); and others—identify key characteristics of innovative organizations. Common findings include:

- **Senior leadership sets the tone for innovation.** Senior leaders prioritize innovation and support the creation of an organizational culture that rewards innovation. In addition, senior leaders often create an organizational structure that is flat in design and nonhierarchical in attitude. They encourage internal innovation champions and change agents who can exert leadership themselves, no matter what their job title is. Senior leaders embrace "heretics" who challenge the status quo and conventional wisdom.

- **Innovative organizations build management and operational processes geared to generate innovation.** Innovative organizations design programs and projects to have both innovation and development visions. They establish an innovation vision tied to clear strategy and exploit the knowledge and intelligence of employees across the organization, as well as from the so-called "extended enterprise" that for a foundation would include grantees, trustees, advisors, other foundations, academic institutions, beneficiaries, and other partners. Everyone in the organization is encouraged to play a part in the idea-generating process. This requires not only clear leadership, but equally importantly, effective systems of coordination between the various units and departments of the organization. The *interrelation* of product, process, market, and organizational innovation is critical. Studies find it is also helpful to create "playful" organizational cultures that encourage creativity.

- **Innovative organizations develop a learning organization.** Development of the learning organisation is a critical success factor in embracing change and thereby fostering innovation.

    > It is not simply learning processes that create value in the business world. It is learning through collaboration—that is, organisational learning. Knowledge and innovation are the result—the by-products—of ongoing collaborative processes that create the conditions for creativity and synergy. This is the vision of the learning organisation. (Laszlo, 2001)

    Learning organizations mix "soft" processes with "hard." Soft processes might include efforts to encourage questioning, and promoting extensive multidisciplinary interaction and networking. Hard processes include a disciplined commitment to evaluation and continuous improvement, mechanisms for knowledge management (for example, knowledge databases), and incentives to encourage employees to share knowledge.

- **Innovative organizations focus relentlessly on "the customer" or end-user beneficiaries.** Studies find that efforts to produce innovations are more successful when they involve customers (or in the context of innovation for development—end-user beneficiaries and other stakeholders) deeply in the processes of brainstorming, prototyping, design, testing, and supporting use. Technology platforms such as the internet and other ICT are key to enabling the engagement of end-users and other stakeholders. The Rockefeller Foundation is among a small handful of grant-makers that have begun to use ICT to help produce Innovations for Development (ASHOKA and Kellogg are others).

- **Innovative organizations understand diffusion, or "impact" pathways necessary to ensure innovations are adopted.** Innovations for Development uniquely rely on the alignment of public policies, educational systems, local networks, and "social-entrepreneurism" to succeed (OECD, 2005). *In short, Innovation for Development typically requires changes in governance systems and accountability mechanisms.*
- **Innovative organizations collaborate with a variety of networks.** Existing studies from Harvard, McKinsey, Accenture, Monitor, and numerous others find that innovation more often succeeds through complex and nonhierarchical—yet still systematic—interactions among networks. Innovation processes based on the "collaboration of networks and institutions that support the creation and diffusion of knowledge while providing a tool for linking the supply of innovation to the market" are viewed as more likely to succeed (Smith, 2000).
- **Innovative organizations embrace failure.** Given the number of variables required to produce a successful innovation, it is not surprising that *most attempts to innovate fail.* Innovative organizations view failure as part of the learning process. They create safe environments that encourage staff to be brave in identifying failures, discussing them, and extracting evidenced-based lessons that will help future attempts to innovate.

Key Challenges

Some key challenges facing innovation for development:

1. Often, innovations for development focus on producing a specific output (for example, a new vaccine, a new financing product, or a new training methodology among numerous others). What too often goes overlooked (or inadequately addressed) is the complementary need to focus on the infrastructure, labor skills, and policy that enable the ability to draw on global knowledge, create knowledge domestically, and disseminate knowledge (Dahlman, 2008).
2. Innovation is risky. Failure is a part of the effort to innovate. Some grant-makers are unwilling to make these riskier investments. Others lack the patience to overcome initial failure (Perrin, 2000).
3. Gender analysis and gender gaps exist, and neglecting women ignores the evidence that women contribute greatly to innovation and solutions (UNESCO, 2008).

4. As noted earlier, innovations benefit from extensive engagement with a variety of networks including end-user beneficiaries, stakeholders representing beneficiary interests, individuals with relevant expertise and capabilities, individuals with the ability to influence adoption of innovations, organizations vital to distribution and awareness raising, policymakers, and entities that will produce or deliver the innovation among others. In developing countries, such engagement is hindered by the dearth of effective mechanisms and governance systems to coordinate stakeholders at the local, regional, national and international levels (OECD, 2005).

5. To paraphrase Schumpeter, innovation can be a process of "creative destruction." This means that a handful of service providers, those in control of germane status quo resources or programs, and those competing to build their own version of a "better mouse trap," may lose status, resources, influence, control, or jobs as an innovation comes on line. Generally speaking, the benefits of the innovation will far outweigh these costs and typically grow the proverbial pie of opportunity. However, the process of innovation must manage a delicate process that seeks the cooperation of those who will also compete against the innovation.

6. Innovations can happen overnight or over decades. While private sector companies strive to reduce the "cycle time" of innovations, typically "breakthrough" innovations can take years to produce. Disseminating (or "diffusing") and innovation can be a lengthy process as well. This requires grant-makers to work within longer-term timelines to deliver measurable impacts from innovation (Perrin, 2000).

7. Evaluating and measuring innovation needs to be a light exercise and needs to be cognizant of the relationship between the grantor and grantee. There should be an understanding of learning, and evaluation should be as useful and valuable to the grantee.[8]

8. Highly innovative institutions often create organizational cultures that are geared to generate innovations. These organizations often balance constructive competition with strong incentives for collaboration, sharing, and learning. They typically value and prioritize stakeholder engagement. They find creative ways to "reward" failure as long as it leads to constructive learning. They prioritize learning and development and allocate extensive resources to innovative process. Finally, these organizational cultures often try to create relatively flat hierarchies. Such characteristics can go against the grain of traditional organizational structures and cultures.

IMPLICATIONS FOR EVALUATING INNOVATION FOR DEVELOPMENT GRANT MAKING

Evaluating innovation for development projects need not take on special complexity or pose unique challenges. At their core, such initiatives can—and often are—evaluated using the same methods and techniques as any other development initiative, however it's important to consider the following when doing 14D evaluations:

1. Evaluation should help determine whether and an investment to generate an innovation was useful, and whether the type of innovation (for example, product vs. process or incremental vs. breakthrough) was appropriate.

    Consider the experience of two sectors that rely on new breakthrough innovation—healthcare and space exploration. Both sectors suffer from urgent need for cost control. Extensive research suggests that a bias toward new, technologically complex, breakthrough innovations crowds out highly cost-effective existing solutions. Grant makers should take care to ensure they do not adopt a similar bias across their programs.

2. Evaluation should ensure that the design of the prospective innovation for development is rigorous enough to avoid "spin."

    The call for innovation can take on the quality of the latest fad. With enough creativity, many traditional programs can be recast as "innovative." In such instances, a program may yield development benefits, but not at the transformational scale and scope of true innovations. Or if a traditional program—cast as innovation—fails to deliver, a grant maker may apply an evaluative criterion that is more forgiving then it should be. Finally, clearer definitions of innovation for development will help build staff understanding and related ability to invest in innovations.

3. Evaluation should help grant makers distinguish the implications for supporting certain types of innovation at certain stages of investment.

    Typically, breakthrough product innovations require more time and money and hold the most potential for transformational impact. However, numerous exceptions to this rule exist. Each type of innovation—be it product or process, incremental or breakthrough—holds the potential to generate substantial development impacts. Grant makers may find it useful to hold a diversified portfolio of different types of innovations. Similarly, innovations can take time to develop. Like venture funds, grant makers can find opportunities to support development innovators at the start-up, mezzanine, or take-off stages of a particular development solution. Evaluation should be calibrated accordingly. To the extent an evaluation is used to judge success, the evaluation method should be calibrated to allow for the variation and nuance an innovative initiative's life-cycle. In addition, evaluation should help grant makers better understand what kind of support will best enable what type of innovative initiative.

4. Evaluation should help grant makers assess the method that a grantee applies to deliver innovation (paying special attention to beneficiary engagement).

Grant makers should invest in those that possess a strong understanding and related processes for producing innovations for development. An essential criterion is a process to effectively engage end-user beneficiaries in the innovation design process.

5. Evaluation should help grant makers assess the process used to diffuse the innovation.

To be successful an innovation must become widely adopted. The development economist William Easterly has recently blogged that a technological advance will fail to advance economic development when countries lack adequate infrastructure to adopt it. The $500 million/year agricultural development innovator, the Consultative Group on International Agricultural Research (CGIAR), refers to this as being able to understand the "impact pathways" that allow an innovation to become adopted. If CGIAR invents a drought-resistant grain, it still must find a way to help a network of national agricultural research institutions to embrace the technology, government ministers to support the distribution of the seed, and technical support institutions to instruct small-holders on how to use it and to encourage small-holders themselves to trust that the new seed is better than alternatives. Too often, a viable innovation fails due to an inability to overcome one or more obstacles related to diffusion.

6. Evaluation should help grant makers to invest patiently and learn quickly.

Innovations typically need time to mature and disseminate. Yet when they fail, it is crucial to assess the reasons why and apply the learning to future grants.

7. Finally, evaluation methods must be flexible to adjust to the breadth of initiatives supported by grant makers.

Some grant makers, such as the Rockefeller Foundation, explicitly possess a program line designed to support innovation for development. Most possess a broad portfolio of initiatives. Some may explicitly seek to create innovations. Others may stumble upon them. This can necessitate two approaches for evaluating I4D. One approach provides basic, core questions for programs that may have one or more elements that feature innovation, but *have not set the goal* for innovation to be the primary output of the program. One can imagine in these instances innovation arising serendipitously—akin to the famous discoveries of penicillin or plastic.

The second approach is for use in programs that specifically aim to produce innovations for development. This would include programs that aim to develop, utilize, test, market, etc. an innovation for development. It is a more comprehensive look into the key areas of evaluation of innovation for development aimed at capturing systematically the role innovation plays in addressing key development challenges.

EVALUATING INNOVATIONS FOR DEVELOPMENT: AN EXAMPLE IN PRACTICE

To understand what such an approach could look like, the following is an example of a model designed for an actual grant maker (Table 9.3). The evaluation matrix below is customized to fit the existing evaluation approach already employed by this foundation. This approach to evaluating innovation is therefore not a "bolt-on," but is built-in to the existing systems staff are comfortable with. The foundation utilizes a matrix based on key performance areas as follows:

- Relevance
- Effectiveness—achieving objectives; the quality of outputs/products
- Influence—specific outcomes; policy influence; influence on industry/sectors
- Sustainability of program outcomes
- Impact
- Risk management

From an I4D perspective, we slightly modify the definition of these performance areas as follows. The first indicator, *relevance* focuses on identifying the rationale, type, and relevance of the innovation over traditional tools and methods that deliver a value-added approach to grant making priority areas for development. There is particular emphasis on the development of the problem and vision that integrates end-user or beneficiary voice. This is based on the research that successful Innovations for Development are highly responsive to the need of beneficiaries or the end-user.

TABLE 9.3

Key Performance Area	Key Question	Subquestions	Indicators-Evidence	Data, Sources and Methods
Relevance (including rationale, niche, value added)	What "problem" is the innovation seeking to address in the grant maker's priority areas (e.g., health, climate change, basic survival)?	**Concept/Rationale.** Is there synergy between the problem, the innovation proposed and grant making priorities?	Clearly articulated problem statement with drivers for innovation. The problem statement should adhere to funding priorities and to its mission to deliver more equitable growth and/or impact resilience	Prospectus, Proposal, Strategy, Mission statement
		What are the vision and goals for the innovation (in addressing the problem statement)?	Vision and well defined goals	Prospectus, Proposal, Strategy, Mission statement, work plan
		Role/Niche: Type of Innovation. Is the innovation a product, process, market, organizations or what combination of these?[a]	Documented assessment of the type of innovation	Prospectus, problem statement, proposal, strategy, interviews
		Is it an incremental, additive, complementary, transformational/ breakthrough innovation?[b]	Documented assessment of the type of innovation	Prospectus, proposal, strategy, interviews
		Does the innovation relate to decreasing costs, increasing productivity, improving accessibility and/or achieving sustainability for the target community/beneficiaries/ end-users?	An articulated understanding of how the innovation has an aim to benefit poor and/or disenfranchised individuals or communities or the grant making priority areas.	Design strategy, prospectus or proposal, business plan

(continued)

TABLE 9.3 (continued)

Key Performance Area	Key Question	Subquestions	Indicators-Evidence	Data, Sources and Methods
Relevance (including rationale, niche, value added) (continued)	To what extent has the "problem" been verified by the innovation's beneficiary/stakeholder/end-user?	**Value added.** Who benefits from the innovation?	A clear model of how the innovation will benefit end users/beneficiaries	Prospectus, Proposal, Strategy, Mission statement, change model
		Relevance to stakeholders. Have beneficiaries or stakeholders been consulted about the need and ability for the innovation to address major concerns by beneficiaries?[c]	Identification of stakeholder engagement process/methodology to consult stakeholders relevant to the "problem" and innovation/needs for change.	work plans, surveys, stakeholder map, interviews, stakeholder meeting minutes.
		Stakeholder Collaboration. Have costs to stakeholders/beneficiaries been anticipated and is there technical or financial assistance for participation by stakeholders?	budget line for technical or financial support	Budget
Effectiveness— Achieving Objectives	To what extent is the "theory of change" producing an innovation?	**Program logic/theory of change** Is there a clear program logic / theory of change for taking an innovative approach?	Clear theory of change or program logic—including objectives. Results chain, linked outputs, outcomes to influence/impact at different levels Assumptions in the results chain identified.	Review of objectives/ strategy documents, Prospectus, Work plan, Interviews with corporate managers
		Situation analysis Is the program logic supported by a context analysis/situation analysis of the broader context of the need for an innovation? That is, does the analysis support the need for an innovative approach?	Data based context analysis—trends, issues, drivers, using respected global and regional analysis. Gender differentiated analysis	Known global analysis documents

(continued)

TABLE 9.3 (continued)

Key Performance Area	Key Question	Subquestions	Indicators-Evidence	Data, Sources and Methods
Effectiveness—Achieving Objectives (continued)		Were key stakeholders—particularly end-users/beneficiaries involved in defining the problem and developing the situation analysis that led to the conclusion of the value of an innovative approach?	Documentation of stakeholder participation in problem scoping, definition. Documentation of approach to translate stakeholder data to innovation design.	Program and project documentation. Interviews with project officers and users
		Clear results—outputs (the what) Is there a definition of the innovation output(s) to be delivered in a specified timeframe? Are there gender-differentiated results where appropriate?	Evidence of progress towards producing and testing innovative design, Evidence of results from the innovation, evidence of adjusting results on a regular basis based on monitoring data, learning events, feedback, evaluations, etc.	Work plan review, monitoring plan, progress reports on results
		Are the innovation outputs and results perceived to be of sufficient quantity, realistic, achievable within the time and resources available?	Results sufficiently aligned with objectives (quantity), budgets/resource allocation and capacity (realistic), timeframe (achievable). Identification of alignment and any gaps Results of interviews with project teams, program managers.	Analysis of work plans and budgets and capacity in relation to objectives Interviews with project managers.
		Have baseline data on current conditions/environment been taken? What qualitative and quantitative indicators are being used to measure progress/impacts and which progress will be measures?[d]	Identification of quantitative and qualitative methods for measuring base line for which progress will be measured against	Baseline data in the form of quantitative, qualitative methodologies.

(continued)

TABLE 9.3 (continued)

Key Performance Area	Key Question	Subquestions	Indicators-Evidence	Data, Sources and Methods
Effectiveness—Achieving Objectives (*continued*)		What is the schedule for data collection against the baseline (daily, weekly, yearly, etc.)?	Plan for data collection.	work plans, design strategy
		Clear and coherent strategy (the how) Is there a clear strategy that operationalizes the work? (Can you tell how work leading to the innovation is to be done?)	Presence of a clear and coherent strategy setting out how results are to be produced/delivered and objectives achieved	Strategy, work plans, project results reports
		Is the strategy aligned with the program logic/theory of change/results (outputs)?	Check for alignment of strategy and results	Strategy, work plans, project results reports
		Will the innovation be trialed on a temporary basis (one week, one month, one year, etc.)	Plan for trial.	Work plan, design plan, learning agenda
		Will the innovation be trialed on a limited scale (e.g., 1 group, 1 community, 2 regions, etc.)	Plan for scale of trial and planned implementation for scale after trial.	Work plan, design plan, learning agenda
	To what extent has learning been integrated into the innovation ideation, design and implementation?	**Monitoring, learning, adaptation** Is there a monitoring plan of performance data that supports learning from success and failure and integrates best practices that allows for course correction, leverage, scaling as needed?	Methods or tools used to understand success and failure and integrate learning into design/development phases for necessary adjustments. Includes gender identification and monitoring tools as necessary.	Monitoring tools, user or test reports, lessons learned reporting

(continued)

TABLE 9.3 (continued)

Key Performance Area	Key Question	Subquestions	Indicators-Evidence	Data, Sources and Methods
Effectiveness—Achieving Objectives (continued)		Is there a methodology for learning from stakeholders that allows for leverage, scaling and course correction as needed?	Methods, tools, process and plan to engage stakeholders into learning agenda and integrate learning.	Engagement process and tools, work plan, reports
		Have there been any unplanned results? Describe them and the circumstances that led to them.	Complete and up to date documentation and explanation of unplanned results	Learning results from trials, progress reports, surveys or interviews.
		Evolution of context and objectives Have there been major changes in context or constraints and opportunities facing the program? Describe them. Has the project teams made subsequent appropriate changes to accommodate these?	Complete and up to date documentation of any major changes in context, constraints, opportunities Revised work plans and strategies.	Progress reports, revised work plans and strategies Interviews with PI and project staff
		Progress in achieving results/objectives To what extent has the project made progress in meeting its stated objectives and delivering its results per the baseline data?	Percentage of results/outputs delivered on time, on budget Perception of key partners on progress in achieving objectives referring to the baseline data	Progress reports, data results, monitoring reports, interviews with project and program managers, partners
Effectiveness—Quality of outputs/products	To what extent are the innovation(s) of high quality?	Describe the methodology and results of the peer review process to ensure that the results are of high quality.	Presence of peer review mechanism Results of peer reviews	Documentation Interviews with project/program managers and partners

(continued)

TABLE 9.3 (continued)

Key Performance Area	Key Question	Subquestions	Indicators-Evidence	Data, Sources and Methods
Effectiveness– Quality of outputs/ products (continued)		To what extent do the outputs meet the quality criteria for developed by the Evaluation team?	Analysis	Quality analysis by Team Interviews with sectoral/regional experts intended users, audiences and stakeholders
		To what extent do managers and stakeholders perceive the outputs to be of high quality	Results of interviews with intended users (other stakeholders).	Interviews with project, program managers and partners
Influence– Outcomes	To what extent can the innovation influence traditional methods/ processes/ products to improve equitable growth or impact resilience for the people, groups, or organizations that it intends to impact and influence?	Measurement of changes in behavior and overall perception of quality of life Are changes or impact of the innovation of knowledge, perceptions, behavior, etc. systematically recorded in the monitoring processes and reporting?	Methods and tools exist and are used for measuring changes. Monitoring reports capture measured changes and discussion around factors leading to or inhibiting the changes	Monitoring tools Tools and methods for measurement of change Monitoring reports Interviews with project/program managers and partners

(continued)

TABLE 9.3 (continued)

Key Performance Area	Key Question	Subquestions	Indicators-Evidence	Data, Sources and Methods
Influence–Outcomes (*continued*)		Sustainability. How sustainable is the innovation's take up over traditional means/method?	Behavior changes recorded cumulatively over time. Evidence that behavior changes are significant enough to contribute to enhancing quality of life and permanently alter development status.	Monitoring and evaluation reports, surveys, interviews, baseline data reports where applicable.
		To what extent are organizational, cultural, and community changes necessary to enable use of the innovation?	Identification of shifts in thinking, behavior, etc. necessary for adoption and sustainable use	Market research, business plan, strategic program plans
		Are there any modifications or assistances needed for use more broadly or to scale the innovation?	Identification for necessary campaigns, communications, PSAs, training, workshops, etc. for adaption and sustainable use	work plans, design plans, strategic program plans
		Research Influence. Is there evidence of transformation of research results into new practices, technologies (devices), organization systems, for development purposes?	Any evidence of the following: New practices, New technology, New intervention that benefits poor and/or disenfranchised communities and/or grant making priority areas.	Interviews with principal investigators, investigators, users, decision makers
		To what extent does a broader "user-market" or audience exist for the innovation?	Research identifying how the innovation will benefit intended end-users/beneficiaries and transferability of the innovation to other end-users/beneficiaries.	Design strategy, prospectus or proposal, business plan

(*continued*)

TABLE 9.3 (continued)

Key Performance Area	Key Question	Subquestions	Indicators-Evidence	Data, Sources and Methods
Influence–Outcomes (*continued*)		Are there other sectors, industries, communities, regions, etc. that may be interested in this innovation?	Expressions of demand for the innovation; research identifying the applicability of the innovation to other areas	Catalogue of demand for broader application of the innovation (including cases with formal requests backed by resources); research analysis.
Sustainability of Innovation Outcomes	Has the adoption and sustainability of the innovation been anticipated?	Have the external enablers and potential barriers to scale the innovation been assessed—for example, as broad as governance conditions, regulations, rule of law, etc.?	Identification of political, environmental, cultural, etc. conditions that enable or disable adoption and sustainable use.	Market research, business plan, strategic program plans
		Have adequate analysis been undertaken to anticipate the needs for uptake and sustainability for beneficiaries/end users (i.e., necessary tools, methods, communications/outreach, necessary for uptake)? Describe.	Identification of other behavior, technical, and other needs to assist in uptake and long-term sustainability of the innovation into the group, community, region, etc.	Research reports, data analysis, interviews, surveys
Impact	Has the innovation provided a better outcome than the traditional method?	To what extent has the impact improved over baseline? Worsened? Remained stable?	Report on change in baseline quantitative and qualitative indicators.	Data sources as agreed for baseline data

(continued)

TABLE 9.3 (continued)

Key Performance Area	Key Question	Subquestions	Indicators-Evidence	Data, Sources and Methods
Impact *(continued)*		Has the impact been verified?	Reports from external sources of the impact of the innovation	Surveys, media reports, external evaluations
		To what extent has the innovation been an improvement over the prior/traditional approach?	Observations on the value of the innovation over traditional methods to address the "problem statement"	Data sources as agreed for baseline data, surveys, anecdotal evidence
Risk Management	Has a governance or decision-making structure been established to assess and monitor risk of the ideation, design and implementation of the innovation?	Has the risk appetite and process for decisions making around risk scenarios specific to design, trial, implementation and sustainability of the innovation been planned for?	Screening processes for decision-making around risk.	Organizational diagram, governance documents pertaining to decision-making and risk
		Is there a decision-making or governance process where assumptions and evidence from the innovation process challenged?	Reviews of data and evidence by internal and/or external bodies and committees.	Work plans, design plans, review committees

(continued)

TABLE 9.3 (continued)

Key Performance Area	Key Question	Subquestions	Indicators-Evidence	Data, Sources and Methods
Risk Management (*continued*)	Have regulatory requirements been identified and accounted for with regard to innovation trial and implementation?	What are the relevant and required regulations and standards that need to be accounted for?	Compliance and standards requirements at the federal, state, and local regulatory levels.	Verified compliance with federal, state and local requirements, work plan and output for tracking and noting any deviations.

a OCED defines four types of innovation in the Oslo Manual for measuring innovation: Product Innovation: This involves a good or service that is new or significantly improved. This includes significant improvements in technical specifications, components and materials, incorporated software, user friendliness or other functional characteristics; Process Innovation, which involves a new or significantly improved production or delivery method. This includes significant changes in techniques, equipment and/or software; Marketing Innovation, which involves a new marketing method involving significant changes in product design or packaging, product placement, product promotion or pricing; and Organizational Innovation, which involves introducing a new organizational method in the firm's business practices, workplace organization or external relations.

b Incremental Innovation—doing more of the same things you have been doing with somewhat better results; Additive Innovation—more fully exploiting already existing resources, such as product lines extensions, and can achieve good results; Complementary Innovation—offers something new and changes the structure of the business/sector/development process/market, etc.; Breakthrough Innovation—changes the fundamentals of the way the business, sector, process or market has traditionally functioned and creates a new industry; product, process, market and new avenues for extensive usability and/or accessibility. (Adapted from Peter F. Drucker, *Managing for Results*. New York: Harper Collins, 1986; pp. 204, 205)

c Innovations for development demand a high level of responsiveness to the priorities and concerns of stakeholders. A process to addresses the concerns, input and feedback of stakeholders should be included in the rationale and intention for innovation. The appropriateness and priority of the development of innovation is legitimate in the eyes of the stakeholder and beneficiary.

d Establishing a credible baseline is a critical part of measuring the impacts of innovations in development. The baseline data should serve as a) record of current conditions pre-innovation; identifies a foundation for comparability of future to be measured; Baseline data should include measures, time frame, assumptions, and comparability. It is important to collect baseline data before the innovation is applied. Baseline data should be quantitative and where not possible, for instance in tracking behavioral changes, qualitative data may apply.

The *effectiveness* indicator is broken into two parts, one that focuses on the innovation's ability to achieve intended objectives and the other on the quality of the innovation output. A heavy emphasis has been placed on the analysis of the problem statement and situation analysis that accounts for a learning process that, again, takes into account beneficiary voice as well as the analysis of impact of the innovation over traditional methods. This indicator also takes into account a peer review and stakeholder perception of the quality improvement of the innovation over traditional methods.

Influence and *sustainability* are particularly aimed at evaluating if the innovation has the ability for achieving dissemination and scale. As indicated earlier, the defining characteristic of Innovations for Development is not only the aim of benefiting the poor and/or disenfranchised, but also the ability for wide dissemination and scaling. These indicators also aim at anticipating capacity needs in order to integrate innovation appropriately and the potential to influence a wider development space.

The *impact* indicator systematizes a way to understand the impact to beneficiaries as well as to understand if the innovation provides a better outcome as it is compared to the baseline data.

Finally **risk management** accounts for the national context of take up of the innovation —any governance, political, or community issues that need to be accounted for in order for wide-scale impact to be created from an innovation. Taking these performance areas, we modify the evaluation matrix that the Foundation has used. Table 9.3 presents this matrix, now modified to evaluate I4D.

SUMMARY

In summary:

- Innovation for development can be defined as: *the process of making changes to something established by introducing something new whether it is an idea, method, or device that is leveraged or harnessed to produce wide spread change that benefits the poor.*
- Innovations for development require well-formed processes and methods to deliver innovations. These processes typically benefit from:
  - Extensive engagement with end-user beneficiaries and other key stakeholders throughout the innovation processes, (paying increasing attention to gender differentiated needs and solutions)
  - Wide engagement of a stakeholder and knowledge networks

- Efforts to create "enabling" infrastructure (including policies, regulations, incentives, awareness-building, capacity building, and governance and accountability reform) that supports adoption of the innovation
- Patient investment capital
- A learning culture that is willing to fail and is able to learn from failure
- Grant makers pursuing innovation for development should:
  - Implement an analytic process to determine when innovations for development are necessary, and what type of innovation will be most appropriate
  - Ensure the definition of innovation for development is rigorous enough to avoid "spin"
  - Build an innovation for development portfolio that focuses on (at least) two criteria—type of innovation and stage of investment
  - Support innovators that possess a strong methodology for delivering innovation (paying special attention to beneficiary engagement)
  - Support innovators that possess a strong idea of how to encourage the diffusion of their innovation
  - Invest patiently and learn quickly

NOTES

1. See the UN Task Force on Science, Technology, and Innovation; The US Department of Commerce's Advisory Committee on Measuring Innovation in the 21st Century Economy; the 2009 OECD Forum for Innovation Strategy; and UNESCO's workshop on Science and Technology, Innovation and Development.
2. Organizations referenced for information provided by their websites: Ashoka, Skoll Foundation, Acumen Fund, Kaufman Foundation, Kellogg Foundation, McConnell Foundation, Learning Innovation & Technology, The National Center for Environmental Innovation (NCEI), SEVEN Fund.
3. Eric Von Hippel, Professor and Head of the Innovation and Entrepreneurship Group at the MIT Sloan School of Management
4. See for example, Branscomb (1993).
5. Interview with Paul Basil, Rural Innovations Network (India)
6. This is noted in our interviews with both Charlie Brown, ASHOKA, and Chris Gerrard, World Bank Internal Evaluation Group as well as in the OECD Oslo Manual.
7. "Microfinance is the supply of loans, savings, and other basic financial services to the poor." (http://cgap.org)
8. Interview with Charlie Brown, ASHOKA

EXTERNAL INTERVIEWS

Todd Barker, Meridian Institute
Paul Basil, Rural Innovations Network (India)
Charlie Brown, ASHOKA
Ted Chen, W.K. Kellogg Foundation
Chris Gerrard, World Bank Internal Evaluation Group
Larry Keeley, Doblin Inc.
Barbara Kibbe, Monitor Company Group LP
Ruth Levine, Center for Global Development
Brian Trelstad, Acumen Fund

ROCKEFELLER FOUNDATION INTERVIEWS

Tara Acharya, (former) Associate Director, Foundation Initiatives
Maria Blair, Associate Vice President & Managing Director, Foundation Initiatives
Karl Brown, Associate Director, Foundation Initiatives
Antony Bugg-Levine, Managing Director, Foundation Initiatives
Samantha Gilbert, Chief Human Resources Officer
Christopher Grygo, Learning and Development Officer, Human Resources
David Jhirad, Special Advisor, Energy/Climate, Office of the President
Peter Madonia, Chief Operating Officer
Nancy MacPherson, Managing Director, Evaluation
Ariel Pablos-Mendez, Managing Director, Foundation Initiatives
Joan Shigekawa, Associate Director, Foundation Initiatives
Gary Toenniessen, Managing Director, Foundation Initiatives\UNL}

REFERENCES

Borden, M., Breen, B., Chu, J., Dean, J., Fannin, R., Feldman, A., & Leopard, O. S. (2008). *The world's most innovative companies.* Fast Company, 16-02.
Dahlman, C. (2008, November). *Innovation strategies of the BRICKS: Brazil, Russia, India China and Korea.* Presentation at OECD-World Bank Conference on Innovation and Sustainable Growth in a Globalised World.
Davila, T. (2005). The promise of management control systems for innovation and strategic change. In C. S. Chapman (ed.), *Controlling strategy: Management, accounting, and performance measurement* (pp. 37–61). New York: Oxford University Press.
Drucker, P. (1993, L). *Managing for results.* New York, NY: Harper Collins.
IBM Global Services. (2006). *Expanding the Innovation Horizon: The Global CEO Study 2006.* Armonk, NY: Author.
Jaruzelski, B., Dehoff, K., & Bordia, R. (2005). *Smart spenders: The global innovation 1000.* Boston, MA: Booz Allen Hamilton.

Kanter, R. M. (1996). When a thousand flowers bloom: Structural, collective & social conditions for innovation in organizations. In P. S. Myers (ed.), *Knowledge management and organizational design*, (pp. 93–132). Boston: Butterworth-Heinemann. (Reprinted from Research in Organizational Behavior, 22, by B. Staw & R. Sutton, Eds., 2000, Elsevier Science)

Laszlo, C. (2001, July). *The Evolution of Business: Learning, Innovation and Sustainability in The 21st Century.* Paper presented at the 45th Annual Conference of The International Society for the Systems Sciences, Asilomar, CA.

OECD. (2005). *Oslo manual: Guidelines for collecting and interpreting innovation data* (3rd ed.). Paris, France: OECD Publishing.

Perrin, B. (2000, November). *How to, and how not to, evaluate innovation.* Presentation to the UK Evaluation Society Conference, London.

Smith, K. (2000, November). *Innovation indicators and the knowledge economy: Concepts, results and policy challenges.* Keynote address at the Conference on Innovation and Enterprise Creation: Statistics and Indicators, Sophia Antipolis, France.

UNESCO. (2008, February). *Expert workshop on science and technology, innovation and development.* Held at the Manchester Institute of Innovation Research, University of Manchester.

CHAPTER 10

FUTURE DIRECTIONS FOR IMPROVING INTERNATIONAL DEVELOPMENT EVALUATIONS

Stewart I. Donaldson, Tarek Azzam, and Ross F. Conner

The chapters in this volume aspire to shed light on some emerging ideas and evaluation practices aimed at improving outcomes for international development initiatives, including larger-scale programs and smaller-scale projects. We focused specifically on how to improve a development initiative's ability to build organizational and evaluation capacity, influence policy, form networks and collaborations, foster innovation, and enhance sustainable development. We learned that each of these outcome areas involves a somewhat unique set of evaluative orientations, approaches, methods, and challenges. Chapter writers were asked to discuss the terms and definitions used to describe their areas, as a first step to understanding the methods, measures, and designs commonly used in evaluating a specific area. The authors were also encouraged to highlight strategies for increasing utilization of evaluation findings, and candidly describe recurring challenges they face when conducting their evaluations.

Emerging Practices in International Development Evaluation, pages 225–241
Copyright © 2013 by Information Age Publishing
All rights of reproduction in any form reserved.

SOME COMMON THEMES

Although the authors of each chapter discussed evaluation within a different outcome area, common themes and ideas emerged across the chapters. Many authors struggled with finding one definition in their area and offered multiple perspectives on the issue before selecting a hybrid definition. Almost all acknowledged the relevance of quantitative and qualitative methods and the power that comes from their combination. Evaluation use was also debated, and the importance of trusting relationships, timing, and the capacity to take action were highlighted as critical factors to increasing the potential for use. Finally, the complexity of the international development context was viewed by all as a major challenge for practicing evaluators. However, potential solutions to this challenge centered on implementing evaluations that are flexible and can anticipate and respond to change, while becoming a natural part of the program cycle and its environment. Some of these common themes are explored in more detail below with an eye toward future directions for improving international development evaluations.

A SEARCH FOR COMMON DEFINITIONS

Across many of the chapters, the initial step of defining the evaluation outcome (e.g., sustainable development, capacity building, etc.) was an acknowledged challenge. Most observed that within each area, multiple potential definitions existed. This was especially salient within the capacity development area, where Peter Morgan (Chapter 4) presented varying definitions of capacity development that ranged from the very broad (e.g., *the ability of individuals to manage their affairs effectively*) to the more detailed (e.g., *the ability of individuals, organizations, and societies to perform functions, solve problems, and set and achieve objectives in a sustainable manner*). Morgan offered these definitions to show the spectrum of possibilities and then selected a hybrid definition that attempted to encompass the others: "*Capacity is that emergent combination of individual competencies and collective capabilities which enables a human system to create value for others.*" Other authors such as Creech (Chapter 6), Raynor (Chapter 7), and Rochlin and Radovich (Chapter 9) present their definitions using a similar process of exploration, followed by a decision to combine elements from different definitions. This process highlights the advantages and struggles associated with finding a common definition. Having multiple definitions allows evaluators to find definitions that best suit the unique outcomes and environment of the program or policy. For example, Peter Morgan's multiple definitions of capacity building can be tailored to programs that narrowly focus on individuals' capacity development, or to other programs that focus on organizational capacity. This would allow for differentiation in what is considered a successful outcome and would be more responsive to the specific evaluation context. However, there is also a challenge to having multiple competing definitions. When different ways of operationalizing an outcome exist, then it reduces the evaluation's ability to compare across programs or initiatives, to find a common standard or measure of program outcomes, and to contribute to the theoretical understanding of how successful programs function. This is why some authors noted that the interplay between definitions and how to operationalize them is a critical first step that sets the tone for the entire evaluation. They suggest that the process of selecting an appropriate definition that fits within the evaluation context should involve stakeholders to help ensure that the methods and measures used in the evaluation are relevant and responsive to the needs of the program and its stakeholders.

EVALUATION METHODS

The authors also advocated for the use of mixed evaluation methods that answer core evaluation questions for the specific program or project, while also helping the evaluation understand some of unique contextual features of the program to help explain outcomes. All the authors believed that, in many instances, a mixed-methods approach was often an optimal option when designing an evaluation, and they had consistent arguments for the relevance of this approach. Lusthaus and Rojas (Chapter 3) stated that mixed methods could bring out values, norms, theories, and belief systems to understanding organizational performance, and believed that this approach offered the deepest insights about the status of any organization. Bass and Bradstock (Chapter 8) argued that evaluations could track attitudes toward the sustainability efforts (qualitative indicator) and expenditure on sustainability efforts (quantitative indicator) as a way to understand the relationship between attitudes and actions. This combination within a sustainable development evaluation may predict the future success of such efforts.

Although there was general agreement on the use of mixed methods, some authors argued for particular methodological approaches that were well suited for their type of evaluations. Carden and Duggan (Chapter 5) recommended the use of case studies as a direct method to describe and track the process of policy influence and the factors that contributed to that influence. They argued that case studies allow evaluators to discover key contextual elements, such as the political goals of different interest groups, that could lead to policy influence. Kumar and Ofir (Chapter 2) also supported qualitative methods in evaluation because they offered an enhanced perspective on the cultural norms, values, and expectations that stakeholders bring to the evaluation process. The qualitative approach was also seen as more responsive to programmatic changes that often occur in developing countries, and better able to represent the program and its outcomes. These authors along with the others also acknowledged that the benefits of qualitative approaches often diverged from some funders' preferences for quantitative methods and measures.

The balance between the methodological needs of the evaluation and the needs of the stakeholders (especially the funders) was viewed as a major challenge when selecting an evaluation's methodological orientation. Some of the discussions focused on the credibility of the evaluation to those being evaluated and to those commissioning the evaluation, and how this would ultimately influence the potential utilization of the findings. In most of the chapters, the "utilization" of findings was an underlying goal of the evaluation process. Some of the authors explicitly addressed this issue, while others incorporated evaluation use within broader discussions of methods and political realities.

Morgan believed that the potential for use is largely determined by the situation and the prescribed position of the evaluator. He suggested that an evaluator should conduct a "situational analysis" by examining the political, social, cultural, and security factors that could help or hinder the potential for use. This analysis may prepare the evaluator to recognize optimal opportunities for use. Similar suggestions were made by Carden and Duggan (Chapter 5), where they recommended an analysis of a policy's history, champions, and perceived impact. They encourage the evaluator to increase the chance for use by building the capacity for use through the development of relationships with key intended users and establishment of evaluator credibility among intended users. These approaches to increasing use were echoed in many of the chapters and emphasized the importance of understanding the context of the program and/or policy and building trusting relationships with potential evaluation users.

CHALLENGES OF UNDERTAKING EVALUATION IN DEVELOPING COUNTRIES

All the authors acknowledged that conducting evaluations in developing countries had challenges that affected the evaluation methods, measures, and potential for use. Within each of the outcome areas, authors cited very unique challenges to doing evaluations in that area. However, there were challenges that cut across all outcome areas and that were well described by Kumar and Ofir (Chapter 2). According to Kumar and Ofir, one of the main difficulties evaluators face when conducting evaluations in developing countries is the presence of complexity and unpredictability, and this chaotic system can directly affect the reliability and feasibility of any evaluation.

Other authors describe this challenge in slightly different tones. Raynor (Chapter 7) states that one of the main challenges in evaluating coalitions is the high level of uncertainty and rapidly changing nature of coalitions and the relationship between its members. Bass and Bradstock (Chapter 8) argue that the ability to measure sustainable development is often hindered by factors that are outside the control of the program or policy and that can move things in different directions, and Morgan (Chapter 4) describes the inherent level of complexity and the need to find ways to design evaluations that are able to offer users a detailed perspective on the outcomes while maintaining the broad view of the program. This challenge impacts evaluations broadly, because it can directly make certain methods not feasible, selected measures unreliable, and ultimate use unpredictable.

Although this was acknowledged by the authors, potential solutions were also proposed. Morgan (Chapter 4) offered the most detailed ideas on how to address this challenge. He argues that the paradigm used in evaluation needs to tackle the complexity issue head on by using new approaches such as complex adaptive systems (CAS). This approach proposes that evaluators should incorporate multiple strategies, cycle times, time horizons, dimensions, and informants, and that there would be no set end point to the evaluation process, but a continuous learning and adapting cycle which guides the evaluation and aids the program. According to Morgan, the ultimate incarnation of this process would produce an evaluation process that is fully integrated within the complex system and acts as a natural part of the system.

This approach is implicitly present in the writings of other authors. Raynor writes about the importance of measuring the intangibles (or "soft") outcomes that are constantly shifting or changing within coalitions. Lusthaus and Rojas acknowledge the need for multiple informants and encourage evaluators to consider the people in developing countries and the values underlying cultural differences across societies. Bass and Bradstock urge evaluators to account systematically for the various time scales when measuring sustainable development. Carden suggests an analysis of the history and culture to anticipate or foresee potential changes to the context and to use these changes to influence policy. Rochlin and Radovich propose that evaluators should consider the unintended consequences of innovation and the impact it has on a community, and Kumar and Ofir encourage evaluators to build relationships with local communities and focus on sustainable evaluation efforts that are seamlessly integrated within program or policy efforts.

POSSIBLE NEXT STEPS

In the preface, Nancy MacPherson provided a funder's perspective and made it clear that the purpose of this volume was to spark a conversation, not provide an authoritative prescriptive statement of how best to conduct development evaluations. We think the chapter authors in this volume have accomplished that mission and provided us with ideas that warrant further reflection and discussion, and could inspire development funders, evaluators, and stakeholders to try alternative evaluation approaches, designs, and methods when conducting complex evaluations, especially in developing countries. We are hopeful that a worthwhile next step will be supporting efforts to keep the discussion going about how to continue to improve the attainment of desired development outcomes using state-of-the-art evaluation approaches.

A second next step might be the provision of training to evaluators around the world that contains many of the ideas presented in this volume. Some efforts along these lines have already begun with the support of UNICEF and others to provide webinars by the chapter authors in this volume on the topics they have presented. Even more recently, a new e-learning program has been created by UNICEF, Claremont Graduate University, and the International Organisation for Cooperation in Evaluation (IOCE), under the EvalPartners initiative, with support from The Rockefeller Foundation and in partnership with UN Women. One series in the program is on "Emerging Practices in Development Evaluation" and uses this volume as a basis for the lessons taught to participants. These capacity development efforts, among others, can be found on the My M&E website at http://www.mymande.org/. These and future efforts to build the capacity of those conducting evaluations in the development context promise to expand further the reach of this volume in its effort to improve the attainment of development outcomes and international development evaluation practice.

Finally, it is important to encourage the use of many of the concepts, designs, and methods presented in this volume in "real" development evaluation practice. After all, evaluation practice is where the real test comes and where the real opportunities exist. One approach for achieving this is to provide short guidance notes for practitioners. In the Appendix following this chapter, the chapter authors have provided brief guidance notes with the hope that these would be helpful for designing future international development evaluations.

CONCLUSION

The authors in this volume have provided us with valuable ideas, concepts, and specific guidance notes to help improve international development efforts, and to improve international development evaluation practice. There are additional capacity development efforts underway including webinar series and e-learning programs that promise to amplify the work of the authors, and the impact of this volume. It is our hope that you are now inspired by what you have read to become part of the worldwide effort to use enlightened evaluation approaches to improve the quality of lives of millions of deserving people in developing countries around the world.

APPENDIX: CHAPTER AUTHOR GUIDANCE NOTES

Organizational Performance Assessment

Charles Lusthaus and Katrina Rojas

Guidance on Definitions

- Organizational performance assessments is: "*A systematic process for obtaining valid information about the performance of an organization and the factors that affect performance.*"
  - The definition could also include social responsibility as an outcome
  - Unit of analysis: individuals, groups, or organizations

Guidance on Methods

- Two main methods can be used in organizational performance assessment, but they are generally dependent on the evaluation's purpose:
  - Evaluations that are implemented for external accountability purposes would benefit from mixed methods which can include case studies and surveys.
  - Evaluations that are implemented for internal improvement purposes would benefit from self-assessment and reflection through case studies and interviews/focus groups.
- The evaluator may utilize an evaluation matrix that can be used to:
  - Organize and identify questions, indicators, data sources, criteria of merit
  - Consider organizational capacity, motivational factors, and the external environment
- An evaluator may also use a balanced scorecard to measure and track the health of an organization.

Guidance on Evaluation Challenges
- Identifying and developing appropriate methodologies for varying contexts
- "Speaking truth to power"
- Gathering and using high-quality organizational data
- Senior managers' general lack of understanding about the role and benefit of evaluation
- Determining who is involved in making the evaluative judgment on the data collected
- Lack of standards of performance across organizational sectors
- The common trade-off between efficiency and effectiveness (i.e., an organization can be more efficient but less effective or vice-versa).

Guidance on Possible Solutions
- Find what works, develop it, and scale it, while also considering the contextual features that contributed to the program's success
- Must consider framework of people in the developing context and the values underlying cultural differences in different societies
- Recognize that methodologies bring out values, norms, theories, and belief systems
- Build and develop the organization's capability for data collection and self-reflection
- Must understand how things operate, to assess the institutional level, in order to develop capacity

Capacity Development

Peter Morgan

Guidance on Definitions
- Capacity Development: *The processes of change that, both intentionally and indirectly, contribute to the emergence of capacity over time.*
- Capacity development can refer to a range of processes apart from an external intervention. These can take place at a variety of levels from the indirect and the global (e.g., national financial crises) to the direct and the immediate (e.g., the influence of the informal networks that actually control the ministry in question).

Guidance on Methods

- There is a need to combine different approaches to evaluation. The challenge is to combine and customize a capacity-focused evaluation to fit a particular situation at a particular time.
- There is a growing need to put country participants at the heart of the evaluation process. Extractive, third-party "expert"-dominated efforts do not contribute much to a legacy of evaluative thinking and acting.
- A complex adaptive systems (CAS) approach encourages the examination of externalities that may directly or indirectly influence the success of capacity building efforts (e.g., political situation, belief structures, or economic stability).

Guidance on Evaluation Challenges

- It takes time for stakeholders to reach agreement on what capacity development should look like when it is achieved.
- Many miss the opportunity to think about capacity development explicitly; however, it is often implicitly considered.
- Capacity development contains various definitions that are often rooted within varying paradigms, beliefs, and ideologies.
- There is a high aversion to conducting capacity development because it is seen as risky in many areas due to the lack of clear definition and measurement.
- There is a strong pull towards measuring the technical (or hard) parts of capacity development and ignoring some of the social (or soft) aspects of capacity development.
- Capacity development is often imposed from the outside.

Guidance on Possible Solutions:

- There should be a common language around this term to help stakeholders understand what it means, and this may also lead to a better commitment to the idea of capacity development.
- Capacity development's political and value-laden definition should be recognized early on in any capacity development initiative.
- The process of determining the definition is helpful because it creates a process where capacity development has to be operationalized and allows participants to think about how to measure it.
- An organization's values and perspectives should drive the definition of what capacity development is.
- There should be a balance between simplicity and complexity when measuring capacity development. The evaluation design should

be complex enough to capture some of the contextual factors but simple enough to communicate its outcomes to the outside world.
- The use of self-reflection as a tool to capture capacity development may be a method of measuring how it has changed stakeholders thinking.

Policy Influence

Fred Carden and Colleen Duggan

Guidance on Definitions

Policy influence can appear through multiple outcomes that include:
- Direct policy change that is guided by research or evaluation findings
- Expansion of policy capacities for decision makers and researchers: This means increasing the capacity of researchers to think about the policy process in relation to their research, and increasing the capacities of decision makers to make use of knowledge.
- Broadening Policy Horizons: This is a process of informing researchers and decision makers of the myriad influences and consequences that affect the decisions they have to take.

Guidance on Methods

- Case studies offer a direct method of describing and tracking the process of policy influence and the factors that contribute to the influence.
- Case studies can also be used to show the key contextual factors that led to policy influence.
- Realist synthesis is also an approach that could be used to represent the relationship between research, the decision context, the overall context, the factors that the researcher can control, and the potential outcomes.

Guidance on Evaluation Challenges

- The presence of hindering factors obscures the evaluator's ability to make a direct connection between research findings and immediate policy change, and these can include:
  - The capacity of policymakers to apply research
  - The nature of Governance or tight government control
  - Economic conditions
  - Stability of decision making institutions
  - Countries in transition

- Competing agendas from different interest groups, who subvert the researcher message (e.g., climate change debate)
- Problem identification, which is the process of identifying the appropriate or relevant problem that the policy change would address.

Guidance on Possible Solutions

- The role of the political process and the role of the evaluator within this process should be articulated and clearly described, along with the associated limitations of the evaluation.
- The presence of an advocacy component could help support policy influence efforts.
- Focusing on what those in power listen to, and understanding how decisions are made could help researchers/evaluators speak to their listening.
- The policy influence model should include varying approaches that respond to varying contexts; for example, how a researcher would approach a policy influence issue in an election year.
- Evaluators should also consider:
  - The time scale needed for change
  - How to utilize the policy influence frameworks when working with grantees
  - The research product and influence strategies should be high quality.
- Learning from evaluations of "successful" development and the factors or conditions that led to their "success."
- Thinking about "power mapping" as a strategy for understanding the influence pathways and the interests of different decision makers.
- "Advocacy progress monitor" could be another tool to detect or measure policy influence.

Networks and Partnerships

Heather Creech

Guidance on Definitions

Rather than attempt to select one term over another, the preference is to use the term "interorganizational relationship" (IOR) to describe networks and partnerships, because this is the most generic description of organizational networks and collaboratives.

Guidance on Methods

- Different approaches to evaluation methods include theory of change, social network analysis and impact pathways.
  - Theory of change is the process of creating a map depicting what the program wants to achieve, how to achieve it, barriers to achieving it, and resources to help achieve it.
  - Social network analysis (SNA) continues to intrigue many knowledge management and networking practitioners because it allows users to create a map that shows the interactions between various partners and how these interactions evolve and change.
  - Impact pathway mapping is a method of showing the step-by-step process of how a program hopes to attain its stated goals and objectives.
- However, the more traditional uses of logical frameworks and identification of performance indicators against stated results, outcomes, outputs and activities continue to prevail in IOR evaluation.

Guidance on Evaluation Challenges

- Networks and partnerships offer the best ways to potentially solve global issues and problems.
- There need to be better evaluations of the governance structure associated with IORs, because this is often where ownership and leadership issues emerge.
- Assumptions about networks may not hold across cultures; for example, there are multiple ways of defining what a "good" coalition member is.
- There are real transaction costs to forming networks, and evaluators should be aware of these costs.
- There are no common bases or standards to measure how well the networks are working.

Guidance on Possible Solutions:

- For the evaluation, there needs to be clarity on the units of analysis used in describing an IOR, and these could include:
  - Individually driven IORs
  - Organizationally driven IORs
  - Mixed IORs
- Evaluation of IORs should attempt to surface the values and beliefs of those who are involved, address the power structure within the networks, assess the ability of the networks to function with the given resources/infrastructure, and recognize the contextual factors that contribute to the success of failure of networks.

- The language of relationship should be increased, and networks should be described using the types of relationships that they have and the formality of these relationships.
- Relying on the native knowledge of participants could be an effective way of strengthening the coalitions in the long term.
- Governance is one of the key factors that need to be evaluated as a measure of network success because it can determine how functional the network will be in the long term.

Coalitions

Jared Raynor

Guidance on Definitions

An organization or organizations whose members commit to an agreed-on purpose and shared decision making to influence an external institution or target, while each member organization maintains its own autonomy.[1]

Guidance on Methods

- Mixed-methods approach is appropriate for most coalition evaluations and commonly includes:
  - Interviews, focus groups, and document analysis methodologies
  - Survey data analysis
- Outcome and impact mapping of the coalition work and process are also part of the evaluation process and can be used to help:
  - Clarify coalition goals and objectives
  - Guide formative evaluations to measure progress towards goals
  - Better understand the values, and capacity of coalition members

Guidance on Evaluation Challenges

- Identifying replicable components of the coalition
- Competing donor interests on the evaluation questions and ultimate outcome of the coalition
- High level of uncertainty and rapidly changing nature of coalitions that can change the original outcomes
- Power differentials that can lead to distortions in data collection or coalition functionality
- Understanding units of analysis in the evaluation: networks vs. individuals
- "Hard" vs. "soft" indicators and having the conviction to make the case for intangibles
- Sustainability of the coalitions across time

- The potential for unintended positive or negative consequences from the coalitions
- Making the evaluation useful to the stakeholders

Guidance on Possible Solutions

- Implement methodologies that are credible to various stakeholder groups.
- Specify early on in the evaluation process the intended outcomes of the coalition and the capacity of its members to achieve these outcomes.
- Request that donors provide space to the grantee so that they can begin to tap their own skills and capacities.
- Focus on governance and develop decision-making rules and evaluate their functioning within the coalitions.

Sustainable Development

Alastair Bradstock and Steve Bass

Guidance on Definitions

- Brundtland Commission 1987 definition: Sustainable development is *"Development that meets the needs of the present without compromising the ability of future generations to meet their own needs"*
  - Important to specify what is being sustained? for example, nature, life support systems, communities
  - Important to specify what is being developed? for example, people, economies, societies

Guidance on Methods

- Use mixed methods, quantitative and qualitative, to attain a richer picture of the environment and its potential for sustainability.
- Organize learning groups composed of national sustainable development champions and decision makers to define sustainable development in their context, identify progress and failures, and generate ways to move sustainable development agenda forward.
- Indicator-based assessments of outcomes/impact can be informed by:
  - A better understanding of local context, culture and resources
  - Indicators that show lack of progress (i.e., indicators of unsustainability), which may appear sooner in the evaluation.
- Narrative approaches such as focus groups, interviews, community forums could be used when quantitative data are incomplete.

Guidance on Evaluation Challenges

- Finding a common definition of sustainable development
- Lack of baseline data and indicators of sustainability
- Sustainable development timeframe—usually long-term, occurring at multiple levels (e.g., local, global, etc.), and complex
- Accessing or influencing decision-makers to support sustainable development efforts
- Lack of single sustainable development evaluation framework
- Determining who owns the sustainable development challenge (whether it is governments or communities, and determining who is responsible)
- The influence of media/virtual sphere on decision makers rather than credible evidence and evaluation results
- Concerns about accepting failure as an outcome of negotiation processes.
- Sustainable development industry as a Western, developed-country concept
- Challenge of evaluating the micro-picture of sustainable development.

Guidance on Possible Solutions

- Find strong champions to sustainable development, because ownership is needed by a global institution that has the ability to enforce/make decisions.
- Bring sustainable development awareness to the organizational level and the governing level.
- Evaluators can emphasize the social "pillar" and reality at the micro-level in their evaluations to measure the on-ground changes that are associated with sustainable development.
- Evaluations should also consider the unintended consequences of sustainable development.
- Evaluation could also do more to recognize the "soft" issues, associated with sustainable development.

Innovation

Steve Rochlin and Sasha Radovich

Guidance on Definitions

Innovation can be categorized using the following typology, with examples:

- Product—new vaccine, Proctor & Gamble's PUR water purification sachet

- Process—Crowdsourcing, ASHOKA innovation for development competitions, Positive Deviancy methods
- Market—Marketing strategies to promote circumcision against HIV-AIDS
- Organizational—Multi-sector collaborative arrangements such as Gobal Alliance for Vaccines and Immunizations, Amazon Fund, Forest Stewardship Council, StopTB Partnership

Innovation for Development Definition

- The change or introduction of new elements (process, product, or market) are leveraged or harnessed to produce change to benefit the poor.
- Innovation for development creates economic, social, political, social, or environmental transformations to improve health and well-being of the poor.
- It seeks to deliver inclusive economic growth outcomes more efficiently, with high levels of growth, scale, and effect in an enduring and sustainable manner.

Guidance on Methods

- Evaluations should utilize methods that are flexible enough to adjust to breadth of initiatives being supported.
- Evaluators should study the usefulness of the innovation, and the level of investment needed to implement it.
- Evaluators should be able to assess/understand the approach that grantee uses to create, deliver, and diffuse the innovation.
- Design for innovation must be rigorous enough to avoid "spin."
- Theory of change is used to better understand the context of the innovation and its potential for success.

Guidance on Evaluation Challenges

- Traditional evaluation measures and approaches might not capture innovation when evaluating an organization or intervention process.
  - Evaluation must tread lightly on grantor–grantee relationship because of failure risks inherent in the innovation.
  - Determine the evaluation focus—is it to evaluate innovation, or to evaluate how innovation makes a difference for development?
- Intellectual property protection comes into play, and it may affect motivations for innovation and the ability to evaluate it.
- The social dimension is often ignored by the innovation field, with too much focus on technology.
- There are unintended positive or negative consequences of innovation.

Guidance on Potential Solutions

- Divide the evaluation focus into two phases or parts:
  - The innovations themselves
  - How the innovation makes a difference
- Understand the power agendas of the context and funders to help navigate the grantee–donor relationship when evaluating innovations.
- Match purpose to type of evaluation. For example, an evaluation focused on the use of innovation may benefit from a developmental or formative evaluation focus.
- Utilize and incorporate qualitative methodologies that get to stakeholder voice.
- Encourage donors to create space for innovation because this could enable existing environments to facilitate flow of innovation; for example, small communities of farmers teach other farmers techniques.

NOTE

1. Mizrahi, T., & Rosenthal, B. B. (2001). Complexities of coalition building: Leaders' successes, strategies, struggles, and solutions. *Social Work, 46*(1), 63–78.

ABOUT THE CONTRIBUTORS

Tarek Azzam is Assistant Professor and Associate Director of the Claremont Evaluation Center at Claremont Graduate University. Dr. Azzam's research focuses on studying the impact of contextual variables on evaluation. He has worked on research and evaluation projects ranging from large multi-year, multi-site studies of reform efforts, to smaller studies of non-profit organizations focused on providing support to underrepresented children. Dr. Azzam is the co-founding chair of the Research on Evaluation Division of the American Evaluation Association, and former chair of the Theories of Evaluation Division. Azzam received his doctorate in Social Research Methodology from the University of California, Los Angeles.

Steve Bass is Head of the Sustainable Markets Group at the International Institute for Environment and Development in London, responsible for IIED's work in economics, business, and market governance mechanisms. He is a forester and environmental scientist with 30 years experience, principally in Southern Africa, Southern Asia, and the Caribbean, and in international policy processes. He has degrees from Oxford and Manchester Universities in Forestry, Agricultural Sciences, and Landscape Planning, and has published several books and over 100 papers on sustainable development, environmental mainstreaming, forest management, and certification. Steve is a co-founder of the Green Economy Coalition and is on its Steering Committee. He chairs the UK's Ecosystem Services for Poverty Alleviation 7-year research program, is a Fellow of WWF-UK, and Honorary Senior Fellow of UNEP's World Conservation Monitoring Centre. Previously, Steve was chief environment adviser at the UK Department for In-

Emerging Practices in International Development Evaluation, pages 243–250
Copyright © 2013 by Information Age Publishing
All rights of reproduction in any form reserved.

ternational Development (DFID). He was awarded the Queen's Award for Forestry in 2001 for services to international initiatives.

Alastair Bradstock is Business Development Director of the IIED. He is responsible for monitoring and evaluation at IIED as well as forging new relationships with donor funding agencies. Last year he started the process of introducing "*results-based management*" to strengthen the institute's focus on outcomes and impacts. He is also working with colleagues to broaden IIED's funding base with a focus on targeting foundations.

Prior to joining IIED, Alastair served as Director of Policy and Research at FARM-Africa for three years, and before that, he lived and worked in South Africa where he investigated the effectiveness of the government's land reform program. FARM-Africa works to reduce poverty by enabling marginal African farmers, herders, and forest dwellers to make sustainable improvements to their wellbeing by effectively managing renewable natural resources.

Fred Carden joined IDRC's Evaluation Unit in 1993 and became the director in March 2004. He has written in the areas of evaluation, international cooperation, and environmental management. His current work includes assessment of the influence of research on public policy, and the development of use-oriented evaluation tools and methods in the areas of organizational assessment, participatory monitoring and evaluation, program evaluation, and outcome mapping. Recent copublications include "Outcome Mapping," "Organizational Assessment," and "Evaluating Capacity Development." He has taught and carried out research at York University, the Cooperative College of Tanzania, the Bandung Institute of Technology (Indonesia) and the University of Indonesia. He holds a PhD from the Université de Montréal and a Master's degree in environmental studies from York University.

Ross Conner is Professor Emeritus, Social Ecology School, University of California, Irvine, USA, Department of Planning, Policy and Design. He had done evaluation work in the areas of health, education, criminal justice and leadership. He has published, usually with co-evaluators, co-authors or co-editors, 11 books plus numerous papers and reports on evaluation project results, as well as on more general topics related to politics and evaluation, context in evaluation, evaluation utilization in program improvement and policy formation, evaluation design, international and cross-cultural evaluation issues, and evaluation training. In addition to his university teaching, he has conducted courses for the Evaluators' Institute and the Claremont Graduate University, plus evaluation workshops in Australia, New Zealand, Russia, UK, Portugal, and the South Caucasus countries of Georgia, Armenia and Azerbaijan. He is Past President, American Evaluation Association

(AEA); Fellow, American Psychological Association and American Psychological Society; National Fellow, W.K. Kellogg Foundation; President (2006-7) International Organisation for Cooperation in Evaluation (IOCE); co-program chair, AEA 2009 annual meeting; and member (2009-10) Special Panel on Impact Assessment, Independent Science and Partnership Council, Consultative Group on International Agricultural Research.

Heather Creech is the Director of Global Connectivity at IISD, responsible for the delivery of IISD's program of work on how technology, in particular communications technology, is supporting and changing how we organize our governing systems, our economies, and our cultures in unprecedented ways. This new program builds on IISD's earlier Knowledge Communications program. Creech and her team focus on three broad areas of work:

1. Networked governance principles and practice, including the management of networks, partnerships and alliances
2. Internet sector engagement and policy support
3. Building capacity for leadership for the networked age

She brings to her work extensive experience in Canada and the South Pacific, establishing networks and providing information and training services in the legal and marine science fields. At the South Pacific Applied Geoscience Commission, based in Fiji, she established the node for the Pacific Islands Marine Resources Information System. As the Law Librarian, University of Papua New Guinea, she managed the Pacific Islands Legal Information Network. Her earliest work at Dalhousie University's Faculty of Law focused on legal information retrieval systems and legal research training.

Creech is an adjunct professor at the Hawke Research Institute for Sustainable Societies, University of South Australia, and the Natural Resources Institute, University of Manitoba. She also serves on the Board of the Canadian Committee for IUCN and the Canadian Commission for UNESCO. She holds a certificate from the Sustainable Enterprise Academy, Schulich School of Business, York University, has studied ocean policy at Dalhousie University (Halifax), and holds an M.L.S from Dalhousie University (Halifax) and a Bachelor of Arts (Hons) from Queens University (Kingston).

Stewart I. Donaldson is Dean, Professor, & Director of the Claremont Evaluation Center at Claremont Graduate University, USA. He leads one of largest university-based evaluation training programs with both residential and distance degree and certificate programs, directs the *American Evaluation Association's* Graduate Education Diversity Internship (GEDI) program, and serves on the Boards of the *American Evaluation Association, American Journal of Evaluation, New Directions for Evaluation,* and *Evaluation and Program Planning,* among others. He has published more than 200 scientific articles, chapters, and evaluation reports and his recent books include *Theory-Driven Program Design and Evaluation: A Practical Guide for Achieving Social Impact* (forthcoming), *Credible and Actionable Evidence: Foundations for Rigorous and Influential Evaluations* (forthcoming), *Emerging Practices in International Development Evaluation* (2013, this volume), *The Future of Evaluation in Society: A Tribute to Michael Scriven* (2013), *Teaching Psychology Online: Tips and Strategies for Success* (2013), *Social Psychology & Evaluation* (2011), *Advancing Validity in Outcome Evaluation: Theory and Practice* (2011), *Applied Positive Psychology: Improving Everyday Life, Heath, Schools, Work, and Society* (2011), *What Counts are Credible Evidence in Applied Research and Evaluation?* (2008), *Program Theory-Driven Evaluation Science: Strategies and Applications* (2007), *Applied Psychology: New Frontiers and Rewarding Careers* (2006), and *Evaluating Social Programs and Problems: Visions for the New Millennium* (2003).

Colleen Duggan is a Senior Program Specialist who has been working with the Evaluation Unit of the International Development Research Centre (IDRC) since 2005. Between 2001 and 2005 she worked with IDRC`s Peace, Conflict and Development Program and with its Women`s Rights and Citizenship Program. Prior to joining IDRC, she spent 10 years with the United Nations system, with the UN High Commissioner for Human Rights in Colombia, with UNDP's Bureau for Crisis Prevention and Recovery in New York and in the field with the UNDP in El Salvador and Guatemala. Her research interests include human rights, gender and transitional justice, peace and conflict impact analysis and evaluation in contexts of violence and fragility. She is the co-editor of *Evaluation in Extremis: Research, Impact and Politics in Violently Divided Societies* (forthcoming, Sage) and has published works on evaluation in the *Journal of Evaluation and Program Planning,* the *International Journal of Transitional Justice,* and the *Journal of Human Rights Practice.* She holds a Masters in International Human Rights and Humanitarian Law from Essex University (UK) and a graduate degree in International Development and Economic Cooperation from the Université d'Ottawa (Canada).

A. K. Shiva Kumar is a development economist, founding member of the International Development Evaluation Association (IDEAS), and Member of India's National Advisory Council. He is also Visiting Professor at the Indian School of Business in Hyderabad and teaches economics and public policy at the Harvard Kennedy School of Government. Shiv's research has focused on poverty and human development, social sector analysis, and the impact of development policies on children and women. Shiv did his Post Graduate Diploma in Management from Indian Institute of Management, Ahmedabad, and his M.A. in Economics from Bangalore University. He also has a Master in Public Administration and a PhD in Political Economy and Government, both from Harvard University.

Charles Lusthaus is one of the founders and a senior consultant and board member of Universalia and an expert in management, organizational theory, and institutional evaluation and change. Dr. Lusthaus has over 25 years of experience in organizational development and assessment in Canada and internationally. He has published numerous books and articles on management and policy development and has made over 100 presentations at conferences and workshops. Dr. Lusthaus is an associate professor in the faculty of education at McGill University. He is one of the authors of *Organizational Assessment: A Framework for Improving Organizational Performance* (IDRC, IDB,2002), which was the culmination of over 20 years of fieldwork and research on this topic. He and his colleagues are now carrying out research on the development and evaluation of international partnerships and networks. Dr. Lusthaus is one of the company stakeholders and a member of the Board of Directors.

Peter Morgan is a consultant on technical assistance and capacity issues, with over 35 years of experience in international development. He has worked for many different development organizations (CIDA, the World Bank, DFID, UNDP, IUCN, etc.) and has written dozens of major reports. He also has extensive experience in Africa. He has written extensively on capacity issues. His work experience has included serving as the research director for the ECDPM study on change, capacity and performance; Program Associate at the European Centre for Development Policy Management, Maastrich; Associate, Institute On Governance; Senior Director, Area Coordination Group, CIDA; Director, CIDA Decentralization Program; Country Program Director for Indonesia; First Secretary (Development) Canadian High Commission, New Delhi, India; Program/Project Manager, CIDA; and Assistant Secretary for Agriculture, Ministry of Agriculture, Government of Kenya.

Zenda Ofir is a former President of the African Evaluation Association (AfrEA), former Vice-President of the International Organization for Cooperation in Evaluation (IOCE) and former Board member of the American Evaluation Association (AEA). A South African citizen with a PhD in Chemistry, she now works primarily in Africa and Asia as international evaluation specialist. She has advised and assisted many international organizations in evaluation policy, strategy and methodology, including the World Conservation Union (IUCN), the Consultative Group for International Agricultural Research (CGIAR), the Rockefeller Foundation and the Global Alliance for Vaccines and Immunization (GAVI). She was a visiting fellow at the University of Hiroshima and for several years presented the Aid Effectiveness module of the International Cooperation course at the United Nations University (UNU) in Tokyo.

Sasha Radovich is a partner and senior manager at AccountAbility and, since 2004, has been instrumental in the development of two innovative programs, the Partnership Governance and Accountability (PGA) program—now titled Collaborative Governance—and the MFA Forum. The PGA program links key research on issues of partnership accountability with AccountAbility's standards and services work. Sasha was the lead developer and author of AccountAbility's Partnership Governance and Accountability Framework and associated publication *Partnership Governance and Accountability: Reinventing Development Pathways.* Sasha also manages the multi-stakeholder partnership, the MFA Forum that works to promote socially responsible and economically viable garment industries.

Sasha has nearly 10 years of experience working on multi-stakeholder initiatives, corporate responsibility and conflict prevention/resolution—as a researcher, advisor and senior project manager for numerous non-profit organizations, as a consultant, and with the United Nations. Sasha has a Masters degree in International Affairs focused on corporate social responsibility with particular emphasis on stakeholder engagement and conflict prevention from Columbia University's School of International and Public Affairs (SIPA). She has worked and lived in Serbia and Ghana.

Jared Raynor is Director of Evaluation at TCC Group. He focuses on evaluation, organizational development (including capacity building and collaboration), and strategic learning. His work has included numerous domestic and international clients, and recent work has focused on advocacy capacity and evaluation, network and coalition capacity and evaluation, and shared measurement platforms. Coming from a background of organizational change management, he has an acute interest in the relationship between evaluation and strategy development and how to foster internal learning organizations. Prior to joining TCC Group, he worked with the NGO Section of the Department of Public Information at the United Nations in New York and the International Rescue Committee in Azerbaijan as well as smaller project work in Latin America and the U.S. Jared is a graduate of the Milano Graduate School at New School University where he received an MS in Organizational Change Management, focusing on community development and the organizational structure of development organizations in humanitarian emergencies. He also holds bachelor's degrees in finance and Spanish from the University of Utah.

Steve Rochlin is a senior partner, director and AccountAbility's U.S. representative. Steve is currently leading AccountAbility's initiatives on the alignment of corporate responsibility with core business strategy such as the Global Leadership Network (GLN, innovative models of collaborative governance, and scaling the ability of voluntary standards systems to impact sustainable development. He has consulted several of the world's leading brands to help them achieve world-class global corporate citizenship performance, measurement, strategy, and stakeholder engagement. Steve frequently delivers keynote speeches on topics related to these issues for events around the world. Steve is a Senior Research Fellow for The Centre for Corporate Citizenship at Boston College. He has co-authored *Untapped: Creating Value in Underserved Markets and Beyond Good Company: Next Generation Corporate Citizenship.*

Prior to joining AccountAbility, Steve worked extensively in the areas of technology-based economic development for the National Academy of Sciences and the Center for Strategic and International Studies in Washington, DC and the Center for Corporate Citizenship at Boston College, where he spent eleven years as director of research and development and as a member of the senior leadership team leading the effort to build one of the premier applied R&D Centers on the strategy, management, measurement, and practice of corporate responsibility. He has also served as associate for an economics and management consulting firm. Steve obtained his master's degree in public policy from Harvard University's John F. Kennedy School of Government and his A.B. from Brown University.

Katrina Rojas is a senior consultant at Universalia who has worked in planning, monitoring, evaluation, governance and other areas of organizational development for the last ten years. Since joining Universalia in 2001, she has carried out assignments for CIDA, the International Development Research Centre, Caribbean Development Bank, Asian Development Bank, World Bank, International Centre for Human Rights and Democratic Development, Foreign Affairs Canada, Television Trust for the Environment, UNCDF, UNIFEM, and the Government of Nicaragua's Program to Support Implementation of the Poverty Reduction Strategy. Between 1994 and 2001, Ms. Rojas lived in Costa Rica and consulted with civil society organizations involved in children's rights, human rights, women's rights and gender equality, health and environmental issues, popular education, and community development in Central America. She was a member of Fundación Acceso, an NGO that provides capacity building services to civil society organizations in Central America. Ms. Rojas is a shareholder in the company.

A. K. Shiva Kumar is a development economist, founding member of the International Development Evaluation Association (IDEAS) and Member of India's National Advisory Council. He is also Visiting Professor at the Indian School of Business in Hyderabad and teaches economics and public policy at the Harvard Kennedy School of Government. Shiv's research has focused on poverty and human development, social sector analysis, and the impact of development policies on children and women. Shiv did his Post Graduate Diploma in Management from Indian Institute of Management, Ahmedabad, and his M.A. in Economics from Bangalore University. He also has a Master in Public Administration and a Ph.D in Political Economy and Government, both from Harvard University.

INDEX

Emerging Practices in International Development Evaluation, pages 251–253
Copyright © 2013 by Information Age Publishing
All rights of reproduction in any form reserved.

CPSIA information can be obtained at www.ICGtesting.com
Printed in the USA
BVOW09s1952241114

376549BV00003B/12/P